"STAND BY TO RAM."

Campbeltown held steadily on her course. In the wheelhouse there was complete silence. Beattie and Montgomery propped themselves against the front of the wheelhouse, ready for the shock of impact. Throughout the ship every man braced himself; in the wardroom Brett's and Purdon's parties sat down on the deck and an unexploded shell, it's red tracer burning in the base, shot through above their heads. Denser and denser grew the black line ahead . . .

THE BANTAM WAR BOOK SERIES

This series of books is about a world on fire.

The carefully chosen volumes in the Bantam War Book Series cover the full dramatic sweep of World War II. Many are eyewitness accounts by the men who fought in a global conflict as the world's future hung in the balance. Fighter pilots, tank commanders and infantry captains, among many others, recount exploits of individual courage. They present vivid portraits of brave men, true stories of gallantry, moving sagas of survival and stark tragedies of untimely death.

In 1933 Nazi Germany marched to become an empire that was to last a thousand years. In only twelve years that empire was destroyed, and ever since, the country has been bisected by her conquerors. Italy relinquished her colonial lands, as did Japan. These were the losers. The winners also lost the empires they had so painfully seized over the centuries. And one, Russia, lost over twenty million dead.

Those wartime 1940s were a simple, even a hopeful time. Hats came in only two colors, white and black, and after an initial battering the Allied nations started on a long and laborious march toward victory. It was a time when sane men believed the world would evolve into a decent place, but, as with all futures, there was no one then who could really forecast the world that we know now.

There are many ways to think about that war. It has always been hard to understand the motivations and braveries of Axis soldiers fighting to enslave and dominate their neighbors. Yet it is impossible to know the hammer without the anvil, and to comprehend ourselves we must know the people we once fought against.

Through these books we can discover what it was like to take part in the war that was a final experience for nearly fifty million human beings. In so doing we may discover the strength to make a world as good as the one contained in those dreams and aspirations once believed by heroic men. We must understand our past as an honor to those dead who can no longer choose. They exchanged their lives in a hope for this future that we now inhabit. Though the fight took place many years ago, each of us remains as a living part of it.

THE GREATEST RAID OF ALL

C. E. Lucas Phillips

With Foreword by
The Earl Mountbatten of Burma, KG

BANTAM BOOKS
TORONTO · NEW YORK · LONDON · SYDNEY

THE GREATEST RAID OF ALL

*A Bantam Book / published by arrangement with
Little, Brown & Company in association with
The Atlantic Monthly Press*

PRINTING HISTORY

*Little, Brown edition published April 1960
3 printings through August 1960
Published in England in a slightly different version by
William Heinemann, Ltd.
Bantam edition / October 1981*

Drawings by Greg Beecham and Tom Beecham.

Maps and figures by Alan McKnight.

ISBN 0–553–20231–6

Published simultaneously in the United States and Canada

PRINTED IN THE UNITED STATES OF AMERICA

0 9 8 7 6 5 4 3 2 1

. . . a deed of glory intimately involved in high strategy

WINSTON CHURCHILL

AUTHOR'S NOTE

"Having been associated with practically all combined operations, from two-man raids to the planning for Normandy, I have no hesitation in saying that the finest and most profitable of the lot was your raid on St. Nazaire."

Thus Lord Louis Mountbatten, as he then was, wrote to Lieutenant-Colonel Charles Newman after Newman's release from captivity in 1945. Yet, of the many exploits of the war, of which this was perhaps the most daring and brilliant of all, few have received so little attention from the investigator. Indeed, no account, official or otherwise, has yet been published which is complete and wholly accurate, even the official casualty numbers being at fault. Captain Robert Ryder's little book, *The Attack on St. Nazaire,* gives an excellent short narrative and still better appreciation, but it is surprising that no full-dress account has yet been written.

The book now presented, accordingly, is an attempt to fill the gap and it will have failed in its purpose if it does not now show that the St. Nazaire raid shines with a luster equal to that of the most brilliant of any small exploit of warfare—small in numbers, but large in achievement. For the gallant six hundred who sailed up the Loire on that cloudy March night in 1942, with guns to right and left and ahead of them, achieved a purpose out of all proportion to their small number and of an extent that was not fully realized until after the war was over. It would be inappropriate to repeat here the comparison made with Zeebrugge in the main text, but it is very apt to quote the verdict of Admiral of the Fleet Sir Charles Forbes in his introduction to Captain Ryder's book.

"Without in any way wishing to belittle Zeebrugge," wrote Sir Charles, "one should now talk of St. Nazaire instead."

These things will appear. On the other hand, no attempt has been made to minimize the less satisfactory features, such as the reluctance of the Admiralty to provide the essential ships, the unhappy collapse of the bombing support program, the loss of the command of the battle through failure of wireless communications and the severe, indeed the heart-breaking, losses among the vulnerable motor launches.

As far as possible, this book has been written entirely from original evidence—British, German and French. No existing account has been taken for granted. In this pursuit I have received generous help from Amphibious Warfare Headquarters and from Lieutenant-Commander P. K. Kemp and Commander M. G. Saunders (particularly for German records) of the Historical Section of the Admiralty. The French Embassy and the Librarian of the Imperial War Museum have also courteously assisted. In addition to a large store of original documents, I have received personal narratives from fifty-three British and eleven German officers and men who participated in the planning or execution of the raid, and in most instances these informants have seen and concurred in those portions of the manuscript that concerned them.

To all these informants, many of whom have put up with much cross-examination, I am very much indebted. For reasons of length, I have been most regretfully obliged to omit a large wealth of detail, particularly regarding the river battle, the escapes and the preliminary planning, with which they have so generously supplied me.

I cannot possibly enumerate, as I should like, all these contributors to the store of information, but for specially valuable or continuous help at many stages I owe particular thanks to Admiral of the Fleet the Earl Mountbatten of Burma; Lieutenant-Colonel S. W. Chant, OBE, MC (who has been a particularly valuable and resourceful aide in the hunt for information); Captain S. H. Beattie, VC, RN; Major R. K. Montgomery, MC, RE; Dr. P. J. C. Dark; Major W. O. Copland, DSO; Mr. R. O. C. Swayne, MC; Commander E. A. Burt, DSC; Mr. R. C. M. V. Wynn, DSC; Commander D. M. C. Curtis, DSC; Mr. T. W. Boyd, DSO; Mr. G. R. Wheeler, MM; Major Anthony Terry, MC; Mr. John Coste, DSC; and Mr. I. L. Maclagan. For the planning and preparation I have been critically guided by Vice-Admiral J. Hughes-Hallett, CB, DSO, MP; Major-General J. C. Haydon, CB, OBE, DSO; Colonel R. D. Q. Henriques, CBE; and Wing Commander the Marquess de Casa Maury; as well as by Earl Mountbatten himself. Mr. H. E. Hewett, Secretary of the St. Nazaire Society, aptly described by Earl Mountbatten as "the most exclusive society in the world," has helped me to make contact with a great number of the gallant "Charioteers" in many parts of the world.

Among German informants, I am chiefly indebted to Kapitän zur See C. C. Mecke, Herr Edo Dieckmann, Dr. Lothar Burhenne, Fregattenkapitän F. K. Paul, Kapitän zur See Mortiz Schmidt and Dr. Herbert Sohler.

Above all, however, I am in debt to Captain R. E. D. Ryder, VC, and Lieutenant-Colonel A. C. Newman, VC, OBE, TD, DL, for their continuous guidance at all stages and for their constructive criticisms of my draft manuscript throughout. Without their help the story of St. Nazaire could not have been told.

From this mass of detailed evidence, official and personal, often contradictory, often incomplete or uncertain, I have done my best to give a true representation of the facts, weighing the evidence in the scales of judgment as best one can. In personal and minor detail, however, some points still remain indecisive, for in the crowded and stirring events of a close action it is not always easy for the participants themselves to be entirely certain of what has occurred. If some small errors have crept in from such causes, this narrative will nonetheless, I hope, stand as witness to an aggregation of deeds of individual heroism that has seldom been excelled.

The title of the book is taken from Hilary St. George Saunders, historian of the Commandos, in his book *The Green Beret*.

The ranks throughout are those appropriate to the time.

C. E. LUCAS PHILLIPS

FOREWORD

_by Admiral of the Fleet the Earl Mountbatten
of Burma, KG_

Of all the operations with which I was concerned in the late war, the successful raid on the battleship dock at St. Nazaire is perhaps the one I am most proud to have been associated with. It was one of those actions which can only be attempted precisely because it must appear, to the enemy, to be absolutely impossible to undertake; and for this reason alone it required courage and determination of a quite unusual order to carry out. What is more, this complicated operation had been planned in greatest detail; and once the forces were committed each individual small ship and each little group of soldiers had to fight it out, guided by orders received at home but entirely in the light of their own initiative.

I know of no other case in naval or military annals of such effective damage being inflicted so swiftly with such economy of force. For in less than half an hour from the moment the *Campbeltown* rammed, all the commando's chief demolition objectives were successfully achieved. This brilliant attack was carried out at night, under a vicious enemy fire, by a mere handful of men, who achieved, with certainty and precision, what the heaviest bombing raid or naval bombardment might well have failed to do. The great Normandie Dock was put out of action and made useless to every kind of ship—and, indeed, was to remain unusable for the next ten years or so. The Germans were prevented from being able to use the only dock on the Atlantic seaboard to which their great battleship *Tirpitz* could go to repair damage sustained in raiding the Atlantic; in fact, this effectively prevented them from operating her against our convoy routes altogether. Thus the main object of the raid was brilliantly achieved.

No fewer than five Victoria Crosses were won at St. Nazaire, out of a total force of six hundred eleven—surely by far the highest proportion of VCs ever awarded for a single operation; and this is the measure of the heroism of all who took part in that magnificent enterprise.

MOUNTBATTEN OF BURMA

CONTENTS

1

WHAT THE FRENCHMEN SAW

Forty minutes before midnight on March 27, 1942, while a thunderstorm was sounding to the north and east and lightning flashed upon a clouded sky, the cry of the air-raid sirens roused from their sleep the citizens of the French port of St. Nazaire. It roused also the German garrison who held so tight a grip on a port vital to the Nazi purpose. The crews of antiaircraft guns and searchlights took post. Another RAF raid was imminent.

A few minutes later, as the German radar station at Le Croisie picked up the leading bombers, the long, chill fingers of the searchlights began to probe the sky. Very soon every window in the town was shaking as the German guns opened fire in a cannonade more violent than any heard before and fountains of red and green tracer were shooting up into the vault, silencing the distant thunder and outshining the lightning of the sky.

Yet no hurricane of bombs resulted. Indeed, only four aircraft released their missiles, one at a time and at long intervals; but a fire was started in the Forge de l'Ouest, hard by the great dock.

On the ground men listened in some puzzlement as the Whitleys circled and maneuvered without bombing. Kapitän zur See Mecke, commanding the German 22nd Naval Flak Brigade, which manned the antiaircraft guns, listening at his headquarters at St. Marc and noting the extraordinary maneuvers of the British aircraft on his radar screen, became more and more suspicious that these maneuvers were merely a blind for "some devilry" not yet apparent, and he communicated his suspicions to all command posts of the German army, navy and air force.

Shortly, however, the raiding aircraft one by one turned

1

away, their engines fading to a whisper in the night, though from time to time others could be faintly heard very high up above the clouds. No object whatever seemed to have been achieved, except that the fire in the Forge de l'Ouest continued to burn fiercely. The guns ceased fire, the searchlights were switched off, and an uneasy quiet settled upon the town and the broad estuary.

Yet no all clear sounded. Gradually, with an irony that none could see, the clouds that had impeded the bombers cleared away at their lower levels and a full moon—the moon that would have guided them surely to their mark—

Submarine pens

shone through the higher nimbus, but shone too late, upon the naked roofs, upon the false peacefulness of the wide estuary, and upon the monstrous concrete kennels where lurked the U-boats of the German 7th and 6th Submarine Flotillas. Still no all clear. No one saw a German patrol boat winking an urgent signal of alarm away at the mouth of the river.

The patient Nazairiens in their cellars and shelters looked inquiringly at each other. Those who had their beds below turned back to sleep. The Germans who had no action stations and the hands from the German ships in harbor, in their separate shelters, fidgeted to return to their bunks and billets. The maintenance hands of the submarines loitered secure within the massive protection of their concrete roof. But the men who manned the guns and searchlights remained at their posts, maintaining, in accordance with new orders that they had received from Mecke, a posture of readiness to react instantly to the totally unexpected events that were to follow.

At 1:30 in the morning of the twenty-eighth, some dwellers in the moonlit Boulevard Wilson, which runs along the sea front southwestwards from the docks, beheld to their astonishment what appeared to be two torpedo boats and a dozen motor launches riding up the estuary, illuminated from both banks of the river by a concentration of searchlights that flung their beams, not upwards as they were accustomed to do, but horizontally upon the sea. They saw a German *Sperrbrecher*, moored in the roads, wink an urgent signal lamp to the advancing flotilla and, apparently receiving no answer, let fly the strikers of her quick-firing guns. They saw the German naval troops who were in their air raid shelters run out from them to fetch their weapons, lie down in the boulevard and open fire with small arms and machine guns upon the flotilla, which vigorously replied.

Thus, without warning of sirens, the Nazairiens heard the artillery break out again on all hands—at first intermittently, hesitatingly and with uncertain note; then, after a few minutes, in a violent crescendo, "a sudden tumult burst." The blast of guns was now accompanied by the new, more menacing sound of shells bursting, bursting at ground level very close at hand. To this was quickly added the sharp rattle of machine guns. Frenchmen who had served their time with the colors could not fail to interpret the notes of this violent orchestra. No air raid this; St. Nazaire was being assaulted from the sea.

The listening French, excitement beginning to mount in their hearts, then heard great explosions, as of mines or very heavy charges, shake the houses. Debris of all shorts spattered down in the streets and on the roofs. Those who could look safely from their windows or come cautiously to their doors saw to their astonishment the flotilla of motor launches, in double column of line-ahead, great fins of water splaying out from their bows as they moved at speed, swing into a dazzling concentration of searchlights in the harbor mouth, through which the streams of colored tracer, like shuttles in an infernal loom, darted in all directions. To this concentration of light under the dim, cold moon was added a series of fierce yellow-tongued conflagarations as, one after another, the motor launches, their naked petrol tanks hit, burst into flames, with violent explosions. The sea itself was on fire as the spilled petrol spread across the surface and clouds of black smoke drifted across the pool of light. "The very sky was alight with these conflagrations and that of the Forge de l'Ouest continued to rage."

For about an hour the Nazairiens listened to this violent clamor. "The confusion was total." It then gradually assumed a somewhat different note as, one by one, a few of the launches—so very few—turned their bows to the open sea and, at full speed, once more ran the gauntlet of the German batteries. Last scene of all, to those who could watch, was that of a lone gunboat, every gun and light concentrated upon her in a tumult of gun flashes, darting tracers, and shellfire, bursting into fountains of water, miraculously escaping, surely under the hand of Providence, through a cloud of her own white smoke.

The gunfire slackened, limited to that of small quick-firing pieces. German lorries were heard driving at speed through the streets of the town, laden with troops, and presently the dominant sounds were those of machine guns and rifles and the sharp burst of hand grenades. Armored cars tore through the streets. An infantry battle was plainly being fought. Was this, Frenchmen asked one another, the beginning at last of the counterinvasion by their Allies?

Before daylight all gunfire ceased, but desultory rifle fire was heard in the streets of the town itself. It must, then, be the Tommies. A German motorcycle combination, its

B.M.W.R. 75

machine-gunner spitting fire at random, was bowled over by counterfire from an unseen hand. Two figures in the old familiar khaki hammered at the front door of a little house and said in garbled French, "Show us the way through to the back." They passed through, climbed a wall, and were gone. Elsewhere the poultry were wakened to a frightened clamor as men dropped astonishingly into their run. At another house a tall, mustached figure in the kilt asked for water for the wounded. Other shadowy figures moved from house to house. Men bleeding from wounds sought shelter in cellars and outhouses.

The morning brought confusion and an atmosphere of terror. There was still a little spasmodic shooting and the Germans, their garrison heavily reinforced, were in a state of high nervous tension. They, too, thought that an invasion was being attempted and suspected that the patriot French would rise in support of it. They picketed every road junc-

tion in the town, firing at shadows and at each other. A
smell as of exhausted fires came from the docks. A convoy
of German ambulances swept in and took away a stream of
wounded. The Nazairiens, of course, were completely in the
dark—and the Germans themselves, angry, bewildered, and
their nervousness soon to be amply justified, almost as much
so. Was this really the prelude to invasion? If not, what had
been the objective of the British?

Sadly the French, as they attempted to go out about
their business, saw small parties of British soldiers and sailors,
many of them very severely wounded, being rounded up one
by one and bundled into lorries—disheveled, bleeding, limping, supporting one another, their badges and rank marks
torn from them by the Germans, but still looking proud,
even gay. From other points along the coast more parties
of British sailors and soldiers, escaping by miracles from the
petrol flames of their sunken craft, were brought in, barefoot
and, except for a blanket, naked. The bodies of others, dead
from gunshots, or drowned, or charred from the fierce flames
of petrol fires, were gathered up from the beaches or from the
sullen waters of the Loire.

But French workmen who went back to their tasks in
the docks saw also another picture. They saw a British
destroyer rammed firm and deep in the gate of the enormous
dry dock, that dock which was the largest in the world and
which would accommodate any battleship of the world's
navies. They saw powerhouses wrecked and burning. And
in the forenoon a mighty explosion shook the town as the
destroyer blew up.

For the British commandos of the Special Service Brigade and for their naval comrades in arms this was the end
of Operation Chariot and the end of the war, save for those
few who astonishingly made good their escapes. But for the
French of St. Nazaire, as one mysterious explosion followed
another long after the raid was over, it was the beginning
of three days of terror and of death, when the delayed-action
results of this most daring of raids stampeded the angry and
bewildered Germans, contrary to their disciplined habits, into
a paroxysm of indiscriminate shootings, in which they shot
down not only innocent French men and women, but also
their own comrades.

Of all these things we shall hear in due place, and hear
also how, in this welter of blood and flames, a blow was
struck for the Allied cause that immediately altered the

course of naval strategy to its advantage. It was a blow far more difficult to deliver, at least equally dangerous, far more successful and deserving even more renown than the famous Zeebrugge Raid in 1918, so closely comparable in purpose. For the Zeebrugge Raid, carried out against a port only eighty miles away, and on the open seaboard, with three times the number of men, was tactically less difficult and strategically not a success, in spite of all its lustrous heroism, since the submarine base was blocked for only twenty-four hours, whereas the Normandie Dock at St. Nazaire was blocked for ten years. Gradually, as the facts disclosed themselves in the next few days to the eyes of the RAF cameras and to the ears of the keenest of intelligence services, the gallant exploit of Ryder and Newman and their companions stood revealed, not as a mere nuisance raid, not as just another sally by a beleaguered garrison, but, in the words of Sir Winston Churchill, as "a deed of glory intimately involved in high high strategy."

Not less memorable were the words spoken to the survivors of the gallant band of Operation Chariot by the French Prime Minister five years later.

"You," said Mr. Ramadier, "were the first to bring us hope."*

*Except when otherwise stated, the quotations in this chapter are from an official report from the Mayor of St. Nazaire to the Minister of Justice in November, 1944.

2

THE BLACK HOUR

To St. Nazaire, as a seaport town, the fall of France in 1940 had brought the bitterness of enemy occupation. The Germans held it firmly in their grasp and the great docks were conscripted to their warlike needs under the Admiral Superintendent of the Dockyard.*

To Germany, still at war with the British peoples—the only combatants of those involved in the hurricane of events of 1940 whom she had failed to conquer—and now freshly at war with America also, the port of St. Nazaire was of great importance, not only in a material sense, but also strategically. Standing on the north bank of the estuary of the great river Loire, which at this point is about a mile wide, St. Nazaire lies six miles back from the open waters of the Bay of Biscay. This wide expanse of water is throughout of shallow depth and patterned with an archipelago of dangerous mud banks, except for a single deep-water channel, known as the Charpentiers Channel, which runs close to its westward shore and immediately under the muzzles of a belt of guns, as may be seen from the map on pages 103–104. Thus the estuary vividly resembles a pair of wide-open jaws, toothed with guns above and below.

Nature and the hand of man had therefore made of St. Nazaire an ideal lair for German submarines; and here the Todt Organization, that paramilitary body of constructional engineers who were molding Hitler's "Fortress Europe" in unnumbered tons of concrete, were building, in the lock known as the St. Nazaire Basin, but which we for greater convenience shall call the Submarine Basin, one of their

---

*Vice-Admiral von Trotha according to most accounts; Mecke thinks it was then Vice-Admiral Rother.

fabulous series of massive, bombproof submarine shelters. At the time when the Charioteers paid their brusque visit in 1942, they had completed nine, with five more still to be done.

Besides these concrete submarine kennels, the docks generally, with their excellent repair facilities, were of great value to the German warships, their tankers and such merchant shipping as managed to elude the British grasp. Above all, and the object to which our attention is to be most closely riveted, was the special dock built for the construction of the great French transatlantic liner *Normandie*. She was the largest ship in the world, and the dock, which to the French was known as the Forme Ecluse Joubert, but which we shall more conveniently call the Normandie Dock, was also of its kind the largest in the world, capable of accommodating a ship of 85,000 tons or more.

To the Germans the special importance of this dock was that it was the only one on their whole western seaboard that would accommodate the new battleship *Tirpitz*, most modern and most powerful warship of the world's navies. To the British, and now to the Americans also, the import of this menacing fact had been seen all too clearly the year before when the *Bismarck*, sister ship of the *Tirpitz*, had broken out into the Atlantic and had presented a fearful risk to our merchant shipping before she was brought to bay and sunk on May 27. It was precisely for St. Nazaire that she had been making for repairs and the port had been specially made ready for her reception. Should the *Tirpitz* sally out on a similar mission, and sustain damage, she stood virtually no chance at all of returning to her home waters by the far northern route, as we should be waiting for her. This Hitler well knew. St. Nazaire was the only port in the world open to her.

Let us see, therefore, in the very simplest light, what was now, late in January, 1942, the strategic threat to our existence with which our naval planning staff, and Mr. Churchill himself, were brought face to face.

Everywhere the fortunes of the Allies were at their lowest ebb. The United States had scarcely begun to collect herself for the struggle imposed on her by the recent affront on Pearl Harbor. The Russians, formerly the fellow conspirators of Germany, but forced into the war against her in the previous June, were being driven back inexorably as Hitler's armies bit deep into their territory. Greece had been overrun by the enemy, and, with the exceptions of Switzerland, Sweden and the Peninsula, the whole of Europe was now in the grip of Hitler and his "Italian jackal."

Britain, having for so long maintained the struggle alone and with her forces stretched to the uttermost over the seas of the world, had suffered grievous reverses by land and sea since the sudden aggression of Japan had added a still further strain on her resources. In the Western Desert, after driving Rommel back for some three hundred and fifty miles, our Eighth Army had in January been forced to retreat in their own turn for half that distance. A much bombed and sorely tired people at home read with rising consternation the daily tale of the sweeping Japanese successes in the Far East, which, on February 15 were to culminate in that most galling of all reverses—the surrender of our great citadel of Singapore. "The crash of external disaster," wrote the Prime Minister, "fell heavily upon us." This month we touched the very nadir of our fortunes.

Away in Norwegian waters, the great *Tirpitz,* having completed her trials, was now beginning to shift restlessly. In company with her were the "pocket battleships" *Scheer* and *Lutzow,* together with a number of heavy cruisers. The notorious *Scharnhorst, Gneisenau* and *Prinz Eugen,* subjected to frequent but unsuccessful bombing raids, lay uncomfortably at Brest, whence they were expected at any moment to sally out (as they in fact did on February 12) to join forces with the Norwegian squadron, either in the Atlantic or in northern waters, preparatory to a sortie against our shipping. If they made such a sortie, the Iceland-Faeroes gap and the Denmark Strait would be barred against their return, but the Biscay ports lay open to them as ready sanctuaries. Of these St. Nazaire was the only one for the *Tirpitz.* Destroy the Normandie Dock, and the *Tirpitz* would almost certainly not venture out into the Atlantic.

Thus the existence of the Normandie Dock and its availability to the *Tirpitz* elevated St. Nazaire, in the eyes of those responsible for directing our naval policy, from being only one of a number of enemy submarine and destroyer bases into a major strategic factor directly governing the dispositions of our ships of war and the whole of our policy for the protection of Allied shipping in the Atlantic.

Indeed the Prime Minister himself, in a minute to the Chiefs of Staff on January 25, had written: "No other target is comparable to it (the *Tirpitz*).... The whole strategy of the war turns at this period on this ship, which is holding four times the number of British capital ships paralyzed, not to speak of two new American battleships retained in the Atlantic."

In defense, everyone knows today, the offensive spirit must somehow be asserted and maintained. Thus a besieged force sallies from its gates to damage and unnerve the enemy as much as possible. Thus in the Western Desert the Eighth Army developed its "Jock columns," to harass and unbalance the Germans and Italians. Such raids and minor exploits, unless related to the commander's main purpose, are apt to be frowned upon by orthodox military authority. They were never once attempted against our own shores by the Germans, to whose doctrine of concentration on the main purpose such exploits did not conform. They dissipate one's forces, distract one's attention from the main design, cause unnecessary losses, and, if they fail in their purpose, are liable to do more harm than good to morale. They are essentially guerrilla tactics and are typically the methods of a force of inferior numbers that has been obliged to adopt a prolonged defensive.

From 1940 onward, for some years, Britain had been in just that position. Except for local theaters overseas, our posture, while we built up our forces, was bound to be one of defense. No one was more determined that that defense should be an offensive one than Mr. Churchill. Partly with these purposes in view, and also for the purpose of training, planning and experimenting for the great day when we should be ready to assault Hitler's Fortress Europe, the Prime Minister had given increasing emphasis to the new interservices organization that had become known as Combined Operations; and in October, 1941, he astonished everyone by appointing as its head a relatively junior naval officer, but one already distinguished for his initiative and courage—Captain the Lord Louis Mountbatten.

Even in that dark hour, when we were at the bottom of the pit, Mr. Churchill was looking ahead to the offensive. Mountbatten, summoned to Chequers, listened, deeply stirred, as Mr. Churchill expounded his purpose. "Your job," the Prime Minister concluded, "is to be offensive. Train for the offensive—work out the craft, the equipment, the tactics, the administration and everything else needed to initiate and sustain the offensive."

With this inspiration to sustain him, Mountbatten was

now installed at Combined Operations Headquarters (COHQ) in Richmond Terrace, which lies between Whitehall and the Thames. His appointment was as Director of Combined Operations, with the rank of Commodore; but as the title was very shortly altered to "Chief" we shall call him that, or CCO, throughout. It was not until after the St. Nazaire operation had been put in train, and just before its execution, that Lord Louis was given his fullest powers and authority and that his organization was developed on the elaborate scale that was to characterize it.

The main purpose of Combined Operations at that time was to carry out raids along the long enemy coastline that stretched from the Pyrenees far away to North Cape in the Arctic Ocean. "One operation a fortnight" was the order that Mountbatten gave soon after his arrival. Sometimes these raids resulted from requests made from one of the Services, or even from a civil ministry, but more often they were of COHQ's own devising.

This interservice planning staff at COHQ was, by normal British standards, a very peculiar one, since it was to a large extent making plans to be carried out by forces not wholly at its disposal. When, as occurred in the St. Nazaire Raid, the enterprise required ships or forces outside CCO's own limited resources, the command of it passed to one or other of the Commanders-in-Chief of the Naval Commands—"our patrons," as Mountbatten called them. Being in command of the operation, the patron obviously had considerable license to amend the plan. The safeguard against any ruination of it was to be found in the Chiefs of Staff Committee, to whom Mountbatten could always refer for a ruling and whose ruling became an order.

The staff for all this busy hatching of plots at COHQ was headed by officers who at that time bore the somewhat pallid title of "Adviser" for each service. As Naval Adviser, and becoming chairman of the St. Nazaire committee, was Captain John Hughes-Hallett. His principal staff planning assistants were Commander David Luce, and Lieutenant-Commander A.N.F. de Costobadie.

The Military Adviser was Brigadier J. C. Haydon, DSO, OBE, an Irish Guardsman. He was Mountbatten's deputy. In addition, pending the return of Brigadier Robert Laycock from the Middle East, he commanded the Special Service Brigade, that formation of the twelve Commandos of which we shall soon be seeing a great deal. The "two hats" that he wore were thus useful on the St. Nazaire committee, for he knew very well the men who would have to attack the targets on shore and was responsible for their training. The Assistant Military Adviser was Lieutenant-Colonel D. W. Price, and in the St. Nazaire planning and preparation a leading part was also taken by Major R. D. Q. Henriques, Royal Artillery. Lean and tall, now a celebrated novelist and successful farmer, Robert Henriques contributed to the common effort a part that was at once imaginative and factual. He was Charles Haydon's brigade major in the Special Service Brigade and thus also personally knew the commandos who were to take part. The Air Adviser was Group Captain A. H. Willetts. All of these at their equivalent level worked entirely as an interservice team concerned with the common interest.

Despite this exemplary co-partnership at COHQ as a whole, these plans and preparations had to be obscured in a night of secrecy. The need to be on one's guard was ever present, and no man must be told more of any affair than he need know for his own part in it. To the staff of COHQ and to the commander appointed for an expedition, necessarily seeking cooperation on many hands, this need not to disclose one's purpose was only too often an obstruction and embarrassment. Only by persistence, or sometimes by craft, were some such difficulties overcome.

This, in broad outline, was the manner in which COHQ handled all these matters at that time; and of all the projects that they devised, none was bolder in conception, none was more heroic in execution and none appealed so much to the heart of Mountbatten himself as Operation Chariot.

3

A PLOT IS HATCHED

An abortive attempt to devise a means of attacking St. Nazaire had begun as early as August 10, 1941, when Admiral of the Fleet Sir Roger Keyes, of Zeebrugge fame, was head of Combined Operations, with the title of Director. On that date the Admiralty requested the Commander-in-Chief Plymouth (Admiral of the Fleet Sir Charles Forbes) to investigate the possibility of an operation, "in consultation with the DCO." Two objectives were suggested for destruction—the lock gates and the U-boats. Sir Charles was a distinguished officer of an old school, of a slight figure, concealing a very shrewd brain beneath a quiet manner, often sitting for a long time hunched up and silent at conferences and then suddenly shooting a penetrating question. He replied to the Admiralty inquiry with a long and highly critical appreciation. The dangerous shoal waters, the risk of detection and attack by superior forces on the long sea passage, the lack of suitable craft that could carry enough fuel for the round voyage, the difficulties of achieving surprise, which was essential—these and other points were emphasized.

Keyes commented shortly a few days later, suggesting the usual technique hitherto employed on commando raids, by which converted cross-Channel steamers (predecessors of the Landing Ships Infantry) proceeded to a point near the enemy coast and there launched the troops in small assault landing craft of the sort known as Eurekas. But the objection to this method, of course, was that it could scarcely avoid detection from the air or sea patrols, and thus would give the show away by its very characteristic appearance. Throughout this stage the operation was considered purely in terms of a commando exploit, all the demolitions to be carried out by troops landed from the assault craft.

14

Shortly afterwards Forbes reviewed the problem in another memorandum and a meeting was held at the Admiralty on September 19. Ways and means could not be found. The meeting was advised by Keyes's military representative that the commando force for the shore destructions alone would have to be at least three hundred strong, plus the demolition parties. No further positive action was taken and on October 29 the Chief of Staff at COHQ minuted: "C-in-C Plymouth has turned this down again." But a further minute of the same date adds, with a significance for our story which, as will appear before long, was almost prophetic:

"The only known change in circumstances since that estimate was made [19th September] is the availability of a lockgate destruction expert in the person of Captain Pritchard."

Even Mountbatten after his arrival at COHQ seems to have regarded the adventure as impracticable; and in November he asked Special Operations Executive if they could undertake the demolitions by means of their secret "cloak and dagger" agents. For SOE, however, though their study of it is reflected in a very long document, it was far too big a task.

There the embryo of this exploit lay, apparently inert and lifeless, but the great dock continued to weigh heavily in the calculations of the naval staff, vitally affecting the strategy of the Atlantic.

One day late in January, 1942 (apparently on the twenty-seventh), Mountbatten had luncheon with his friend Captain Charles Lambe, who was Deputy Director of Plans at the Admiralty and about to become Director. During the meal Lambe brought up the matter of St. Nazaire; he was a good deal worried by the problem and disappointed that the project had been turned down. Could Combined Operations examine it in a fresh and unconventional light?

It so happened that at Richmond Terrace on that same morning Hughes-Hallett had been "running my eye down the French coast" in the course of the search for targets, together with Dick de Costobadie. St. Nazaire, Bayonne and a smaller target had caught their attention as worth examining. What had appealed to Hughes-Hallett in St. Nazaire, he said, was "the flaw in the defenses that permitted vessels of light draft to approach over the mud flats at high water of extraordinary spring tides."

This Mountbatten heard when he returned from lunch-

ing with Lambe and summoned his staff. He sent also for the
half-forgotten file that had originated in August, but it could
not immediately be found, for someone was "sitting" on it.
To his staff he said, "I think this is worth going into again.
Let us get out something unconventional."

Thus what might have been approached as a mere raiding objective was now revealed to be an operation "intimately involved in high strategy." It was by far the most
important task that Combined Operations had yet tackled.
From its inception and ever afterwards Mountbatten, amid
all his other preoccupations, took the closest personal interest
in it, for its high purpose and its daring conception appealed
at once both to his imagination and to his strategical sense.
His eyes were wide open—more so than those of some other
men—to the multiple perils that threatened those who were
to carry it out. If he did not think of Balaclava, nonetheless
that wide, gunfringed mouth of the Loire only too obviously
resembled the jaws of death into which an amphibious Light
Brigade was to be ordered to charge. Paradoxically, however, he saw that not the least chance of success was, in his
own words, the very fact that to the enemy the exploit must
appears "absolutely impossible to undertake."

From then onward things moved with speed. Haydon,
Hughes-Hallett, Willetts and their subordinate staff officers
proceeded to a joint examination in detail. Technical specialists
were called in and of these the most important for our story
was Captain W. H. Pritchard, the Royal Engineers officer
already mentioned, whose consuming purpose was the destruction of dockyards. Casa Maury was asked if he had any intelligence material and replied:

"St. Nazaire! Yes—heaps!"

He produced a very fat file of exceptional value, collated
for the greater part from various sources when he had been
Intelligence Officer of 19 Group, Coastal Command, at
Plymouth. It contained not only air photographs and such
other material as one might expect, but also exact technical
information, photographs and detailed engineer drawings of
of the great Normandie Dock gates which were the very
kernel of the nut to be cracked. There were also complete
details and drawings, originating from our secret agents, of
the submarine pens. In addition to this paper information,
Casa Maury also produced a very fine model of the docks
constructed by the modeling section of the RAF Photographic
Reconnaissance Unit. This was to prove of incalculable value

not only to the planners but also to the commandos who, on that coming night in March, would have to move about the docks with even more confidence and certainly with more speed than those who worked in them daily.

In the study of this file and this model the planners' chief attention was directed early to the Normandie Dock.

They learned that, as we ourselves have already seen, the Normandie Dock was the largest structure of its kind in the world, serving as a lock when filled with water or as a dry dock for the repair of ships when empty. Begun by the French Government in 1928, it had taken four years to build, measured 1148 feet long by 164 feet wide and could accommodate a ship of more than 85,000 tons. It lay roughly north and south. To control the flow of water in or out of the dock there were at each end of it, north and south, two enormous sliding steel gates, measuring 167 feet long, 54 feet high and no less than 35 feet thick, each built in the form of a great sectional steel box with compartments that could be filled with water to any extent necessary to withstand various pressures. Lock gates of this description, which slide in and out rather than swing, are technically known as "caissons," and this term we shall adopt to distinguish them from other lock gates in this dockyard.

To move these massive portals, either for the passage of ships or for the emptying or filling of the dock, powerful gear was obviously necessary. The method of operation was to wind the great caissons laterally on rollers in or out of deep sockets, technically called "cambers," situated on the west side of the dock. Each of the two caissons was wound in and out of its camber by means of large twin wheels, which, with the motors that actuated them, were housed at the extremity of each camber. We shall refer to these small buildings as winding-houses.

When it was desired to use the Normandie Dock as a dry dock instead of as a lock, it was, of course, necessary to pump out all the water, and for this purpose there was a large pump house, with its motors at ground level but with its pumps, of massive strength, deep in a cavern some forty feet directly below; safe enough, one might have thought, even from a commando. This pump house and the two winding-houses were all on the west side of the Normandie Dock.

From air photographs in Casa Maury's intelligence file the planners also noted with satisfaction that the southern caisson, which was the one open to attack from the sea, was

not protécted by a boom, though an anti-torpedo net, suspended from its floats, hung like an underwater curtain some
fifty yards outside. Nor was there any barbed wire anywhere
to be seen. In the shallows of the estuary there was no evidence of any mines, "so," in Hughes-Hallett's words, "we
decided to assume that there were none."

The caisson was a most formidable nut to crack. It
might never have been possible to have planned the job with
complete confidence, in spite of the very detailed intelligence
file, if it had not been for one very fortunate circumstance.
It so happened, the committee were delighted to learn from
the encyclopedic Casa Maury, that the caissons of the Normandie Dock were of almost identical design and construction to that of the great King George V Dock at South-
hampton.* Thus it was not long before, in answer to an
urgent request, an engineer of the Southern Railway, who
were the owners of the King George V Dock, arrived within
the doors of COHQ, causing some little flutter because, in the
middle of a battledress London, he arrived silk-hatted and
morning-coated, en route to an investiture at Buckingham
Palace. The silk-hatted visitor, bearing plans and specifica-
tions, revealed all and offered his help for any technical calculations; if he made some shrewd guess that it was St.
Nazaire that the committee were interested in, and not the
"K.G.V.," he kept his thoughts to himself.

In addition to the Normandie Dock, the St. Nazaire
planners also looked at the great concrete submarine kennels
in the Submarine Basin, but these, so fabulously solid that
they could withstand a direct hit by the largest known bomb,
were a target that no small raiding force could hope to
destroy. The dock was the thing. However, if the waters of
the Submarine Basin could be made tidal, by destroying the
lock gates that controlled their flow, then the use of the U-
boat pens, it was hoped, would be considerably interfered
with. There were six of these gates—two on its eastern side
in the original, nineteenth-century entrance, called the Old
Entrance, and four more in the long channel of the new or
Southern Entrance of 1907 date, embraced within long,
clasping arms that stretched out into the waters of the Loire.

These, however, were by no means all the destructions
that would have to be tackled by a raiding force, for they

---

*It had been built by the Furness Shipbuilding Company after
study of the Normandie Dock with the Southern Railway engineers.

would also have to assault gun positions that threatened them and destroy all bridges by which the enemy could bring up forces for a counterattack. Another tempting target was seen in the underground oil fuel tanks that lay to the east of the Normandie Dock. Though the planners kept the Normandie Dock steadily before them as the main objective, the number of targets of all sorts that had to be attacked finally reached the formidable figure of twenty-four—eight lock gates, four bridges, six power installations and six gun positions (thirteen guns), apart from purely fighting tasks. We must bear these figures well in mind when we come to see what a tiny force was to be expected to do it.

This formidable program of havoc called for a highly detailed and technical plan of demolition by means of explosives and the planners were therefore fortunate to be able, at the very outset, to seize upon the young Royal Engineer officer whose "availability" the Chief of Staff had noted on October 29. Captain Pritchard, by a remarkable chain of circumstances which will be narrated later, had made a plan for these very tasks long before the strategic requirement had arisen.

With these and other helps the interservice planners formulated their preliminary proposals remarkably quickly. The means of carrying them were also soon agreed upon. A powerful force on conventional lines to fight its way through was neither available nor appropriate. The utmost economy of force was demanded. The planners therefore decided to attack the main target—the southern caisson—by what has aptly been called the "terrifying solution" of ramming it with an "explosive ship." By this was meant an old destroyer (no smaller ship would make sufficient impact) with her bows packed with high explosive, which should be detonated by a delayed-action fuse after she had been evacuated. The shore targets were to be destroyed by parties of commandos landed from the destroyer and carrying prepared charges according to a plan formulated in. its technical needs by Pritchard under Haydon's direction.

Whatever the targets were, and however they were to be attacked, the force had to be got there. The course to be followed at sea, the methods of avoiding enemy forces there and other related factors were not for COHQ to decide, but for C-in-C Plymouth, Sir Charles Forbes, who would automatically be "patron" of this enterprise if the Chiefs of Staff sanctioned it. Hughes-Hallett and his co-planners, how-

ever, looking speculatively at those dangerous, wide-open
jaws of the Loire estuary, saw at once that the deep-water
Charpentiers Channel, running under the very teeth of the
guns on the best bank, must be avoided, and that therefore
the craft to be employed must be able to negotiate the large
expanse of the only less dangerous shoal waters, which, even
at high tide, gave a maximum depth of water of only ten
feet.

Quite clearly, to escape destruction from the guns that
lined the jaws of the estuary and, still more, the massed dual-
purpose weapons assembled in its throat at St. Nazaire itself—
an analysis of which is given in Chapter 10 and the locations
of which may be seen in the map on pp., 102–103, 111—
some means of surprise or deception was an imperative requirement. Granted that the force escaped observation at sea,
how could it expect to sail through those last six miles of
highly sensitive and protected waters, past batteries of guns
and searchlights, ram the caisson and actually land its troops
unseen and unheard?

To carry out the whole operation, however, it was not
enough to have an unopposed approach. What hope was
there that the commandos, if landed, could penetrate several
hundred yards into a dockyard full of Germans and proceed
to blow up lock gates, bridges, guns and powerhouses under
their noses?

It had been remarked by several observers that an air
raid, or even the expectation of one, was apt to blind the
force attacked to anything that was happening on the ground.
This phenomenon had been observed by Mountbatten himself
at the bombardment of Cherbourg by HMS *Revenge,* when,
although no air raid was in progress, the Germans' searchlights remained directed upwards. "I know myself," he said
on this point, "what happens when explosions go off and
you don't know what's up. I am jolly sure that if there are a
lot of bangs going on the Germans will look up in the air and
won't think of the sea, when no reason at all exists to
imagine that an attack from the sea is likely."

Henriques also, going out into the streets during raids
on London, had found the same thing. "You could," he
said, "go into any house, commit any crime, do anything you
liked, and no one would take the slightest notice of you."

What was proposed, therefore, was that Bomber Command should be asked to support the operation by a raid
which should not only cover the approach of the ships up

the estuary of bombing the docks, but which should also be continued while the commandos were actually at their demolition tasks ashore, during which the bombing should be on the town instead of the docks. By this means, it was hoped, the enemy's guns and searchlights would be so occupied with engaging the aircraft overhead that both ships and men would be able to steal swiftly in unobserved. This bombing raid was, of course, an integral and essential part of the whole operation, as essential as the fire of its artillery is to infantry in the assault.

These critical factors demanded also a close study of the tides, the moon's phases, dates and times. The tide must be at high-water springs. The advantages of a moonlight night were preferred to those of a dark one. To these requirements of high tide with full moon were added the need to keep out of sight of land until night fall and to be away out of sight again on the following morning; and this meant that the attack could not take place much before midnight and must be over not much after 3:30 A.M. British Summer Time (which is the time used throughout this narrative). These conditions of a full tide and full moon at St. Nazaire between midnight and 2 A.M. were found to exist in the last week of March, the best date being the night of March 29 and 30. After that period, in view of the shortening nights, there would be no suitable opportunity until the autumn. There was not much time to lose.

On January 31, after "looking at the thing again," Mountbatten had instructed Hughes-Hallett, as chairman of the committee, to draft a plan. It was ready by February 6 and the next day Mountbatten sent a draft of it to the Vice-Chief of Naval Staff, Vice-Admiral H. R. Moore, and asked for his views. This was the plan:

A gutted and "expendable" destroyer of light draft, carrying a commando force, was to cut through the anti-torpedo net and ram the outer caisson. A large weight of explosives would be packed at the point of impact and the ship blown up by delayed-action fuses. Through the breach thus made a specially adapted motor-torpedo-boat—the very peculiar MTB 74, commanded by a cheerful young daredevil named Micky Wynn—was to pass and attack the inner, or northern, caisson of the lock. The troops in the expendable destroyer would meanwhile have landed and would proceed to destroy with explosives all lock gates leading into the Submarine Basin, with the intent of making it tidal. Bomber Command would be asked to engage the attention of the enemy's guns, search-lights and radar by a bombing operation to be begun before the expedition entered the estuary and to be maintained throughout the assault. Finally the commandos and the skele-ton crew of the expended destroyer would withdraw in a second destroyer, which would have followed up and proceed-ed alongside.

This was the core of the plan originally devised in this revival of the St. Nazaire enterprise. It was simple and audacious, counting on the achievement of surprise, on the resolute handling of ships and bold leadership of the troops to be landed. In retrospect one may say that it was certainly the best plan of all, but, paradoxically, it was the Admiralty itself which upset it, although its essential features of an ex-

M.T.B. 74

plosive destroyer and bombing support were stuck to tena-
ciously by the COHQ planner all through.

Returning from Scotland, where he had gone to watch
the final dress rehearsal for the invasion of Madagascar,
Mountbatten became immediately absorbed again in Chariot.
To his concern, he found that the Admiralty, having themselves asked for the job to be done as a matter of high strategic importance, were now showing the strongest reluctance
to providing the means. The naval staff, admittedly hard
pressed for ships in their innumerable tasks in the oceans of
the world, grudged the loss of even one for purposes to their
own benefit. The only suitable craft that they could suggest as
the explosive ship for ramming the caisson was the *Ouragan*,
belonging to the Free French.

As for the second destroyer, for the withdrawal of the
commandos and the crew of the first destroyer after the
demolition, that was quite out of the question.

This was the major topic of discussion at a critical
conference of the Chariot committee and Admiralty staff
officers on February 19 at which Mountbatten presided. Haydon having outlined the assault plan and Hughes-Hallett having explained the naval requirements, the meeting discussed
an amendment to the plan in which the second destroyer was
replaced by a flotilla of twelve motor launches; some of
which, if the *Ouragan* was used, would have to be French.

The employment of these little craft—the famous "Fairmiles" of "our light coastal forces"—was not much to the
liking of the Chariot planners, particularly to the naval members. Their small fuel capacity gave them a very limited range.
They were extremely vulnerable and inflammable, being built
of mahogany and run on petrol, so that if hit they were
liable, in the phrase of one young officer who took part, "to
go up like a box of matches." They were also highly vulnerable to aircraft, having nothing to fight them with but a light
"twin Lewis" machine gun of the previous war's vintage. For
surface action their only armament was an antique little
Hotchkiss three-pounder, of Boer War date, quite inadequate
against the shore batteries by which they must expect to be
engaged on the way out. When Hughes-Hallett observed,
"We may lose every man," Mountbatten replied thoughtfully,
with a slight movement of the shoulders:

"I'm afraid you're right, but if they do the job we've
got to accept that."

There seems, however, to have been no alternative, since

Combined Ops' own assault craft were out of the question. Two measures to improve the motor launches, however, were now proposed. To enable them to get to St. Nazaire and back, extra petrol tanks were to be fitted on deck (thus increasing their inflammability also). For armament, in order to give maximum defense against aircraft while the force was at sea, the Hotchkiss was to be sacrificed and replaced by two Oerlikon guns. These were light automatic-cannon firing a 20-mm., half-pound explosive bullet at 470 rounds a minute, capable of engaging air or surface targets, and it was calculated that the concentrated fire of twenty-four of them from twelve MLs would see off most aircraft.

The decision to employ these vulnerable motor launches meant that the plan for bomber support from the air became even more important. "It should," as the minutes of the meeting of February 19 record, "take the form of a really heavy bombing raid on the dock area, later moving to the town itself for the period troops area shore." The details of this bombing support had still to be worked out by Haydon and Willetts after the meeting, but we may note here that Bomber Command were asked to provide not less than three hundred and fifty aircraft. Observe carefully also, that at this stage—and until nearly the last minute—the bombing in the second phase was to be on the *town*.

Before the conference of February 19 closed, Hughes-Hallett was instructed to embody the decisions in a formal Outline Plan for submission to the Chiefs of Staff. This plan Mountbatten forwarded on February 24, and on February 25 the Chiefs of Staff gave their approval.

"This," said the First Sea Lord, Sir Dudley Pound, "is a most important operation—worth an army corps."

"You mean," Parried the quick-witted Sir Alan Brooke, "two battleships."

The Chiefs of Staff were not, however, in favor of the idea of using a Free French ship and Sir Dudley undertook to try to find a British one. The Prime Minister was also informed of the plan and was well pleased. The audacity of its conception and the calculated acceptance of known risks heartily appealed to him. The King also was informed and took the greatest interest in the operation.

So far, however, all was merely paper. Combined Ops could supply no more than the troops to carry out the shore demolitions; it could provide no expendable ship and no motor launches. Only the Navy could provide these and the men to man them. Their provision and the method of executing the plan, with the great volume of detail that that was to involve, would now become the concern of Sir Charles Forbes, with continued co-operation from COHQ.

Before C-in-C Plymouth came into the picture again, however, Hughes-Hallett began negotiation with the Admiralty for the necessary craft and officers, doing so verbally or by private note. Clearly it was important that the officer who was to command this daring exploit of high importance, this "enterprise of great pith and moment," should be appointed and briefed as soon as possible. Accordingly, almost immediately after the Chiefs of Staff had given approval, Hughes-Hallett telephoned Captain L. A. Ashmore, Naval Assistant to the Second Sea Lord who dealt with officers' appointments, and said:

"I want an able Commander for a special job. He must be a really first-class man."

4

ROBERT RYDER

Meanwhile, a frustrated young naval officer was sitting at the headquarters of Southern Command at Wilton House, near Salisbury, the ancestral home of the Earls of Pembroke. There he was Naval Liaison Officer on the staff of General the Hon. Sir Harold Alexander, his duties being to advise the Army on naval matters affecting the shore defenses against invasion.

This officer was Commander R. E. D. Ryder. He did not at all care for his tame shore appointment, to which he had been assigned after having lost a ship, thereby "incurring the displeasure of Their Lordships" of the Board of Admiralty. However, this time-honored pronouncement of official displeasure was seldom taken seriously by officers of spirit, and what bothered Ryder was simply the fact that he was not at sea.

Robert Ryder, whose initials led inevitably to his being called "Red," was then just thirty-four years old, below middle height, dark-haired, clean-featured, and of determined and forthright character. He had just married Hilaré Green-Wilkinson. At fifteen he had gone sailing with an elder brother in a converted Fleetwood fishing smack and thereafter sailing ships became the call and rule of his life. He joined the Navy by public school entry and grew up to be what a fellow-officer describes as "a man of calm and rocklike reliability, with immense reserves of courage and endurance."

In 1933, after three years in submarines, he spent his leave, together with four other officers, sailing from China to England the ketch *Tai Mo Shan*, built specially to their order at Hong Kong. He then, when only twenty-six, volunteered and was selected for command of the research yacht *Penola*, an auxiliary topsail schooner fitted out for a long expedition

27

to the Antarctic, led by John Rymill, the Australian explorer. For three years, from 1934 to 1937, Ryder was on this very hard service in the stormy waters and icy winds from Cape Horn to the South Pole, commanding a ship's company made up mostly of young men from the universities, with a bearded ex-Guards officer, the memorable James Martin, as boatswain. For this service Bob Ryder wears the rare ribbon of the Polar Medal.

At the end of this period of semi-independence, the Admiralty, in Ryder's own words, "thought it was high time I came back to naval discipline" and he found himself back again in big ships. The war found him serving in a Mediterranean flagship, "a service to which I was totally unsuited," and when he received a signal from Vice-Admiral Gordon Campbell, the famous Q-ship VC of the First War, asking if he would like to join him, he eagerly accepted, without knowing what was afoot.

Before long he was given command of one of the new Q-ships, a Cardiff tramp named *Willamette Valley*. In her, with guns concealed beneath dummy deck cargo, according to the practice of the First World War, he went out as bait for German submarines. But in the dark of a June night in 1940 he was suddenly attacked by two U-boats and sunk two hundred miles west of Ireland. Some twenty-five of the crew got away safely in a boat, but his old Guardsman-boatswain James Martin, who was serving with him again, was lost and Ryder himself was left in the sea clinging to one of the large wooden chocks that wedge ships' boats on deck. To this he clung for four days without food or water, steeped in oil and his life jacket perished by its action. A ship ironically named *Empire Courtesy* passed him by. After this feat of endurance, he was picked up, just alive, by a British tanker. He was taken below by a deck hand who, having put him in dry clothes, offered him some rum, which Ryder declined. Having drunk a good swig of it himself, the rascal inquired:

"What are you, mate? Fireman? Seaman?"

"No, master of a tramp ship," replied Ryder.

"Master! Blimey! Don't tell the Old Man about that rum, will you?"

There followed the command of the frigate *Fleetwood* for six months and promotion to commander before Ryder was appointed to command the *Prince Philippe*. This was a Belgian cross-Channel ship that had been fitted out at Penarth to carry infantry and their special landing craft for raids on the Norwegian coast. She had scarcely been commissioned and manned, however, before, in the summer of 1941, she was rammed in thick fog off the Firth of Clyde by the *Empire Wave* and sank. Then had followed the letter of "displeasure" and the months of tedium with the Army at Wilton House while the winter draggegd its course.

Then, one day in February, 1942, he received a surprise signal from the Admiralty ordering him to attend a conference at the headquarters of Combined Operations at three o'clock on the twenty-sixth. Wondering what it could all be about, he took a train to London.

5

"A TRUE SOLDIER APPEARETH"

An officer in another service, though more actively employed, was also fretting at prolonged frustration.

Lieutenant-Colonel A. C. Newman, a Territorial officer of the 4th Battalion the Essex Regiment of sixteen years' standing, was by normal profession a civil engineering contractor. Thirty-eight years old, he was married and had a small family. He was of middle height and solid build and his fair hair was beginning to retreat from his forehead. His face, of which his pipe was almost a permanent feature, was illumined by a lively intelligence and a quizzical good humor. He had a genial disposition and brought to the business of war, not a grim intensity, but the temperament of what Bridges has called a keen-hearted sportsman, "whose joy danceth on peril's edge." Few commanding officers can have enjoyed so much as Charles Newman the warm affection of all who served under him. His own affection towards them glows in his diary, where, at the start of the war, he writes of his "desire to soldier with one's friends, to have under one's command all these lads from Barking and East Ham and outer London whom we had trained; we knew all their families and loved them all."

Newman was at this time commanding No. 2 Commando, one of the twelve Commandos that constituted the Special Service Brigade, under Brigadier Charles Haydon, which had been raised specially from picked volunteers for the "offensive defense" that we have discussed. The unit had had its origin in No. 3 Independent Company, which Newman commanded as a major and which had been blooded in the brief campaign in Norway in the early days of 1940. In the autumn of that year the Independent Companies were absorbed into the new Special Service Battalions, within the Special Service

Brigade, which Haydon was appointed to command.

The Special Service Battalions, however, did not last long. Over one thousand strong, with fifty officers, they were too large and unwieldly. They were accordingly divided up into smaller units now officially designated "Commandos," though Haydon's headquarters, under whose command they remained, kept its title of Special Service Brigade. On March 5, 1941, 1 Battalion was split into 1 Commando and 2 Commando, Newman being promoted to lieutenant-colonel and appointed to command 2 Commando.

The command of a battalion or its equivalent is a moment in an officer's life which is at once critical, anxious and inspiring. Newman, like many others at such a moment, made a searching examination of himself and the objectives that he would set for his new command. These he embodied in what he called his "ideal" for the Commando unit, covering several sheets and set out in twenty-two points. It embraced complete efficiency in all the techniques of the soldier's trade, the special skills demanded of the commandos in cliff-climbing, the handling of boats, swimming in full battle order, moving across country by night with complete confidence, the use of explosives, and the attainment of that "extra scruple of endurance" that often makes the impossible possible. He would be ruthless in getting rid of any man not dedicated to the fighting spirit and eager to attack the enemy closely. Officers and men must be very close to each other, enjoying "mutual respect and friendship" and with "complete understanding and confidence in each other, so that men would follow their officers in complete faith." Otherwise the outward forms of soldierly discipline were strictly observed. Least of all was there any doubt at all about "spit and polish." Men were at all times expected to be correctly and smartly turned out, with webbing scrubbed and all brass parts polished.

The "Jocks," however, presented a special sartorial problem, for, although it was forbidden on operations and on exercises when concealment was important, the kilt was normally allowed to all ranks entitled to it. Needless to say, it was worn with *brio* in all its color variations of Argyll, Black Watch, Gordon, Cameron, Seaforth and others. These Highland troops together formed 5 Troop under Captain D. W. Roy, Cameron Highlanders, a young officer of great dash and *élan,* perhaps the most colorful figure in 2 Commando, tall, heavily mustached and known throughout it as "the Laird."

However, even this apparently orderly arrangement had
its serious problems, for in 5 Troop, not content with a common Scottism, the sparks of antique tribal rivalries were re-
kindled and old Highland fueds broke out into flames. Campbell and Gordon were at each other again.

Newman was very angry. He had the whole troop out
and told them that this sort of nonsense had got to stop. "You
must make up your minds," he said, "whether you are going
to fight each other or the Germans. If each other, back you
all go to your units tomorrow."

Donald Roy, very stiff, erect and troubled, said, "Colonel,
you can rely on us."

"I mean it, Donald. This sort of thing can't go on. I
shall RTU every man jack of you if you don't stop it."

"Returned to Unit" was the most dreaded phrase to
every man, for throughout the commandos virtually the only
punishment ever imposed was to return him to the unit
whence he had come.

Newman was extraordinarily fortunate in having a second-in-command who was in every way his complement in
personal qualities. Major W. O. Copland, a Territorial of the
South Lancashire Regiment, was works manager of a large
engineering firm in Warrington. A veteran of the First Great
War, he was forty-four years old, yet he stood up to the rigors
of commando training with complete equanimity. As hard as
the nails he manufactured and of incredible vitality, "Major
Bill" was quite fearless, unexcited by a crisis, inclined to be
be severe and had a most convincing presence.

About midsummer, 1941, Commando went off to Scotland, where they remained, training very strenuously in the
mountains and in the cold seas until, after several disappoint-
ments of raids promised and canceled, Hopper's troop and
half Birney's took part in the successful Vaagso raid in De-
cember.

A sudden call took Newman to London to get orders
for another operation, but the long journey was wasted, for
yet again the operation was no sooner planned than it was
canceled. He took his Commando off for stiff winter landing
exercises in the Outer Hebrides in HMS Prince Charles and
then back again to the normal location at Ayr in mid-Febru-
ary. He was beginning to be a little "browned off," but he
had no sooner set foot in Ayr than he was summoned by
Charles Haydon to a training conference at Irvine. The
conference over, he was told to stay behind and when they

were alone Haydon ordered him to take the train to London that very night and to meet him at COHQ the next morning.

More significantly, he gave orders for a hundred picked men from Newman's Commando to be specially trained in street fighting by night and for a squad to be sent to Burntisland, in the Firth of Forth, for a course in demolitions. "You must make it perfectly clear," he said, "that it is a case of 'No questions, no answers.'"

Speculation and excitement ran high in Newman's orderly room when he went back to Ayr to give the necessary orders for these details, but he himself was slightly cynical. On arrival in London, he took a room, by a quirk of chance, at the Normandie Hotel and soon afterwards made his way in the cold winter sunshine to COHQ. He found that Haydon had not yet arrived, but his pulse quickened as he listened to veiled remarks by the staff.

"Do you know what the job is?" asked one of them.

"I haven't a clue," Newman answered breezily.

Another said, "What a very, very lucky chap you are."

A third handed him a fat file and said, "Perhaps you would like to look through this, sir, while you are waiting."

It was the St. Nazaire intelligence file. While he was still wondering what it was all about, Haydon arrived and they went together into a private room, where Haydon broke the great news.

After outlining the plan he said, "The dock demolitions are to be carried out by combined demolition squads from the Brigade that Pritchard is to train at once. Your Commando is to provide the fighting troops for the operation and you are to be the Military Force Commander." He added. "This is by far the biggest job yet attempted by the Commandos."

Newman was electrified. "I was," he says, "filled with elation. Here was a goal as exciting as any man could wish for."

He was then firmly locked into a small room and there he gloated eagerly over the air photographs, the plans of the great caissons, the spottings of enemy defenses, the information from sercet sources and, above all, the beautiful little model of the docks made by the RAF, which he took wholly to his bosom till he had learned it by heart so well that he could have walked about the docks blindfolded and placed his slabs of explosive unerringly on the vital spots.

Then, with a smile of anticipation, he awaited the conference that had been called for February 26, when he was to meet his co-driver of this "chariot of fire."

6

THE LEADERS MEET

No such easy briefing was given to Robert Ryder.

We have seen him, chafing at Wilton House, receive a sudden signal to attend a conference at COHQ at three o'clock on February 26. Normally punctilious in being on time for any engagement, he arrived at Richmond Terrace fifteen minutes late through the aberrations of wartime transport. He moved quietly into the room to which he was conducted, took an obscure seat at the back and beheld to his surprise an imposing gathering of twenty or more senior officers of all three services, headed by an Admiral of the Fleet, in whom he recognized Sir Charles Forbes. He saw also Rear-Admiral A. J. Power, Assistant Chief of Naval Staff, Home Waters.

Mountbatten was in the chair. There was a model of some sort in front of him. He was outlining to the meeting some operation that was to take place clearly a raid on some port in which commando troops were to be landed for demolitions and aircraft were to drop bombs. Ryder listened with interest but with limited comprehension. What had all this to do with him?

Towards the end of his exposition of the plan, Mountbatten said tersely:

"The Naval Force Commander appointed for this operation is Commander R. E. D. Ryder." Then, looking up: "That all right with you, Ryder?"

To which the startled officer replied, "Certainly, sir."

Mountbatten asked, "Has this been mentioned to you yet?"

"No, sir," Ryder answered, "but I'm quite ready to take it on."

Mountbatten having finished his outline, Sir Charles

34

Forbes was invited to give his views. Before the meeting he had made it very clear to Mountbatten (very much his junior) that the operation still found no favor with him. He thought it extremely rash and likely to end in total loss. "It is not," he said with emphasis, "an operation of war. But as it's got to be done, we must make the best of it."

To the meeting he put two problems of particular concern. First of these was how to plot a route to St. Nazaire that would be free from German attack, especially air attack, but one which would not be too long. The second was the still intractable problem of the ship that was to ram the caisson, since the Chiefs of Staff were opposed to the use of the French *Ouragan* and since the Admiralty, in spite of Sir Dudley Pound's assurance to the Chiefs of Staff, still obstinately hung back from providing even the one essential explosive ship. Why not, it was now suggested, an old submarine? To this Hughes-Hallett immediately opposed critical objections: a submarine could not keep pace with motor launches, was a bad platform from which to land troops, might not be able to penetrate the anti-torpedo net and would not have sufficient impact on the caisson.

Nor was the explosive ship the only essential at which the Admiralty jibbed. It was even most improbable, Admiral Pound said, that any escorting destroyers could be found for protecting this very vulnerable force during its sea voyage; but he would see what could be done.

The meeting over, Haydon introduced to each other the two men who were to be so closely bound together in this exploit and upon whom all now centered—Ryder and Newman. It was a memorable meeting in their lives and a vital one for those whom they were to lead, for the fate of the expedition might well have depended on their relationship. As it was, the two men shook hands, sized each other up and were satisfied.

The moment they met, Newman subjected Ryder to a barrage of questions—how do you propose to do this and what do you think of that? But as soon as he could get in a word, Ryder himself asked:

"Look here, where the hell *is* this place we are supposed to attack?"

For throughout the time that Ryder had been present at the conference the object had not been mentioned.

Newman laughed. "Good heavens! Haven't they told you? It's St. Nazaire."

"Nobody's told me a damned thing. What are we supposed to do at St. Nazaire?"

"Blow up a lot of dock gates and so on. A really saucy job."

"Are you in on it already?"

"Rather, Brigadier Haydon has briefed me. Outline plan, big intelligence docket and a splendid model. Quite a plateful for both of us."

Ryder thought a minute, the immensity of his task beginning to dawn on him. Then: "God! Where do I start? I've no staff, no office, not even a clerk or typewriter."

This was to be one of Ryder's most vexing handicaps. Unlike Newman, who had a second-in-command, an adjutant and a small office staff, Ryder was a lone hand, with no status, no apparatus for executive action, and actually no authority to give orders to anyone, for he commanded no unit or formation.

There followed for both of them several weeks of desperately hard work, the days and nights spent in a whirligig of journeys, conferences, specialist consultations, arguments, long hours of hard thinking and the study of charts, plans, air photos and intelligence reports. There was only a month to go. Newman summoned his adjutant Stanley Day, to come up from Scotland to help with the multitudinous detail, and he sent to Copland, without revealing anything, special instructions on the types of training on which the picked men were to concentrate—night movement, street fighting, weapon training.

For several days the whole prospect was bedeviled by the Admiralty's stubborn objection to providing the explosive ship. Two days after the meeting Rear-Admiral H. E. Horan, who directed Combined Ops' Landing Craft and Bases, told them on Mountbatten's behalf that a submarine really would not do and that if no suitable surface craft could be definitely allocated within two days, the CCO "intended to plan the operation with the use of coastal craft [motor launches] alone."

The destroyer was provided at last. Mountbatten would have fought it out through the Chiefs of Staff, but he had to leave London and in his absence a telephoned signal was made on his behalf to Admiralty that, unless a destroyer were provided, the operation would be canceled as far as Combined Operations were concerned. Time was desperately short and thus the matter was brought to a head. In fact, the Chariot committee knew privately that a destroyer had already been earmarked should the issue be forced. This was HMS *Campbeltown,* formerly the American destroyer *Buchanan* ("old Buck" to those who had sailed in her under that flag), one of those fifty ex-U.S.A. obsolete four-funneled ships for which, in a time of dire need, we had bartered away to the Americans the use of certain of our Caribbean ports for a hundred years.

There is one final and important COHQ conference at which we must look in before we leave London to see the plan—still far from complete in its details—being translated into action. This was on March 3. Ryder and Newman—the latter unaccountably very nervous—explained their own plans for carrying out their tasks. But by far the most important matter discussed was the air plan. Significantly a representative of the Director of Plans, Air Ministry, was present (Wing Commander J. M. Tomes), but a certain amount of unease was experienced by many, especially by Newman. It was becoming clearer that Bomber Command was not as keen as had been hoped. The aircraft that they were prepared to offer rapidly dwindled under the stresses imposed on their own program of operations. For the time being, the plan held that the bombing attack should be directed to the docks until just before *Campbeltown* rammed and should then switch to the *town.*

Newman particularly asked that some low-flying aircraft be put in at the critical period of fifteen minutes before zero (as it was then called) until fifteen minutes afterwards. "After all," he said, "*we* are going in pretty low." But he received an arid answer. It was perhaps after this meeting that he said to Robert Henriques, and was to say again later:

"I don't believe this bombing will come off."

Paper now began to be translated into action. There was a mountain of work to be done in very little time. The resourceful Intelligence machine produced nimble answers to the many problems of detail that still bothered Newman in particular. Most insistent of the tasks were the drastic modifications to *Campbeltown,* whose strange metamorphosis from a "four-stacker" American to a bogus German we shall shortly witness. Quantities of stores had to be collected under the veil of secrecy. Naval stores officers could be given no reason or "authority" why extra petrol tanks should be sent to

Poole and Appledore, nor why the country had to be scoured
for the scarce Oerlikon ammunition. No one must be told
why special explosives of curious shape and sizes were demanded. Specialists must not know the purposes for which
their brains were being picked. Doubts had to be referred to
many and sometimes peculiar consultants—such as the
gentleman at the Admiralty with the Canute-like title of
Superintendent of Tides, the officer at the War Office known
even more mysteriously as the Controller of Deception, the
Inter-Services Security Board, Home Office experts on the
killing range of explosive blasts (lest our own men ashore
should suffer when *Campbeltown* blew up), the Director of
Signals for secret information on German naval signal systems,
and so on.

On March 10 *Campbeltown* arrived at Devonport Dockyard, where her conversion was to be carried out, and on that
day Ryder and Newman attended a conference at Fort Egg
Buckland, Forbes's headquarters nearby, with Sir Charles himself in the chair. Chariot was now under his command and
he gave to its problems all his experience and the services of
an able staff.

But a figure even more significant to the grand design
was also met at this conference. Lieutenant N. T. B. Tibbits
was a product of that establishment which the Royal Navy
calls HMS *Vernon*, where they study not only torpedoes but
also other forms of explosive destruction. He had been hand-
picked as the specialist officer to devise the means of blowing
up the *Campbeltown* after she had rammed the caisson, and
it was the greatest good fortune for the expedition, if not for
the officer himself, that he should have been selected. Nigel
Tibbits was twenty-eight years old, of middle height, fair,
with a long, intelligent face and a slow smile. The son of an
admiral Robert Roxborough prizeman cadet, winner of five
firsts in the sub-lieutenant examination, Ogilvie medalist in
torpedo gunnery, he had also a "passionate interest" in mathe-
matics, the higher abstractions of which he would discuss with
verve and gusto and often with great bursts of laughter. His
intellectual grasp of things was instantaneous and sure.
Through all the searching tests that Ryder, so meticulous in
detail, was to put him, he was found to have an easy mastery
of technical detail and a resourceful answer to any problem.
He was one of several who on the eve of this exploit was to
have that queer premonition of death that men sometimes do
before battle.

Ryder had now thankfully finished with London, and he presently repaired to Falmouth, where, it had been decided at the COHQ conference of February 26, the combined force should assemble. "The only way," said Ryder, "to get anything out of the Admiralty is to get as far away from them as possible and make signals." Newman, however, had to go back there for a while. He sent Stanley Day off to Ayr to rejoin the Commando and said with it to Falmouth in the *Princess Joséphine Charlotte,* one of the "carrying ships" for commando landing craft. Then he, too, quitted London by car, but before doing so had an interview with Mountbatten which Newman was always to remember. They met on the steps of Richmond Terrace as Newman was about to walk down to his car and Mountbatten called him back. Lord Louis was always very forthright.

"I want you to be quite clear," he said, "that this is not just an ordinary raid; it is an important operation of war."

Nothing could have enchanted Newman more. Mountbatten went on:

"It is also a very hazardous operation. I am quite confident that you will get in and do the job all right, but, frankly, I don't expect any of you to get out again.

"If we lose you all, you will be about equivalent to the loss of one merchant ship; but your success will save many merchant ships. We have got to look at the thing in those terms."

Deeply impressed, Newman listened on.

"For that reason, I don't want you to take anyone on the operation who has any serious home ties or worries. No married men. Tell all your men that quite openly, and give every man the opportunity of standing down if he feels he should. Nobody will think any the worse of him and we must have that quite clear, too."

Newman promised soberly to obey, but he knew without the least scruple of doubt what the answer would be. No doubt Lord Louis did also.

Noting ironically that it was Friday, the thirteenth, Newman drove off to Falmouth.

7

THE DESTROYERS

While Newman, Ryder and the staffs of COHQ and Plymouth were working hard at their plans and preparations, the officers and men of eight Commandos were preparing themselves for their adventure. In Ayrshire the hundred picked men of 2 Commando, knowing nothing yet of what lay ahead, were training intensively under Copland, especially on the craft of street fighting by night. This was but a continuance of the sort of work they had long been practicing, but over on Burntisland, in the Firth of Forth, a very special form of training was going on.

On orders issued from Haydon's Special Service Brigade headquarters at Castle Douglas, seven Commandos, in addition to Newman's, had sent to Burntisland small, selected parties of officers and men for specialized study and practice in the destruction of dockyards. These were 1, 3, 4, 5, 6, 9, and 12 Commandos. To all of them, about ninety in number, it was just a "course" in another type of task that commandos might be called upon to do.

The guide and tutor of these men was perhaps himself the most remarkable of them all, and one to whose memory there is owing a tribute too long unpaid. Captain W. H. Pritchard was a Territorial officer of the Royal Engineers, aged twenty-eight. He was tall, strongly built, dark-haired, dark-complexioned, with brown eyes. He had great charm of manner and, in the words of Bob Montgomery, who knew him intimately, had "a wonderful smile and mischievous eyes." This Celtic fire and charm broke through the surface on the least occasion; to quote Montgomery again, he was both a romantic and a fanatic, born a hundred and fifty years too late.

Bill Pritchard was the son of Captain W. E. Pritchard,

MBE, Dock Master of Cardiff. He had thus not only been brought up in docks but also, on apprenticeship to the engineering branch of the Great Western Railway, had spent five years in their dockyards. In September 1939, he had gone to France with the British Expeditionary Force and had won the Military Cross for the demolition of a bridge under fire during the withdrawal to Dunkirk. It was the Dunkirk evacuation that first filled him with enthusiasm for dock demolition. "Why the hell," he asked, "didn't we blow up all the Channel dock before we left them to the Hun?"

On return home Pritchard was posted as an instructor to Aldershot and there met, as a fellow instructor, Captain R. K. Montgomery, young Regular officer of the Royal Engineers, who became his fast friend and disciple—indeed, his hero-worshiper. When home on leave in Cardiff Pritchard witnessed a heavy air raid on the docks, and became more than ever a fanatic for dock destruction by engineer methods. He said to Montgomery on return to Aldershot:

"You'll never destroy docks by bombing. It's a complete waste of time. You make a lot of big holes and create a nuisance but you don't stop the dock from working. The only certain way is to send chaps in and place explosives right on the vital parts."

Thus we very soon find him going to the Transportation branch (which is a Royal Engineer branch dealing with docks, canals, railways, etc., not motor transport) at the War Office, and, junior though he was, getting himself listened to. What he put up to them and what they were interested in, was the destruction of our own docks in the event of invasion. He was told to study the problem and began to do so in company with Montgomery. He was given the plans of a dockyard which, by one of those dramatic coincidences that seem too unlikely for an authentic narrative, were the plans of St. Nazaire itself. By a further coincidence Montgomery had himself been at St. Nazaire immediately before the British evacuation. On these plans the two officers worked night after night before at last they put up their demolition proposals to Transportation. It is of particular interest that they proposed the use of two destroyers, though all the demolitions were to be carried ut by troops lands from them.

In 1941 the two friends were separated, Pritchard being posted to a Transportation unit in London, Montgomery to 3rd Division. Later Pritchard trained a party of twenty-six Royal Engineer NCOs for three months in dock demolitions and an association with COHQ began. Late in January, 1942, he was posted to a unit in Leith, but was intercepted en route and told to report to COHQ at once. A day or two afterwards he telephoned his friend Bob Montgomery and said:

"It's on. Would you like to come?"

Thus, having "prised himself loose" from 3rd Division, Montgomery returned to help his friend in the study of a problem with which both were already familiar. Under Haydon's direction, Pritchard had already completed a plan setting out the weight and shape of plastic explosive for each target, the precise spot on which each was to be placed, the number of men required for each, the manner in which they were to carry it out and the detailed load for each. To a large extent, he was merely putting into effect the plans already put up to Transporation after cautious consultation with technical specialists. The explosives, "tailored" for each job, were made up by Major David Wyatt at the Stevenage SOE depot, each charge "boosted" with a dry guncotton primer and wrapped separately in waterproof sheeting, with detonating cord sticking out for quick attachment to the firing system.

Many of these charges were of a like nature, such as those for blowing up the several hinged lock gates and the dockyard bridges, by the destruction of which the commandos would seal themselves off against counterattack from beyond the Submarine Basin. Others were of different and special natures, such as those for the big impeller pumps in the pump house. For the destruction of guns, "sausage" charges were to be fixed round the barrel. Similar charges were to be wrapped round the pipes of machinery, blowing inwards. There were magnetic "clams" for attacking ships and small "limpets," also magnetic, for blowing open doors; and for motors in powerhouses there were charges that lifted the machinery off its bed.

For major tasks several charges were required to be linked together in one firing system, comprised of a length of the instantaneous and waterproof detonating fuse known as "cordtex," a detonator, a short length of the slow-burning "safety fuse" and a hand igniter. A length of the cordtex was attached direct to each charge and each length secured by a clove hitch to a "ring main," also of cordtex, so that all charges went off simultaneously.

For the two big caissons, a very special charge, known as a "wreath," had been devised. This resembled not so much a wreath as the steering wheel of a car, on the spokes of which magnets were fixed, so that the wreath would cling to the internal perpendicular face of the caisson and blow a hole in it. There were twelve wreaths for the interior faces of each wall of both caissons and others were to blow holes in the internal decks or floors. Thus the wreaths required descent into the inside of the structure. For the wet, outer surfaces (both walls of both caissons would be wet if the dock were filled), twelve eighteen-pound charges, looking in their waterproof wrappings like large plum puddings, were to be suspended twenty-seven feet below water.

All these charges were connected to a ring main of cordtex, so that the whole formed one firing circuit. The ring main was laid out by one man, while the others fixed the wreaths and lowered the underwater charges by lengths of ordinary cord, secured these cords and then connected all the cordtex fuse leads of the charges, which were always doubled, to the cordtex ring main. Quite obviously, this was a complicated and tricky job. There was well over a thousand feet of fuse and cord to handle; and to put all this correctly into position under fire without becoming hopelessly entangled needed not only a practiced and a steady hand, but also unshakable determination.

Remember that the farther, or northern, caisson was positively designated as a commando task, but also that the commandos had to be prepared to attack the more important outer caisson, should *Campbeltown* not succeed or should the caisson be found to have been withdrawn into its camber. These two tasks were in due course to be assigned to teams from Harrison's 12 Commando, largely from Northern Ireland, and Sanguinetti's 5 Commando, who were mainly Regulars and reservists from the Dunkirk divisions.

The orders for their special training having been issued by Brigade headquarters, Pritchard went to Burntisland for the "course" and there walked his students round the bleak Rosyth dockyard.

Under his tutorship they became immediately enthralled, for he had, said one of them, Ronald Swayne, "a great gift of commanding men and getting them to do just what he wanted." Nearly all were subaltern officers or NCOs.

Without doubt the most remarkable of them all was Tom Durrant, a Regular sergeant of the Royal Engineers, who acted as sergeant-major and who was destined to win in death the only Victoria Cross ever awarded to a soldier in a naval engagement.

Like Swayne, Durrant came from Glendinning's 1 Commando and he was, Swayne tells us, "without doubt the most loyal and efficient NCO I ever encountered." Aged twenty-three, Tom Durrant was of average height, well set-up, well-knit, strong, as dark as a gypsy, with a thin line of mustache. He had a granitelike determination, was himself a very fine technician and was steeped in that high code of soldierly integrity and devotion which is the hallmark of his Corps. But he had also a strong strain of independence and self-reliance and when his opinion was asked by an officer answered like an equal. Again in Swayne's words, he was "a formidable character and was treated carefully by all ranks, yet his charm and good humor were evident to everyone in his infectious smile." Durrant, who came from the village of Green Street Green, in Kent, had been a butcher's boy and a builder's laborer before enlisting in the Royal Engineers on February 1, 1937.

The training was quickly mastered and the pace accelerated. The young destroyers learned the difference between a caisson and the type of double lock gates that fold or swing back on hinges, they studied the machinery for opening and closing them, examined steel bridges and power stations. Using plasticene for practice purposes, they learned how to mold the new plastic charges to the most vulnerable part of any equipment, choosing, wherever possible, a metal casting as the point of attack, since castings were irreparable (the castings of the big impeller pumps below ground at St. Nazaire being irreplaceable in less than a year), and choosing, on all targets that were identical, the same point of attack, so that subsequently the enemy should be unable to interchange parts. They learned the simple lighting by fusee of slow-burning "safety fuse," which looks like a length of cord and burns at two feet per minute, and then firing by a percussion igniter by pulling out a pin to strike a spark. Gaining confidence and dexterity in the handling of all this dangerous material, they were taught how the safety fuse, when ignited by fusee or percussion igniter, burned for its set distance till it set off the small, tubular No. 27 compound-explosive detonator into which it was crimped, thus initiating a detonating wave through the instantaneous cordtex and thereby blowing the main charge.

Thence they went on to learn that, for any major task, everything must be duplicated—two cordtex leads for each charge, two initiating points for firing the charge, two directions of impulse through the ring main, provided by means of a cordtex switch across the loop. Thus, whichever initiating point fired first, and whichever way the detonating wave went, the plastic charges would go up. Destruction by fire with "tar babies," "firepots" and petrol ampoules also had its part; and for delicate machinery sledge hammers and axes, duly insulated against electric shock, were adequate.

At the end of February the demolition course split into two parties, one going under Pritchard to his home ground at Cardiff and the other to the shattered docks of Southampton, where Montgomery had gone soon after joining, to meet Mr. M. J. McHaffie, the Docks Engineer, and to study the King George V Dock.* Although the guise of normal training was maintained, various security precautions were taken, such as the removal of Commando shoulder flashes, and when some pompous official at Cardiff inquired what right they had to obstruct roadways with their queer and apparently senseless bits of string, they quietly folded up their gear and melted away. Dockers and other onlookers gazed indulgently at the silly soldier games as, hour after hour, officers and men played with funny brown paper parcels, handled with care and precision, all tied together with long coils of wet string.

The object was to train each man to complete nearly every demolition in the dark in under ten minutes. Each task was reduced to a drill for a set party and in all exercises men were dropped as casualties as they ran up to their objectives, so that, if necessary, one man could do at least the most vital part of the whole task. They learned the drill first by day, then carried it out blindfolded and finally by night. The sheer physical effort required for these performances may be judged by the fact that the average load of the explosives, carried in rucksacks by officers and men alike, was sixty pounds per man, and in some cases as much as ninety pounds. This heavy encumbrance meant that none of them could carry any arms except a Colt automatic pistol as a personal weapon, and strongly armed protection squads were therefore to be provided by 2 Commando to cover them as they worked.

After about a week the Cardiff and Southampton parties changed round, so that all should be familiar with every task. The time came when Pritchard was able to report by telephone to Newman that all parties were now thoroughly competent to do their tasks in less than the time allotted, in

---

*The plans signed for by Montgomery are still there.

complete darkness and under the full adversity of casualties. Accordingly the two parties assembled at Cardiff on March 12 and thence journeyed to Falmouth to meet their comrades of the fighting parties from No. 2 Commando newly arrived in HMS *Princesse Joséphine Charlotte*.

8

THE GATHERING OF THE FORCES

By March 13, in a spell of warm spring sunshine, nearly all the elements of the mixed naval and military force had assembled at Falmouth, ignorant of what was afoot and ignorant even that they had anything to do with one another. In the old-fashioned, unwarlike *Princesse Joséphine Charlotte,* which we shall abbreviate, as the troops did, to *P.J.C.,* speculation was inevitably afoot among the soldiers, but as they gazed over the rails and saw the trim motor launches with their flared bows and workmanlike cut gliding over the quiet, sunlit waters of the harbor, they took small notice. That was not the kind of chariot by which the commandos were accustomed to being carried into battle. For the first few days the *P.J.C.* stayed berthed at the quayside, while quantities of stores poured in by every train, and then she moved out and anchored in the Sound, well isolated from the shore.

The MLs, for their part, were equally unsuspecting. The modifications which they had just undergone in the form of extra petrol tanks and Oerlikon guns fore and aft suggested nothing more than some mission that required extended cruising. They sailed quietly in, enjoying the fair weather and the mellow sun, moored or berthed and awaited the call for orders. Red Ryder, a pile of burdens on his shoulders, settled himself in the conservatory of "Tregwynt,"* which was the Falmouth Naval Headquarters, and was provided with a chart table and the bare necessities of an office, and here he collected together as best he could all the secret gear that must not yet be disclosed—the German ensigns, the special explosives, the charts, the intelligence material and much else. He had not only to complete his own detailed orders, much

---

*Together with "The Haven," now the Membley Hall Hotel.

of which depended on decisions still to be made by the C-in-C, but also he had, in scarcely more than a fortnight, to mold into an expeditionary force the mixed assemblage of craft and men that had been allotted to him.

The little force had swollen considerably from the early conception of one destroyer and eight motor launches. A "Combined Operation Order," finally formulated on March 16, had been worked out by Mountbatten's and Forbes's staffs jointly. One result was that the force was to be considerably strengthened and improved by the additions of two Hunt class destroyers as escorts while at sea and of a motor gunboat as a small "headquarters" ship for Ryder and Newman. Four more motor launches had been added to accommodate the additional soldiers who were needed for the formidable list of harbor demolitions; and now, after arrival at Falmouth, a further four were provided by Forbes at Ryder's special request. No provision had been made in the COHQ plan for offensive craft to deal with unexpected emergencies or any chance encounter with enemy patrols, guard ships or "examination vessels" such as are to be expected at the approach to a defended harbor. Forbes therefore fortified him with four motor launches equipped with 18-inch torpedoes, but time did not allow the mounting of Oerlikons and they therefore retained their antique Hotchkiss three-pounders. Thus there were now sixteen motor launches in the expedition, plus others we shall notice presently.

These motor launches were "B" class Fairmile boats provided from three Motor Launch Flotillas of Coastal Forces— the 7th, which provided the four torpedo craft, and the 20th and 28th. They came from that service whose little ships kept a coastwise watch off the shores of Britain, maids of all work on the sea's fringe, fighting fierce little battles with the en-

Class B Fairmile

emy's small craft in the narrow waters, protecting merchant convoys, hunting submarines and rescuing from death the crews of wrecked aircraft. Though very handy and seaworthy, their hulls were built of two thin skins of mahogany, with a lining of calico between, so that they would not resist even a rifle bullet, though some light plating round the bridge and a few coir-filled splinter-mats were provided.

Measuring 112 feet by 19 feet 6 inches, these little boats were powered by two 650-h.p. Hall-Scott petrol engines, giving them a maximum speed of eighteen knots. From the well-equipped little bridge the captain, usually a lieutenant, passed his helm and engine orders by voice pipe to the small wheel-house, a few steps down and forward of the bridge, where the coxswain stood at the wheel, and where also were to be found the engine-room telegraphs, which rang down to the engine room the speed ordered from the bridge, the two engine revolution counters and the control for actuating the Foamite fire extinguishers below deck. The boats of 20 and 28 Flotillas were fitted with an additional wheel on the bridge.

The wheel itself actuated a Lockheed hydraulic steering gear, which we shall see being put out of action again and again as shells or splinters smashed its oil-filled pipes. When this occurred, the only manner of steering was by hand—a very exposed and dangerous performance not to be attempted by the chicken-hearted. For this purpose an iron tiller had to be fitted onto the rubbed head on the open deck, and the helmsman, standing completely unprotected, then actuated the tiller by hand on orders shouted back from the bridge.

Besides their new Oerlikons, the "B" class Fairmiles were armed also, as we have briefly mentioned earlier, with a "twin Lewis" light machine gun of the previous war's vintage, intended primarily to be used against low-flying aircraft and sited amidships. In the wings of the bridge there were "stripped Lewis" guns, fired from the hand as in infantry work. They were equipped also with depth charges for use against submarines and with a projector for tossing hand grenades at aircraft. They had wireless, of course, as well as signaling lamps and flags, but no radar.

Normally manned by two officers and ten ratings, their complement was increased for the St. Nazaire operation and, in addition, each of the troop-carrying boats took about fifteen commandos, so that the total of all hands on board amounted to about thirty. They were then very crowded and the upper deck was much encumbered by the extra 500-gallon petrol tanks and the Oerlikons. The deck tanks also sharply increased the boats' already high inflammability, in spite of being covered in self sealing material of crêpe rubber laminations, and Ryder accordingly ordered that these tanks were to be used up first and then filled with sea water through the fire hoses. He also ordered that, in order to make room for the after Oerlikon, every motor launch was to land its dinghy.

All motor launches, and similar Coast Forces craft, were designated by a Navy List number, but, as these numbers are liable to confuse the reader, we shall identify them instead by the names of their commanding officers or by the simple tactical numbers by which they were designated in their cruising order; thus Stephens's boat was ML 192, but for our purposes it will be No. 1. A record of their Navy List numbers is given in Figure 2, page 99.

Such were the little ships that assembled under Ryder's command at Falmouth in that sunlit March. He very soon discovered, however, that an unexpected difficulty faced him. For none of these craft had ever before maneuvered together in large formations. "I realized at once," said Ryder, "that it would be a great mistake to underestimate the difficulties of handling this untrained and heterogeneous force. Their weakness in signaling and their inexperience in maintaining contact at night had somehow to be remedied, and remedied in a fortnight. So I determined to work them as hard as I could in that woefully short time."

But of one thing Ryder, unlike Wellington, could not complain—the quality of the human material allotted to him. Himself a lover of small ships, he took an instant liking to these young men of Coastal Forces and found, he said, "their attitude most refreshing." There was nothing stuffy or conventional about them. Unlike the commandos, the officers and ratings of the motor launches and of all the naval force were not volunteers or picked men. They were simply the augmented crews of the craft on everyday Coastal Forces duties. Yet, if there had been a selection board, it would have been difficult to have found a gathering of young men more excellently suited. Nearly all of them were "hostilities only" officers and ratings of the Royal Naval Volunteer Reserve—a force ideally suited to the companionable service of small ships.

Such were the motor launches destined for St. Nazaire and such the men in them. To these were added two other small motor craft of peculiar interest.

The first, arriving at Falmouth on March 14, was that very peculiar and temperamental little craft which was included in the very first plan of all made by the Chariot committee. This was MTB 74, commanded by Sub-Lieutenant R. C. M. V. Wynn—Micky Wynn to most people and Popeye Wynn to his intimates. "Mad as a hatter," Casa Maury had said when he brought him to the notice of Hughes-Hallett, "but he has a very useful toy."

Wynn, a young Welshman of Merionethshire, was a complete individualist. He had been a Regular officer in a cavalry regiment, but found that the Army was not his avocation and he had quitted it early in the war and signed on as a deck hand in a civilian motor boat for the Dunkirk evacuation before joining the Navy. He was not at first much liked by the commandos, a few of whom had met him before at Dartmouth, because of his derogatory remarks about "pongos," but that all changed later. He was equally disparaging about admirals.

Wynn was fair-haired and stockily built, with a face in which you could easily trace the lineaments of a quiet stubbornness. Withal he had a quick eye for a pretty face—even a German one, which he was to find much to his cost when, having successfully escaped from prison in Germany, the hailing signal customary on such encounters was intercepted by the fräulein's boy friend.

Wynn's first lieutenant, and his "dear and personal friend," was Arthur O'Connor, a New Zealander. Their "toy," MTB 74, was a small Vosper-built motor boat, which, as the outcome of a wild suggestion by Wynn after a hilarious guest night, had been specially modified for a clandestine attack upon the *Scharnhorst* in Brest harbor. For this purpose the torpedo tubes had been dismounted from their customary positions in the boat's hull amidships and mounted on top of the fo'c'sle, the intent being that the torpedoes, gutted of their engines, stuffed with 2,200 lb. of explosive and fired at extremely close range, would jump over the anti-torpedo net with which the battle-cruiser was surrounded, sink to the bottom and go off on a time fuse. Clearly a "suicide job."

When *Scharnhorst* had escaped from Brest early in February, the disconsolate Wynn appeared to be out of a job. However, the Chariot committee at COHQ saw in him a very useful desperado for some task of destruction. After several suggestions, these tasks were finally determined in Forbes's Operation Order of March 23; if the outer caisson were found to be open, the MTB was to enter the lock and attack the inner caisson, or, if she were able to pass through the Old Entrance, she was to fire her delay torpedoes at the U-boat kennels.

These, however, were not the only peculiarities of Wynn's Weapons," as the MTB became known among the Charioteers. Smaller even than an ML, she was of doubtful seaworthiness in rough weather. She had no fewer than five engines, but they were so temperamental that a defect in any one of them communicated itself to all the other four, like measles among children. For some very mysterious reason, she was incapable of any speed in between a sluggish six knots and a furious thirty-three, so that, when sailing in company with other craft, she had to keep leapfrogging and waiting. Moreover, she consumed vast quantities of petrol, so that she had a very short range, and, if taken on Chariot, would have to be towed most of the way.

Small wonder, therefore, that when Ryder was offered this odd craft he gave it a cold welcome. When he learned of a serious engine defect a few days before sailing, he gave a decisive "No." Undefeated, Wynn, entirely off his own bat, and against official resistance, obtained a new engine just in the nick of time; under the guidance of Chief Motor Mechanic Lovegrove, with only improvised lifting gear, the little crew worked all the last night to install it and, a few hours before the expedition was due to sail, Wynn reported to Ryder:

"Ready for sea, sir."

Much more orthodox in character, but in fact much more important to our story, was the second of the two special craft added to the force. McCrum, of Sir Charles Forbes's staff, had seen that some sort of "headquarters ship" would be essential for Ryder and Newman and the C-in-C therefore provided them, at the last minute, with MGB 314. From this memorable little ship we shall see a great deal of the battle.

MGB 314, which belonged to the 14th MGB Flotilla, was a "C" class Fairmile motor launch, differing a good deal from the B class. Two feet smaller both in length and beam, she was powered by three 850-h.p. supercharged Hall-Scott engines, giving her a maximum speed of twenty-six knots. She had a long and rather deep keel, three screws and twin rudders, with a poor turning circle. Her hull was built of two skins of thin mahogany, like those of the "B" class, but was of "hard chine" design, so that she rolled with an irregular

rhythm and the sea slapped noisily against her angular but
graceful hull. Her engines and petrol tanks took up so much
space that accommodation was very cramped and uncom-
fortable and permeated by the condensation from human
bodies. The ship's company got so used to their food being
flavored with paraffin, which was the sole means of cooking,
that they complained when the flavor was lacking. Bridge and
wheelhouse were arranged in much the same manner as in
the B class, but in the 14th Flotilla it was customary to steer
from the bridge and not from the wheelhouse. The three engine-room telegraphs were also on the bridge, usually operated
by the captain himself, who stood to port.

As one might expect from her designation, the gunboat
was quite strongly armed for a small craft. Forward she carried a two-pounder hand-operated Vickers pom-pom, very
exposed and prominent, capable of firing about a hundred
and twenty rounds a minute. Aft there was another two-
pounder, this time a Rolls semi-automatic, and amidships two
twin power-operated heavy machine guns of half-inch caliber,
but these and the Rolls were to be out of action for the whole
battle.

What made the gunboat particularly suitable as a headquarters ship was that she was also equipped with a radar set
and an echo-sounder. She was thus well-fitted to lead a force
of small ships over the shallows of the estuary, the echo-
sounder telling her the depth of water underfoot among the
dangerous shoals and the radar giving warning in the dark of
the proximity of enemy vessels or other objects, though the
radar proved of little value, for it was a primitive type fixed
fore and aft.

With all these advantages of speed, armament and navigational aids, however, the gunboat, like Wynn's MBT, suffered from a very short radius of action. By some adroit
quick thinking, extra petrol tanks were secured on the very
eve of departure, but she would nevertheless have to be towed
if taken on the expedition.

For the great raid the crew of the gunboat was augmented to a total of twenty-four, all hands. Her young captain was Lieutenant D. M. C. Curtis, an Old Etonian who
wore a red-gold beard. His gay and easy disposition seemed
to belie his trade as an international lawyer but was very well
suited to the cloak and dagger traffic in which he had been
hitherto engaged of running Allied agents to or from remote
parts of the French coast by night. He had actually just re-

turned from a mission in which he had taken off the patriot Pierre de Vomecourt and the traitress Mathilde Carré, who, it was alleged later, on suppositions for which this narrative will show that there are no grounds, had "alerted" the Germans by disclosing to them a British request for information on the St. Nazaire defenses. Dunstan Curtis had also, though he did not know it at the time, ferried over several times members of the *réseau*, or group, that had been responsible for providing much of the intelligence information used in preparing the Chariot raid.

If we now move from the bridge of the gunboat and go forward to the Vickers pom-pom, we shall meet the entirely different man who was destined on that dark March morning to win in death the Victoria Cross. Able Seaman William Savage, to quote the words of an old shipmate, Donald Mackenzie, "always looked a proper sailor with his stocky build, his beard and his pipe." He was twenty-nine years old and was the youngest of a large family who lived in Smethwick, where his parents kept a general store. He was employed by the brewing firm of Mitchell & Butler and was essentially a quiet, steady fellow whom everyone liked, married, a member of his firm's water polo team and secretary of the local darts club.

Just before she sailed, a very special hand joined the gunboat. This was Leading Signalman F. C. Pike. He had been employed in that secret department of the Admiralty which has certain dealings with enemy wireless signals and he had been sent to Ryder's force in answer to a request for someone who could signal in German.

Another specialist whom Ryder was particularly glad to get was Lieutenant A. R. Green, an officer of the Regular service and a specialist in navigation. It would be his business not only to pilot the little fleet at sea but also to guide it over the dangerous shoal waters of the Loire estuary and at the last moment to direct *Campbeltown* onto her target.

The inevitable gossip in a small port about "what it was all in aid of" constantly haunted the two leaders. Falmouth did not have a good name for secrecy, and it was said that there was a known spy there. Moreover, it was not a purely naval port and was open to mercantile shipping, including foreign ships, and indeed a convoy arrived while the Chariot force was assembled. In the naval boat yard and among members of the new force itself, speculation was inevitable.

The first precaution to be taken, therefore, was to keep the khaki and the blue well away from each other as far as possible. Ryder, who had a keen sense of "security," devised a special "cover plan" to account for the new craft and, with the C-in-C's approval, a bogus command was established under the title of the Tenth Anti-Submarine Striking Force.

It was put about, in order to explain the additional petrol tanks and the extra antiaircraft defense, that the flotilla's mission was to carry out long-range anti-submarine sweeps in the Bay of Biscay. For such a mission Falmouth was a perfectly natural base. Thus Ryder was able to make and receive signals freely and to obtain stores, and the naval headquarters staff, including the Wrens who handled the signals traffic, were presented with a plausible answer to their speculations. A few bogus signals also helped and tropical kit was issued openly in the technique of the double bluff.

20 mm Oerlikon

Under cover of this plan the motor launches were put through a stiff program of training. They carried out antiaircraft practice with their new Oerlikons. They were taken out to sea to practice station-keeping in formation, at which they were very bad, they were exercised in maneuvering after dark and, under Ryder's exacting eye, were drilled again and again in running their craft alongside jetties at night, not knowing that it was operational practice and thinking that it was only a Regular officer's tiresome insistence on the smart handling of their craft. On March 16, after having put about a suitable "training" pretext, they went for a two-days' cruise in vile weather to the Scilly Isles and back, taking the commandos with them and "vomiting till it hurt." It was the first time that the commandos and the men of the motor launches had come together and they took to each other immediately.

They came together again on March 21 for the final and much more significant Exercise Vivid, in which, under a suitable cover plan, they carried out a night raid upon the Devonport defenses as a rehearsal for the real thing. Haydon and Henriques were present and valuable lessons were learned.

But the blinding dazzle of the massed searchlights, in which the boats could not satisfactorily navigate, keep station or land their troops, was a vexation to which they knew no answer and a foretaste of sharp realities to come.

"THE SAUCIEST JOB SINCE DRAKE"

On the evening of March 18, the day after the return from the Scilly Isle cruise, while the men were off duty in the mess decks below, the thirty-nine officers—an enormous proportion for so small a force—were summoned to a CO's conference in the wardroom after dinner. They trooped in and sat down round the big table. In a corner they saw a blackboard on which had been drawn the map of a river mouth. Beside the blackboard stood their Colonel Charles in very good form, smoking his pipe, laughing and talking to Copland and Day. When they were all in, he ordered the door to be locked, put his pipe aside and began to speak.

"Gentlemen," Newman said, "I know jolly well you have all been wondering what we are up to down here, and now I'm going to tell you. You will all be delighted to know that we have been selected for a really lovely job—a saucy job—easily the biggest thing that has been done yet by the commandos. You could say it is the sauciest job since Drake."

You could have heard a pin drop. There was not a man whose heart did not quicken its beat. In dead silence and with rapt attention they listened as Newman went on:

"Look at the blackboard. That is the map of a French port. I am not going to tell you what it is—not until just before we sail. But you have all got to learn the geography of the port by heart, with the help of that very fine model over there, so that you will be able to move about in it in the dark as though it were your own back garden. The code name of the operation is 'Chariot,' and you are not to discuss it with a single soul except among yourselves—not even with the Navy, who don't yet know anything about it."

He went on to explain the background and conception of

the operaiton and, using map and model, described in general terms the purpose of the raid, pointing out the targets and emphasizing that the primary one, to which all others were subsidiary, was the outer caisson of the big dry dock. He explained also how what at first apepared to be a preposterous undertaking was immediately made feasible by a surprise approach and a diversionary bombing attack. Coming to the "method," Newman went on:

"As there are about twenty-four objectives, the detailed plan is a fearfully long one. I shan't attempt to go into the detail tonight. You'll be getting an Operation Order of forty-odd pages of foolscap, and I shall take you all through your separate parts later on. All I shall do now is to give you the general outline of the military plan.

"This is essentially a mission of demolitions. Our job is

Colt .45 M 1911 A1

to blow things up and, as we have got to do so right in among the Jerries, the chaps doing the demolitions must be able to do so undisturbed. So the military force is to consist of two types—demolition troops and fighting troops. The demolition chaps will not be expected to fight, as they will be too heavily laden to carry any arms except a Colt.

"The fighting troops, who will be provided by 2 Commando, have got to do two jobs. The first is to assault enemy gun positions and hold a perimeter of bridges until they are blown, against counterattack from the town side of the docks." He pointed out on the blackboard the bridges at the northern and southern ends of the Submarine Basin and the main caisson, which was itself a road bridge. "These assault parties will be the first ashore and have got to be pretty slippy. You, Johnny Roderick, have got to be off like lightning, because you've got to tackle a gun position right slap alongside *Campbeltown* after she has rammed the near caisson.

"The second job of the fighting troops is to provide protection squads for the demolition tears. They will stick close alongside the demolition chaps and guard them against interference while they lay their charges.

"That is the general idea of the military plan. The parties will be awfully small—only about a dozen in each assault party, one officer and four men for most of the demolition jobs and the same number for the protection squads. What Brigadier Haydon calls 'boy scout parties.' If we make up our minds to be quick in and quick out under cover of the bombing diversion, we shall have done the job before the Jerries realize that we have paid them a visit at all."

At about this point, we are told—and we may scarcely wonder—it came from to Newman's audience, despite his buoyant and confident manner, that the raid was not merely "the sauciest job since Drake," but also an extremely difficult and dangerous one. To more than one of these highly intelligent young officers it had all the appearance of so many "suicide jobs."

"So much for the general idea. Now a few words on how we are going to tackle the job. To make the thing manageable, all these targets have been divided into groups, which will correspond to the most suitable landing places for them. Those on the left, or south, situated on the Southern Entrance, will be Group One, under you, Bertie Hodgson." He looked towards his friend, the leader of No. 1 Troop. "Those in the center, a rather mixed bag, stretching right up to the Penhouet Basin, will be Group Two, under Micky Burn. Those on the right, which are associated specially with the big Dock, will be Group Three, under Major Bill Copland. All these groups include assault parties, demolition chaps and their protection squads." He went on to enumerate the other tasks in outline.

"Now about getting there," Newman continued. "Groups One and Two are to make the passage in MLs—in fact, in the MLs in which we made yesterday's seasick trip to the Scillies, although they don't know it yet. So don't go talking to them. We shall enter the river in two columns of MLs—Group One in the port column and Group Two in the starboard.

"Group Three, however, is to take passage in the destroyer, HMS *Campbeltown*, whose job is to ram the near caisson and to blow herself up by delay fuse, after we have all gone. Not, I hope, before. The further caisson, as well as the pump house and the winding-houses, which house the machinery for operating the caissons, are our birds. The near caisson—the really important job—will be our bird too if anything should go wrong with *Campbeltown*.

"Each of these groups will have a separate landing place. Group One is to be landed at the Old Mole, here, where there is a landing slip, Group Two in the old Entrance, here, and Group Three will land from the bows of the destroyer onto the caisson itself.

"I myself, with Stan Day, will be with Commander Ryder, the Naval Force Commander. For the outward passage we shall be in HMS *Atherstone*, one of the escorting destroyers, and on the second night we shall transfer to an MGB as headquarters ship. My headquarters after landing will be this building beside the Old Entrance and close to the bridge marked G. Bill Pritchard will have general control of the demolition tasks, except for Group Three, which will be looked after by Bob Montgomery."

Newman paused a while, as though to emphasize the close of a phase, then he continued:

"As you can imagine, in a party like this communications will be very important but limited. Once ashore, Sergeant Steele will open up from my headquarters with three other stations—Commander Ryder in the gunboat, Major Bill and the Beachmaster on the Old Mole. For this purpose we have been issued with some new and extremely hush-hush portable

GREAT

ENGLISH...

Plymouth

400
Falmouth

Scilly Is. The Lizard

1911 A

26 MARCH

B 2300
Ushant

Bres

BRITTANY

BOYD, HORLOCK
WALLIS

Lorient

La Roche
Bernard

Belle I.

St.
André

St. Nazaire

0700 C
U-Boat action

Rendezvous point
Atherstone, Tynedale

Z 2215
Sturgeon

'D - French Trawler
sunk 1204

27 MARCH

E 2005

BAY OF BISCAY

radio sets with a microphone operating on the larynx. They must on no account fall into enemy hands.

"Well, gentlemen, having done all our jobs, we have to get home again, and smartly, too. As each demolition team completes its job it is to come in to my headquarters to report. When they are all in I shall give a withdrawal signal by means of thirty-five-star rockets to the assault parties still out on the perimeter—green for those on my right, red on my left. We shall then all assemble at the butt end of the Old Mole and re-embark in the MLs under the orders of the Beachmaster, Lieutenant R. E. A. Verity.

"One last thing, and this is awfully important. Remember that we shall all be milling about in the dark, with Jerries all round us. In fact, in this show the danger of shooting up one's own chaps will be at the maximum. So recognition will be terribly important—faces clean, not blacked, all webbing equipment scrubbed and blancoed white. Secondly, every man is to carry a blue pinpoint torch. Thirdly, the answer to any challenge will be the name of the officer in charge of the particular sub-group. Fourthly, I've concocted a password that I defy any German to pronounce who is not an expert English linguist, even if he ever finds it out." He smiled. "The password will be 'War Weapons Week' and the countersign 'Weymouth.' A good mouth of W's!

"But, apart from these devices, there will be the characteristic silhouette of our tin hats. And remember that, as we shall be wearing the new-issue rubber boots, the sound of any hard-soled boots will be as good as a loudspeaker shouting. 'Here comes a Jerry!'

"I think that is enough for tonight. Tomorrow I shall talk to the men and then you will all have some jolly hard work to do practicing your parts until you can do them blindfold."

The next morning Newman broke the news to the men, mustered on the mess deck by RSM Moss. He told them to sit easy and then began, Sergeant Butler tells us, with the words:

"Well, chaps, this is it!"

As he unfolded the story in simple terms they listened in the same electrified silence as the officers had done. They were filled, Sergeant Butler records, with "a spirit such as I had never before experienced—a sort of swelling that our bodies were too small to contain. Before he had finished it came home to us how difficult it was going to be ever to return, but this did not detract from the general determination one bit. I felt proud to be there."

That evening Corporal Wright, as he wrote up his diary in the mess deck, said of the plan: "A most audacious one; it almost takes one's breath away (like the rum that I am now drinking).... Everyone is happy, this is real commando stuff. Tonight most of us are speculating about the scheme and looking forward to the leave that will follow.... This is a strange life—as I sit writing a lieutenant is playing draughts at my elbow and our other 'two-piper' is drinking tea at the bottom of the table. And so to my hammock."

From then onwards, except for Exercise Vivid, on March 22, the commandos plunged into an intensive concentration on their various tasks. Newman had each of the "boy scout" parties into his cabin, the model on his bed and the map and air photo above it, and went through its task in detail, with Pritchard in attendance for demolition matters. The squads went away and rehearsed their own tasks again and again, squatting on deck in little groups all over the ship, putting test questions to each other. "You would have thought," wrote Swayne, "that a dozen conspiracies were going on at the same time." The model, the air photographs and the maps were burned into every man's mind, so that each knew exactly where he ought to land, where else he might have to land, the route from that point to his objective, the buildings that he would meet in the darkness and the ways round them, the places where the enemy was to be expected and the route back to the point of re-embarkation at the Old Mole.

For the demolition parties the orders to be studied were minutely detailed. From Pritchard's hand there were exact descriptions of the docks equipment and how they were operated, precise instructions where to place each charge, the weight and nature of each charge, where precisely and how to fix them, the manner of their firing, together with lists of what each individual officer and man in the demolition parties had to carry of explosive, adhesive tape, cordtex, detonators, sledge hammers, firemen's axes, ML flares for burning out electric windings, boxes of fusee matches, "tar babies" for setting oil on fire, rubber gloves for those who would have to handle electric apparatus, and so on in infinite detail.

Quantities of stores were coming on board—bamboo scaling ladders, grapnels, explosives, weapons and ammunition, special clothing, the new type of rubber-soled boot with rubber crampons, emergency rations and a multitude of other items that kept Regimental Quartermaster-Sergeant Seaton working day and night. The ordinary web equipment had to be altered to take the formidable amount of ammunition, grenades and trench-motor-bombs that men in the fighting parties were ordered to carry, special pockets being added for the extra Bren and tommy gun clips and the whole equipment "built to the man." Blue sweaters were issued to every soldier, a box of morphine Syrettes to every officer and a haversack of shell dressings to a trained first-aid man in every party.

The day after Exercise Vivid—March 23—it was the turn of the naval force to be admitted to the secret.

In contrast to Newman's orders, which had to be minutely detailed, Ryder's were short and simple. He briefed only the commanding officers and first lieutenants of each vessel, taking six at a time. They in turn were to brief their own ships' companies, but not until after sailing. The main requirement was that they should be able to recognize their proper landing places in the glare of the searchlights with which they had had such a trying experience the night before. These searchlights Ryder simulated with electric torches placed in the model, while the officers looked at the harbor approaches at eye level.

The probable date of departure, Ryder told them, was Friday, the twenty-seventh—only four days hence—and zero hour—the hour at which *Campbeltown* was to hit her target—was fixed for 1:30 A.M. two nights later.

On that day Forbes's operation order was issued. The routes laid down for the outward and return passages had

Hunt Class Destroyer

been skillfully calculated and timed in order that the force
should escape enemy observation aircraft, on the movements
of which he was particularly well informed, or, if observed
by chance aircraft or ships, that its direction and demeanor
should give no clue to its purpose. By day the flotilla was to
adopt the broad arrowhead cruising order of an anti-submarine sweep. The force was to part company with the escorting destroyers at Point E at 8 P.M. and thence proceed on its
own. In order that Green should have a precise "fix" of his
position on the chart, vital for the final run-in over the shoals,
HM Submarine *Sturgeon,* commanded by Lieutenant-Commander M. R. G. Wingfield, was to serve as a "navigational
beacon," surfacing at Point Z, forty miles from St. Nazaire,
to meet the force at about 10 P.M.

On that same day also—March 23—the two escort ships
sailed into Falmouth. These were the Hunt class destroyers
Atherstone (Lieutenant-Commander R. F. Jenks) and *Tynedale* (Lieutenant-Commander H. E. F. Tweedie). Ryder, together with Green, moved his headquarters to *Atherstone,*
where he felt much more at home. The motor launches were
now anchored in Cross Roads and, as a result of Vivid, had all
been repainted that shade of mauve known as "Plymouth
Pink" or "Mountbatten Pink" to make them less conspicuous
under searchlights. Throughout the whole force there was now
a throb and bustle as the last-minute preparations were made.

Other late arrivals came in about the same time. Two of
these were French-speaking liaison officers for whom Newman
had specially asked for reassuring civil inhabitants and seeing
that they kept indoors. These "French faces" were Captain
Vicomte Peter de Jonghe (in fact a Belgian and a well-known
steeplechase rider) and 2nd Lieutenant W. G. Lee. Soon after
them there came two press representatives sent from the Ministry of Information in the persons of Mr. J. M. G. Holman and
Mr. E. J. Gilling; Newman interviewed them on board and
allotted Holman to the headquarters gunboat and Gilling to
the motor launch of Wallis, the Australian. Almost last of all
came Captain Anthony Terry, a liaison officer from the War
Office.

And now at last, on March 25, HMS *Campbeltown* arrived, astonishing the older naval hands who saw her in the
distance. For from a little way off she looked very like a German destroyer of the *Möwe* class, with two rakish, cut-back
funnels of unequal size, instead of her normal four. Even

stranger changes had taken place on her upper deck. All her guns were gone, their places usurped by a little twelve-pounder forward and eight Oerlikons mounted high on "band-stands." Her bridge and wheelhouse superstructure were sheeted with armor plating as a shield against small-arms bullets. Less obvious, riveted to the deck amidships, were long, low armor-plate fences behind which the commandos were to lie down as they faced the hail of close-range fire before they clambered ashore.

Equally strange sights were to be seen below deck—her bows packed with high explosive ready at short notice to be made alive, her torpedo tubes and all other heavy gear not essential to her task removed, her magazines emptied, her fuel oil and boiler water reduced to the calculated minimum for reaching her objective. Riding very light in the water, she was stripped and ready for the last race of her life. She drew only eleven feet of water, or twelve feet at the stern when moving fast, but even that was risky for her ride over the dangerous shoal waters, for the tidal calculations had shown that she would have only ten feet of water.

These sweeping changes in her cut and trim had been made in phenomenal time by the hands of Devonport Dock-yard, giving her new captain a few days in which to take her to sea and handle her. He found that, like all these old American destroyers of her class, she was anything but easy. Compared with our V and W class destroyers of the same date, she was, in his own words, "a bitch." At a cruising speed of twelve knots she had a turning circle as wide, it seemed, as a battleship's. Only when reaching about seventeen knots did she handle with the suppleness of an ordinary destroyer. Moreover, ruthlessly lightened as she was, she skidded badly, needing frequent corrections to her helm.

To his own distress, *Campbeltown's* former captain, a thoroughly able officer with whom Ryder would have been perfectly happy to sail, had been displaced, as, in the Commander-in-Chief's opinion, his years were against him. In his place Forbes had appointed Lieutenant-Commander S. H. Beattie. Nothing could have delighted Ryder more, for he and Sam Beattie were old friends and shipmates, cadets of the same team in the training ship *Thunderer* when they had joined the Navy together as boys from school.

In him Ryder had complete faith, for Beattie perfectly suited the part. In his early thirties, he was tall, slender, black-

bearded, blue-eyed. With his handsome presence he matched
a charming personality and a retiring manner. Nothing rattled
or ruffled him and he could be relied upon to carry out with
a calm precision the great test of nerve and fortitude to which
he was committed.

Beattie was the son of a Herefordshire parson, and had
taken no small risk to his career in marrying very young. Indeed, he had had at first to hide his wife, as it were, from
senior officers. He and Philippa Beattie were devoted to each
other, and already had three small children. At home he was
a completely domesticated animal and was as ready to deal
with nursery tasks as he was to con a ship.

This was the officer chosen to lay his ship upon her
sacrificial altar. For the final act of destruction Tibbits had
meanwhile been working at an explosive scheme that seems
to have been almost entirely his own, consulting with Pritchard from time to time. COHQ's first tentative plan of placing
the explosive after the ship had rammed was too chancy and
there was very little experience to go upon. No one knew, for
example, how far back the ship's bow would buckle. Since
Campbeltown's immolation was the kernel of the whole business, Ryder demanded an absolutely foolproof scheme, designed to meet every foreseeable contingency.

"How can you be sure," he demanded to know, "that the
charge will be in intimate contact with the face of the caisson
but yet not be smashed by the impact? What happens if we
run into heavy fire and the fusing system gets shot up? Or the
chap responsible—that's you—gets shot up? If the delay action has to be long enough to save our commandos from
being blasted when ashore, how can we prevent the Germans
from disarming the fuses when they board the ship after we
have gone, as they certainly will? How do I know that this
cordtex stuff is really waterproof? Demonstrate it to me."

To all these and other posers Tibbits supplied answers,
conferring with Pritchard on methods of fusing. In the outcome the explosive charge was placed immediately abaft, or
behind, the steel column that supported the ship's most
forward gun, on the argument that this was the first obstacle
of strong resistance to the momentum of the ramming impulse. The charge was made up of twenty-four Mark VII
depth charges, as used for attacking submarines, weighing
four hundred pounds each, so that the total charge weighed
four and a quarter tons. It was enclosed in a special steel tank

on top of the fuel compartments and cemented in, as shown in Figure 1. The fuses used were the Army's new long-delay "pencil" fuses, set to act after eight hours, at least three being inserted in the charge, and the whole connected together with cordtex. To safeguard against casualties to vital personnel, the fuses would be actuated at about 11 P.M., before the ship entered the estuary, and to safeguard against disarming by the enemy the ship was to be scuttled after ramming.

Some mystery still remains today on exact points, and particularly as to whether the alternative two-and-a-half-hour fuses were ever used. A paper inquest was held after the raid on this point, but the only men who knew the answers, were dead.

The time was drawing very near. There was no more shore leave. Personal affairs had been settled. Wynn and Boyd had "dated" some Wrens for a party on a night after their return. Stuart Chant had put his Lakeland terrier, Spiff, into the care of his friend Mr. George Green, the Falmouth Docks Manager, and the crew of "Wynn's Weapons" had entrusted their Scruffy to the Wrens of the duty boat (though he got away from them and actually took part in the raid in another boat and was shipwrecked and rescued).

On board the *P.J.C.* the soldiers listened to a very poor lecture by an officer from London on the technique of escaping should they fail to get home in the motor launches, but were given none of the customary escape aids. Newman, to his relief, received at the last moment, a clear direction from COHQ, through Henriques, defining the priorities of the tasks and emphasizing that if only the big lock were destroyed the mission would have been fulfilled. If necessary, everything should be sacrificed to that aim. By the same letter Henriques told him the final bombing plan and passed on to him the considerations that Haydon had laid down for abandonment if that should appear necessary.

Away in London, meanwhile, no little anxiety was being experienced at COHQ over the proposals for providing support by bomber aircraft. Up to the last minute these proposals were clouded with doubts. The "really heavy" support that had been asked for early in February, and the seventy aircraft that had later been "considered adequate," dwindled week by week as Bomber Command, hard pressed for ma-

chines for their own campaign and obliged to transfer some
to Coastal Command, found itself more and more reluctant
to spare any forces for an operation not within their own
scheme of things.

Moreover, a new dilemma had arisen about the target
that was to be selected for bombing while the commandos
were about their business in the dockyard. As late as March
16, when the Combined Plan was issued, the bombing in this
second phase was to be on the *town* of St. Nazaire. About
that time, however, Mr. Churchill himself gave a direction
that, in order to avoid casualties to Frenchmen, the town was
not to be bombed.

Thus on March 22—four days before the Charioteers
were to set out—we find Air Vice-Marshal Robert Saundby,
Senior Air Force Officer, Bomber Command, having received
the Combined Plan, forwarding to COHQ the suggested new
basis of bomber participation. In this the number of aircraft
to take part had shrunk to thirty-five and the target for the
second phase—"Target B"—has been changed to the northern
end of the Penhouet Basin and the adjoining building slips—
more than a mile away to the north of the selected landing
places.

This proposition was received at COHQ with concern.
In conjunction with the reduced number of aircraft, it altered
the whole complexion of the affair. On March 24 Haydon
urged strongly that thirty-five aircraft were quite insufficient
and that the change of Target B was also very unsatisfactory;
the purpose of bombing in this phase, he observed, was to
draw the enemy's attention away from the docks and not to
them.

"I recommend very strongly," he wrote, "that we should
hold to our original request—even though it may run counter
to political opinion."

Haydon was further disturbed by Forbes's proposal that,
if bad weather prevented the bomber force from starting, the
naval and military force should still go in, if it had not been
spotted on passage. The essence of the military plan, however,
was that the enemy would be unable to take counteraction
against the commandos quickly; if no bombing took place
enemy reaction would be swift and would be far too strong
for the very small and scattered commando parties. "I do not
consider, therefore," Haydon wrote, "that the assualt without
air support is a fair proposition. I therefore recommend the

recall of the force should air support be impossible."

Henriques speaks of the "ferocity of our arguments" at this stage on the bombing needs. This was not just another Lofoten or Vaagso pinprick; it was a saber cut of serious strategic importance. "If we only drop soda-water bottles on the town," Haydon said, "or harmless objects that will scream through the air, that would serve the purpose. Anything to distract or mystify the German defenses in the vital two hours."

Such unorthodoxy, however, received no welcome.

The attempt to change Target B therefore failed. As Willetts pointed out, nothing short of a Cabinet decision could permit Bomber Command to accept the bombing of the town.

Other representations, however, succeeded. That same day—the twenty-fourth—Mountbatten attended a meeting of the Chiefs of Staff and he emphasized that "the success of Chariot depends very largely on the success of the diversion created by air bombing." He asked for a ruling as to what should be done if weather prevented bombing aircraft from participating and the Committee agreed "that Operation Chariot should not be undertaken unless the diversionary air bombing could be carried out." Mountbatten appears, however, to have been reluctant to abandon the operation altogether and, in the event, the orders received by Ryder and Newman, from Forbes, gave them discretion to press the operation if they had not been spotted at sea.

The urgent request for more bombers was also successful. Bomber Command responded to it by raising the number to sixty-two. When their Operation Order was issued on March 25, however, very severe restrictions were imposed on pilots. They were to bomb no other targets than those specified, they were not to come below six thousand feet and they were to drop their bombs singly on separate bombing runs. Moreover, in the subsequent briefing, it was impressed upon pilots that they must not attack at all unless they could clearly identify their targets and they were told nothing at all about the main operation, or the critical importance of it, beyond the fact that "a night operation by naval and military forces has been planned."

Thus, although provision had been made for cancellation of the expedition if the bombers should be unable to take off, and although Bomber Command laid on a modified program should some of the airfields be fogbound, no provision was made for advising the two force commanders what was to be done if the pilots were able to take off but were unable to see their targets on arrival.

"I bet you anything you like," Newman said when bidding good-by to Henriques after Exercise Vivid, "that the bombing won't work."

Down at Falmouth everything was now ready, ahead of time. The statistics of tide and moon had shown that the first night of the most favorable spell at St. Nazaire was that of March 28–29, which would have required sailing from Falmouth on March 27. The suspicion of a break in the weather, however, the arrival of *Campbeltown*, and the impulse to be gone, moved Ryder to suggest to the Commander-in-Chief that they should leave a day earlier. Forbes agreed.

On March 25, therefore, with all safely "locked up," Newman caused his commandos to be mustered in the *P.J.C.* and he told them their destination.

Reminded to make their wills, most of them did so—the soldier's pay-book will, which needs no witness. Barling, the doctor, who had a fractured ankle, ignored the hurt. Every man bathed and put on clean underclothes, to lessen the chance of infection from wounds. All badges were removed, except those of rank. Kits were minutely examined to make sure that each man carried all that he should and nothing that he should not. Grenades were primed with all due care. Webbing equipment was blancoed white. When all was ready and done RQMS Seaton and Corporal Crippin, the orderly-room clerk, earnestly appealing and inventing quite unnecessary jobs for themselves, persuaded Newman to allow them to join the great enterprise for which they had worked for so many sleepless nights and days.

Just after nine that night Newman received the signal from Ryder: *Can you come over to* Atherstone *with your magnifying glass?* He went at once and found Ryder in the captain's cabin studying a set of new air reconnaissance photographs taken that morning. Robin Jenks, *Atherstone's* commanding officer, was there, too. Pointing to one of the photos, Ryder said, "Look at that, Charles."

There in the Submarine Basin, right alongside the spot chosen by Newman for his battle headquarters, were berthed four German destroyers of the *Wolfe/Möwe* class. These, as we learned later, were part of the 5th Torpedo Boat Destroyer

Figure 1. Sectional view of one section of *Campbeltown*'s charge; there were six such sections. Thick lines show steel plating; light shading shows concrete filling and heavier shading wood blocks.

Flotilla, commanded by Korvettenkapitän Moritz Schmidt and consisting of *Seeadler, Falke, Kondor, Jaguar* and *Iltis*. They were to play no small part in the Chariot story.*

Newman looked at him quizzically. It was characteristic that to him they were not a new menace but a new opportunity; fresh victims for his bag. He said cheerfully:

"We'll slip on board and sink them with limpets." Then reflectively, "How many men should I need to capture them, Bob?"

"Well, now, how many have you got in reserve?"

"Twelve."

"Then I suggest, Charles," said Ryder with a smile, "that you will probably need all of them."

Ryder just had time next morning (March 26) to go ashore to telephone this troublesome news to Pat McCrum at Plymouth. There was nothing that the Navy could do about the ships while in the docks, but McCrum promised to ask the Commander-in-Chief to procure two more destroyers to reinforce the escort on the return voyage. The signal *Prepar-*

---

*Referred to sometimes as torpedo boats and sometimes as destroyers, they will be called destroyers in this book, to mark their comparative relation to the Hunts and the sharp dissimilarity from our motor torpedo boats.

ative Chariot, which required the expedition to be at half an
hour's notice for sea, was received from Plymouth at 9:30
A.M. At 11:03 Ryder in *Atherstone* signaled to Newman in
Princess Joséphine Charlotte:

Request troops may be sent now.

At 12:30 P.M. came the executive order from Forbes:

Carry out Chariot.

A few minutes after one o'clock, Copland, last to leave
the *P.J.C.,* climbed aboard *Campbeltown* and signaled to
Newman now in *Atherstone:*

All troops embarked.

At two o'clock, under a genial sun, with a light breeze
from the east-northeast, and with Spitfires circling a few feet
above the water, the Charioteers sailed quietly out into the
English Channel, followed by the three destroyers an hour
later. They numbered, apart from the escorts, six hundred and
eleven souls—three hundred and forty-five naval officers and
ratings, one hundred and sixty-six all ranks in the fighting

Spitfire

parties from 2 Commando, ninety-one all ranks in the demolition teams of the combined Commandos, together with the
medical party, three liaison officers and two press representatives.

Had the spirit of Hotspur been with them, he would surely have said as he did of old:

"Our plot is a good plot as ever was laid; our friends true and constant—a good plot, good friends, and full of expectation."

10

THE ENEMY

Very soon now we shall meet the enemy. Hitherto his defenses have been spoken of only in general terms, but it is essential for our narrative that, without further delay, we should look more closely at the men, the weapons and the ships that defended the stronghold which Ryder and Newman were about to assault.

Not all the information now presented, which is taken from German documents, maps and personal reports, was in the hands of our planners at that time. Our information on the enemy's fixed coast-defense gun positions was good, but it was far from complete on the locations of all the small, rapid-firing guns of Bofors and Oerlikon types, which were not only difficult to spot among buildings in air photos, but which were also liable to be moved from day to day. Nor were the planners or leaders able to assess the opposition that might be met from ships in harbor at the time of the attack. The positions of these ships is shown on Map 3, and were taken from the German maps and lists used by the German naval staff in their subsequent tactical study of the operation.

The defense of St. Nazaire and the seaward approaches to it were entirely in the hands of the German Navy, being manned by what the Germans describe as "naval troops," organized on an army basis and dressed in the field gray of the army, but wearing gilt-colored naval buttons and badges. The Germans had no "marines" as we know them. The defenses were under the command of the See Kommandant Loire, Kapitän zur See Zuckschwerdt, whose headquarters were at La Baule. Under him were a battalion of coast-defense artillery, a brigade of flak, or antiaircraft artillery, and the minor forces of the Harbor Commander.

The coast-defense guns were manned by 280 Naval Artillery Battalion under the command of Korvettenkapitän Edo Dieckmann, with headquarters at Chémoulin Point. He disposed of twenty-eight guns, of calibers of 75 mm., 150 mm. (5.9 inches), 170 mm. (6.6 inches) and a powerful battery of 9.5 inches (240 mm.) on railway mountings at La Baule. All these guns were to be engaged in the action, though the big railway guns fired only a few rounds on account of their slow traverse.

The antiaircraft, or dual purpose guns were manned by 22 Naval Flak Brigade under the command of the shrewd and able Kapitän zur See C. C. Mecke, with headquarters at St. Marc. He had three battalions in position in and close around St. Nazaire—703 Battalion commanded by Korvettenkapitän Thiessen, 809 by Korvettenkapitän Lothar Burhenne and 705 Battalion by Korvettenkapitän Koch. The German maps show forty-three guns of 40 mm. and 20 mm., with a few 37 mm. The 40 mm. and 20 mm. were very similar to our Bofors and Oerlikon guns and for the convenince of the narrative we shall use these terms, although they were not always so called by the Germans. In addition, the enemy had some heavy antiaircraft batteries, but these could not engage surface targets. Many of these guns were mounted on the tops of concrete bunkers, on rooftops or on flak towers, formidable objects to attack, and extraordinarily difficult to hit from water level.

The ears of all this artillery were provided by two main radar stations—one at Le Croisic and another, for seaward observation, under Dieckmann's command at St. Marc. Mecke's flak brigade had also three other radar stations, for air shooting only. At Chémoulin Point was a naval signal station.

Harbor defense appears to have been the responsibility, at least to some extent, of the Harbor Commander (Hafenkommandant), Korvettenkapitän Kellermann. He commanded no troops other than guard companies and the like, but disposed of some small harbor defense boats (*Hafenschutzboote*), of which four were in harbor on the night of the battle (and came into action) and two on patrol at the mouth of the estuary. Kellermann himself was on leave at the time of the raid.

Besides these forces under the command of Zuckschwerdt, various other forces were available in St. Nazaire on the night of the battle. These included 2 and 4 Works Companies, small units of naval technicians who had an emergency role as infantry, and a few other small detachments. Much more important, however, were the crews of ships in harbor. These included, besides the four harbor defense boats, five ships of 16 Minesweeper Flotilla in the Submarine Basin, the same number of 42 Minesweeper Flotilla in the Penhouet Basin and the crews of three German tankers —the *Passat, Schledstadt* (both actually in the Normandie Dock itself) and the *Uckermark.*

In addition, anchored two cables east of the East Jetty, directly in the course to be taken by the Charioteers, was a ship hitherto described as a flakship, but which we now know to have been *Sperrbrecher* 137, formerly the *Botilla Russ,* a ship of 996 tons, armed with one of the dangerous 88-mm. guns and several Oerlikons. These Sperrbrechers ("barrage breakers") were very stout ships used for dealing with magnetic minefields. This ship was clearly seen on the air photos used by Ryder and Newman, but not identified.

In the submarine pens on March 28 there were nine U-boats, mainly of the fully operational 7 Submarine Flotilla under Kapitänleutnant Herbert Sohler, and partly of 6 Flotilla, then in process of formation under Kapitänleutnant Wilhelm Schultz. Only their maintenance and headquarter hands were there and though their chief duty was to defend their ships (or to blow them up if threatened by an enemy landing) some of them appear to have manned machine guns in the action. The operational crews, who were very precious to Hitler's purpose, were billeted out of the danger area in La Baule and were under orders to be evacuated inland in the event of a British landing.

Altogether, we learn from Dieckmann, there were about five thousand troops and hands in the defenses and ships in and around St. Nazaire and about another one thousand, chiefly his own, disposed along the shores of the estuary. A balloon barrage unit was provided by the Luftwaffe.

Such was the citadel that was to be assaulted by an old destroyer and by two hundred and fifty-seven soldiers, carried into battle by light wooden motor launches.

Eight miles westward of St. Nazaire lay a cluster of headquarters that might critically affect the battle. Here, among the sand dunes and the pine trees that fringed the Atlantic coast, was the fashionable seaside resort of La Baule. Here, in addition to the headquarters of Zuckschwerdt, were the Corps headquarters of General Ritter von Prager. Under his command, 333 Infantry Division was stationed to cover the area St. Nazaire-Lorient, one of its brigades being stationed at towns a few miles inland from St. Nazaire, and the head-quarters of the brigade being just west of La Baule itself.

Entirely unsuspecting, secure in their hold upon France, reveling in the successes of the German armies in Russia, Hitler's forces on the Loire went about on their normal rounds while Ryder and Newman were slipping quietly out to sea.

11

TO SEA

Ryder shaped course southwesterly at thirteen knots to
follow the long route ordered by the Commander-in-Chief,
giving the Lizard a wide berth to keep out of sight of land.
He was quite happy about the weather prospects. The easterly
winds prevalent at that time and the bright sun, making the
land warmer than the water, promised him a protective haze,
with low cloud and patches of fog off the western coast of
France. This was precisely the weather that he wanted. He
was in HMS *Atherstone* as guide of the fleet, standing on the
bridge with Robin Jenks, her captain, Green, his specialist
navigator and staff officer, and Sub-Lieutenant J. E.
O'Rourke, his Canadian signals officer. With them were Newman, glad to have a few brief hours of ease after the exhaust-
ing days and nights of preparation, Stanley Day, Terry, the
War Office representative, and Gordon Holman, the journalist.
Immediately astern, in tow by *Atherstone*, they could see
Dunstan Curtis's MGB 314, the headquarters ship to which
the two Force Commanders would transfer for the approach
and the assault, and in which were the remainder of Newman's headquarters party. Astern of *Atherstone* was *Tynedale*, followed by *Campbeltown* towing "Wynn's Weapons."
On either hand of the destroyers were the two flotillas of
motor launches in line ahead, that on the port hand carrying
the soldiers for the Group One objectives, that on the starboard those for Group Two. A strange force, one might well
say, for "the counterpoise of so great an opposition," composed of more than sixty guns and six thousand troops. A
single Hurricane continuously circled the little fleet at nought
feet, knowing nothing of its purpose.

In the *Campbeltown* the ship's company had been reduced to seventy-five, all ratings not required having been

Hurricane

transferred to the *P.J.C.* at the last moment. Sam Beattie mustered the reduced ship's company on the quarter-deck and broke the news to them.

The sun shone. As the afternoon wore on, the breeze freshened to Force 4—a moderate breeze of eleven to fifteen miles per hour. The motor launches rolled a little and from time to time their bows lifted out of the moving sea. As a precaution against observation by enemy aircraft, the commandos were not allowed on the upper deck unless wearing oilskins or duffel coat, of which they had been provided with a small supply, and steel helmet. One or two borrowed from the sailors the white sweaters that the Navy calls submarine frocks.

Ryder presently hoisted the signal (F Pendant One) to

adopt the broad arrowhead formation of cruising order No.
1, in order to simulate a normal anti-submarine sweep. Speed
was reduced to ten knots. In order to avert the danger of
wireless signals being picked up by the enemy, no ship-to-
ship signals were allowed except visual signals—by flag or
Aldis lamp by day or a screened and subdued light by night.
Newman, on *Atherstone's* bridge, watched absorbed as the
signal was repeated back along the line by ship after ship,
and then, when all had received it, he watched with delight
the "fine sight of each vessel changing speed and direction to
take up her new position" on the screen two cables* apart,
with the three destroyers astern. Tired though he was from
the laborious time at Falmouth, Newman was too absorbed
to seek sleep, though from time to time he retired to the charthouse to smoke a quiet pipe. Day, however, was worn out
from nights without sleep, and turned in.

Dunstan Curtis in his gunboat astern of *Atherstone*,
which had often been his parent ship in operations off the
French coast, had the same sense of unreality. "We sat about
gossiping," he said, "as though it were a pleasure party, helping ourselves to the raisins that I always had in saucers on the
bridge."

Everyone, Ryder records, was feeling "pretty confident."
Neither he nor Newman now concerned themselves great-
ly with the discretion given them to abandon the operation if the bomber support raid did not materialize. What
gave greater concern to Newman was the realization that he
was now cut off from the troops he commanded and that he
could no longer influence or co-ordinate the dismembered
fragments of his complicated jigsaw. Now was there any possibility of changing the design as might be required by the
unforeseen. Such pitiably small parties!

Others also had their small misgivings or anxieties. The
burly Tom Boyd in ML 8 admitted that he set off with apprehension, because "I felt that the Force, as regards the
Navy, was insufficiently trained, and this was borne out by
the frightful stationkeeping." Ian Henderson, in ML 14, remarked to Swayne that he thought motor launches were
"hardly the best vessels for this sort of job." Swayne himself
experienced the sensation of being watched all the time by
some malevolent eye, expecting a German aircraft to drop
out of the clouds at any minute.

---

*A cable is approximately two hundred yards.

Thus the golden afternoon wore on. At 3:30 Horlock, the "spare commanding officer," took over ML 13, since Platt had to lead the port column in the absence of the sick Wood. Ryder rebuked the motor launches for excessive lamp signaling. Newman similarly made the signal: *Too many obvious soldiers on deck in all boats.* On board the little MTB 74, in tow by *Campbeltown,* Lovegrove and his engine-room hands, after a night without sleep, were tuning and adjusting their new engine; and the remaining hands labored to remove the warhead of one of their special torpedoes and to fit a new fuse, obtained at the last minute by Mickey Wynn's pertinacious independence "and the influence of a certain admiral, in an effort to prolong our lives."

Soon after seven o'clock on the evening of March 26, as night approached, having reached Point A in his orders, Ryder altered course almost due south. A haze had developed over the sea and the breeze abated, to the greater comfort of the motor launches. Just before dusk the lone Hurricane, forever circling, straightened out and roaring low above the little fleet, flew away northwards into the gathering gloom.

As darkness fell, Ryder made the signal to change to the night cruising order, and as all ships took it up, they maneuvered gradually into three columns, the destroyers in the center column, one and a half cables astern of each other, and the motor launches out on either hand, a cable between each. Speed was increased to fourteen knots, in order that it might be reduced the next day; for heavy wash from the vessels by day would instantly attract the eyes of scouting aircraft.

To Ryder's disappointment the morning of Friday, March 27, opened to a brilliant dawn with a cloudless sky and limitless visibility. This was particularly the day when he would have welcomed heavy clouds or a light fog. He and Newman, who, "much against my will," had taken a few hours' sleep, were on the bridge before daylight and again Newman watched the little fleet obey the signal to swing out into the anti-submarine formation. He chuckled, and every soldier in the force chuckled with him, when the three destroyers, though not the motor launches, were seen to hoist the German ensign. It was now the last day.

By seven o'clock in the morning the fleet had reached point C, some one hundred and sixty miles to the westward of St. Nazaire. In accordance with his orders, Ryder altered course to 112°. Five minutes later *Tynedale*'s Gunner sighted an object, possibly a submarine, on the port beam, seven and a half miles distant at a bearing of 37°.

Ryder ordered *Tynedale* to close and investigate and he himself, after the gunboat had been cast off, followed her at speed in *Atherstone*, with Nock's and Falconar's MLs in company. As *Tynedale*, still wearing German colors, closed the distant object, Tweedie, her captain, identified it as a submarine, surfaced and apparently stationary. When she had closed to about five miles, the submarine saw her coming bows-on and fired a rocket of five white stars as a recognition signal. *Tynedale* replied with five long flashes of her signal lamp—a pure guess.

The U-boat seemed to be satisfied and she remained innocently on the surface until 7:45. *Tynedale* had now closed to about five thousand yards and Tweedie, hauling down the German colors and breaking the white ensign, opened fire with the forward mounting, much too soon. Columns of water spouted up around the submarine, which immediately crash-dived.

Tynedale, continuing at speed till she had reached the submarine's estimated position, dropped a pattern of depth charges thirteen minutes later. The shock forced the U-boat to break surface again and *Tynedale* opened fire on her a second time at short range and with all the guns that could bear. The U-boat, said the watching Newman, was enveloped in "a mass of large columns of water," but she was on the surface for only a few seconds before diving again, apparently hit.

The expedition was not out after submarines, but what concerned Ryder was the chance that, before diving, she might have seen them and might later make a sighting report by wireless to the German Naval Commander-in-Chief West (General-Admiral Alfred Saalwächter). He therefore ordered *Tynedale* and *Atherstone* to carry out a "square search," but *Tynedale's* asdic went out of action and contact was lost. After two hours Ryder called off the hunt. As both the submarine herself and the launches lay low in the water, with limited horizons, he hoped that she would have seen only the destroyers. Tweedie thought it looked probable that she had been sunk or mortally injured. Ryder, however, was far from convinced and, with a shrewd instinct, he ordered the two destroyers to steam off on a southwesterly course, so as to deceive the U-boat, should she have them under observation from her periscope.

This quick-witted decision had a vital effect. Had it not been made, the whole expedition would surely have been imperiled, for the submarine, which postwar evidence showed to have been U 593, homeward-bound, had in fact sighted some of the motor launches before she had been attacked but had not reported them, not supposing that they could conceivably be British. Nor had she been sunk. After the attack she remained submerged for five and half hours and at 1:47 P.M. reported by wireless:

0620 (7:20 A.M. B.S.T.) *three destroyers, ten MTBs, 46° 52'N., 5° 48'W. Course West.*

The effect of this report, which was received at German Group Command West, at 2:20 P.M., and the error in judging the course of the Charioteers, was to cause the enemy to suppose that the British force was withdrawing after a mine-laying operation, or else that it was on passage to Gibraltar. "An imminent attack from the sea on a port on the French west coast," we are told in the report of the German naval staff, "was never anticipated." This was exactly what Ryder wanted, but it had been a very near thing.

After abandoning the hunt, *Atherstone* and *Tynedale* rejoined the force by a circuitous route. *Atherstone* once more took the gunboat in tow. Ryder felt sure that, as a result of the encounter with the submarine, he must very soon expect enemy reconnaissance aircraft to appear, but he had now to turn his glasses to a new cause of apprehension. On the port bow there appeared a fleet of French fishing trawlers.

He had given careful thought to this likelihood, for he was anxious to do no avoidable harm to French interests or to any other innocent parties. It was, however, known or believed that the Germans sometimes put observers equipped with wireless sets on board French fishing boats and Ryder had therefore decided that any that were met would have to be sunk. On this occasion, however, shortly before noon, he was confronted not with one or two fishing vessels but a whole fleet. Their appearance so soon after the encounter with the submarine was suspicious; they may have had a rendezvous together.

Two, however, were widely separated from the rest and he dispatched *Tynedale* to sink one of them, which was the trawler *Nungesser et Coli*, and *Atherstone*, with the gunboat in company, sank *Le Slack*. The skippers and crews, throwing their hats in the air with delight at this totally unexpected appearance of the white ensign, which the destroyers hoisted, accepted the decision with perfect good will and cheerfulness. They were taken on board the destroyers and made much of, involuntary participants in the great enterprise. At its conclusion, they were taken back to England to their great delight, where most of them joined the Free French Forces. From the skipper of *Le Slack* Ryder learned that the fishing fleet, which was from Le Pallice, carried no wireless or German observers and he decided to sink no more.

To the relief of all, the sky had now become completely overcast with low cloud, but Ryder remained apprehensive of the danger of observation by enemy craft, particularly from the air. The encounters with the submarine and the fishing craft were disturbing, a clear sign that the nearer they approached the French coast the greater was the danger of unforeseen encounters. This apprehension was increased by news received from Plymouth soon after midday of the moves of the five German *Wolfe/Möwe* class destroyers, commanded by Moritz Schmidt, which he and Newman had spotted from the last air photographs of St. Nazaire docks. Just after the trawler incident Ryder had been relieved to hear from Plymouth that these destroyers had moved up to Nantes the day before, but at 5:18 P.M. a second signal from Plymouth reported that they were now back at St. Nazaire and "might be met."

This was disturbing news, as they were a very much superior force to Ryder's. In point of fact, however, the German Group Command West, after receipt of the submarine's report, telephoned the information to the Luftwaffe and to the admiral commanding the Protective Forces and then, on the supposition that the force had been engaged in mine laying, ordered the destroyers to carry out a "mine reconnaissance" along the U-boat routes off St. Nazaire *that night*. The submarine's report therefore worked unexpectedly to the advantage of the Charioteers, for, at the time when Ryder was beginning to steal over the shoal waters of the Loire, Schmidt's flotilla, following the orthodox Charpentiers Channel, was already at sea.*

---

*Six weeks later Schmidt, in *Seeadler*, was sunk by an MTB near Dover, and, he tells us, "had to swim for my life in the cold water of the English Channel."

Of these movements Ryder, of course, knew nothing. He was expecting extensive air reconnaissance at any time, and he knew that once spotted, he would be kept continuously under observation even if not attacked. The wisdom of the course selected was therefore now apparent, for, as they were now heading, they might be supposed to be making for La Pallice, a good way south of St. Nazaire. Even so, the presence of the enemy ships anywhere near St. Nazaire was a menacing factor, if only for the subsequent return voyage home, and therefore Ryder took comfort when another signal came from Forbes, telling him that two more Hunt class destroyers, the *Cleveland* and the *Brocklesbury,* had been sailed from Plymouth to support the withdrawal.

Many years later he was to learn that, that very day, as he was moving towards his objective, Admiral Doenitz, C-in-C of the German submarine forces, having left his headquarters at Kernval, near Lorient, was himself visiting the threatened docks of St. Nazaire. He had come to inspect the submarine base and during the course of his inspection he asked Kapitän-leutnant Herbert Sohler, commanding the 7th Submarine Flotilla:

"What are you going to do if the British attack this place?"

Sohler replied that plans had been made for that unlikely event and embodied in an Emergency Order. "However," he added, "that is considered here to be highly improbable."

"I should not be too sure," Doenitz commented.

For, only four days earlier, Hitler had issued his personal order on "Command Organization on the Coasts." In this order (Directive No. 40) he warned all higher commanders that British landings with limited objectives were to be expected. Our strategic reasons for such operations were perfectly well understood by him. He therefore ordered that "special attention must be paid to British preparations for landings. ... Large-scale parachute and glider operations are likewise to be expected."

Ryder continued to take every precaution, the antennae of his senses stretched in every direction. Earlier that afternoon he had again rebuked the motor launches for too much lamp work and had ordered Tillie in ML 4: *Go round MLs telling them all by hailer to reduce Aldis signaling.* Later, as evening approached, he instructed the whole force: *Glass on wheelhouses most conspicuous at night. Must be covered with paint, paper or grease on outside.*

The commandos, however, were little concerned with these anxieties. For the last time, they cleaned their weapons, checked their gear and ammunition, and rehearsed their tasks. Sergeant Steele, in the gunboat, satisfactorily netted his new 38 radio sets with the operators of the other three stations that were to be set up. Throughout the fleet the commandos shared antiaircraft duties with the naval ratings, and in the motor launches they practiced the use of the Oerlikons and twin Lewis guns, fitting themselves to take part as integral mem-

Twin Lewis Guns

bers of the ships' companies in their fire plans; but otherwise they had little to do. They played brag in the forecastle or sat about on deck in oilskins or duffel coats. Their only inconvenience was a prohibition of washing and shaving, since the fresh water supplies were severely strained by so many extra hands and a strict water discipline was necessary. The officers gossiped with the troops or kept company with the naval officers on the bridge.

In the *Campbeltown,* with more room to move about, the soldiers were even more comfortable, though here also the number of soldiers allowed on deck was limited. The scaling ladders and ropes for use in the disembarkation were brought out and put into position. The two 3-inch mortars with which the commandos were to supplement the fire of *Campbeltown*'s weapons, under Proctor, were mounted on the fo'c'sle. Action stations were practiced under Gough, the first lieutenant. Final rehearsals were held.

Nothing stimulated the hilarity of the troops so much as the ensign of the Third Reich. Draped in all manner of "fancy dress," picked out from ship's stores that would never now be wanted, they grouped themselves aft, mocking the ensign with the Hitler salutation, and were photographed by cameras illicitly brought by one or two. Gunner Milne, Roy's soldier-servant, looked on the emblem with a deeper design, biding his time. Above all, however, the most ardent occupation of soldiers and ratings alike was to eat. For security reasons, the ship had been provisioned on more or less the normal scale at Devonport and there were large quantities of food on board, and of sorts that the commandos, on home rations, had never seen in such abundance. Eggs, hams, "real butter," sausages and other fare liberally supplemented the ample meals served from the galley. And after eating their fill they sat about in groups and sang songs.

The canteen was likewise well stocked. For some time the ratings and other ranks solemnly went on paying for their wares in the normal way until someone said; "Hey, the ship's going to be blown up tonight—accounts and all. What are we paying for?" There after, everything was "on the house." Nor did the fun stop there. From these doomed canteen supplies bright spirits made sandwiches filled with tooth paste, shaving soap, and hair cream to be offered to unsuspecting friends. Copland had allowed the soldiers a rum ration the day before, but on this last day he would not sanction it. The thirty-six-hours holiday was soon to end. They knew that they ought to get some sleep before their tasks of the small hours, but most of them were much too excited to do so.

Operationally only one small mishap disturbed the ordered routine. At 6:30, when the sun was very low, the port engine of Douglas Briault's ML 10 went out of action, and although one of the flotilla engineer officers, Sub-Lieutenant Tom Yenloll, came to his assistance, nothing could be done in time. In accordance with the prescribed plan Falconar's ML 15, one of the spare vessels so fortunately added late in the day, took over her troops, who consisted of Hodgson's assault party and Barling's medical party. Putting on full speed, Falconar caught up the remainder of the force two hours later, taking station last in the port column of troop-carrying boats. The unfortunate Briault followed on one engine as best as he could the blue hand-light put out for him by Nock, but the port engine was not repaired until 10:20 P.M., when all chance of catching up had long gone. Sadly Briault turned about and returned to England alone.

No further encounters took place and no German aircraft flew. Under the clouded sky, the Charioteers sailed on at a quiet eight knots. The second night drew on. At eight o'clock, just after darkness had fallen, they reached Point E and turned northeastward, shaping now straight for the open jaws of the Loire. Here the whole force stopped and finally maneuvered in the dark into the special cruising order in which they were to make their attack. Wynn's MTB was east off from *Campbeltown* and her engines pulsed sweetly into action under Lovegrove's care. For Ryder and Newman the time had come to say good-by to *Atherstone*. Curtis's gunboat was cast off and came alongside. Ryder, accompanied by Green and O'Rourke, and Newman, accompanied by Day, Terry and Holman, after cordial "good luck" wishes from Jenks and his officers, jumped on board.

It was indeed a dramatic moment. As the little gunboat began to move away, *Atherstone*'s company lined the rails and gave a warm cheer that seemed suddenly to people the dark and empty sea with friends. Jenks, remembering *Atherstone*'s old status as parent ship to the little gunboat, called out: *"Don't forget whose father I am."*

Very much stirred, Curtis took his gunboat to the head of the line. Astern of him the motor launches moved silently as night moths into their columns and the solid bulks of the escort destroyers slid away on either hand. Then, with *Campbeltown* two and a half cables astern, with the two columns of motor launches close in on either hand, the torpedo-carrying boats of Boyd and Irwin leading them to starboard and port respectively, and with Wynn's MTB in the tail of all, he moved on at twelve knots into the clouded night. Only seventy-five miles now.

Grenade

There was only one more check point to pass now; at Point Z they were to make contact with Mervyn Wingfield in the submarine *Sturgeon,* acting as a navigational beacon from which Green could get a pinpoint chart position for the last run. She would be displaying a masked white light showing to seaward only and intermittently flashing the letter M. To broaden the chance of safely keeping their ocean rendezvous, *Atherstone* and *Tynedale* stayed near them for a little while, taking station about a mile on either beam. But so precise was Green's pilotage that, at 10 P.M., the double dashes of *Sturgeon*'s light were sighted, winking from the dark waste two miles exactly ahead.

As they came closer in the phosphorescent gloom they saw the *Sturgeon* half-submerged, nothing more visible than her conning tower, looking like a mere tub afloat in the ocean, and inside it the small, dim figure of her commander.

As they passed close to her Ryder thanked her through the loud-hailer. Wingfield called back "Good-by and good luck," and, as the boats further astern came up: "Good luck, boys!"

The two destroyers turned away, to begin an all-night

patrol off the mouth of the Loire, and to await such as might return the next morning. The Charioteers watched their dim shapes fade into the night, watched the submarine slip below the sea. They were alone.

12

INTO THE JAWS

Forty miles to the goal.

Glancing back from time to time to see if all ships were keeping proper station, Ryder saw the shapes of the two leading torpedo-carrying motor launches two hundred yards away on either quarter, and astern of them the troop-carrying MLs stretched back for a mile in two orderly columns, gradually diminishing in size so that the farthest were scarcely discernible as faint black marks upon the somber gray seascape. Falconar, with Briault's troops, had just caught up. In the very tail of all, "Wynn's Weapons" continued to hang back and leap forward by her queer jerks. The haze persisted and thickened. The clouds grew denser and it began to rain a little. The tall bulk of *Campbeltown* astern, five hundred yards away, became blurred with a thin veil of moisture. This, thought Ryder, was just the weather he wanted to avoid being seen; it did not, perhaps, occur to him in his preoccupation with the immediate present, that it was just not the weather for the bombing support that was of such critical importance.

Newman, going below, found Private Kelly slipping down his trousers and about to put on the kilt. The Scot looked up a trifle guiltily, saying, "Can I, sir?"

Smiling good-naturedly, Newman answered, "All right, if you think you'll fight better that way."

All hands had already had their last meal and in *Campbeltown* the officers thought regretfully of the doom of their excellent La Ina sherry in the wardroom and they all had a glass or two before supper. At eleven o'clock Nigel Tibbits, assisted by Able Seaman Demmelweet, activated the eight-hour pencil delay fuses that were to set off the great explosive charge, starting the flow of the acid that would gradually eat through the copper. Their known margin of error made it possible that one of them might turn out to be a six-hour fuse, so that the charge would go up at five o'clock next morning, and it should not, in any case, go off later than nine o'clock.

Just before half past eleven, while they were still several miles out to sea, the throb of our bombers was plainly heard coming over to attack. Mecke, the German antiaircraft commander, had in fact given the alert at 11:20 and a few minutes later the horizon ahead of the Charioteers leaped into life. The sky became illuminated with the probing fingers of searchlights, followed very soon by the sharp flashes of many guns, seeming at that distance like the flickering of innumerable torches or the flashes of some army of crazy photographers. The streams of colored tracer were seen climbing into the sky with little pin-points of bursting shells at their extremities. Almost immediately afterwards they heard the muffled crump of bursting bombs, not in showers, but only one at a time. The battle of St. Nazaire had begun.

Midnight passed and it was Saturday, March 28.

Half an hour later, exactly on time, the little force entered the estuary of the Loire. At a quarter to one, in the vicinity of Le Chatelier Shoal, they had their first glimpse of land, the low line of the northern shore being dimly discernible. Green thought that the set of the sea must have carried them a trifle further to the north than he had expected and he altered course a little. They were now in the dangerous shoal waters and speed was reduced to ten knots, in order to minimize *Campbeltown*'s draft as much as possible, for she settled by the stern when at speed. Navigationally, this was the most difficult part of the passage, for the destroyer, head and front of the whole enterprise, had nothing whatever to spare beneath her keel.

Accordingly, ordering *Campbeltown* to steer a course of 50°, which made allowance for a strong northerly set, and to act as guide of the fleet, Ryder himself moved off on either bow to locate shoals by the echo-sounder and to take ranges to the shore by the radar equipment. He found, however, that the radar, primitive as it was, able to read only directly fore and aft and subject to false echoes from the adjacent ships, was of little value.

The destroyer did in fact ground twice. Each time, Donald Roy tells us, "we felt her churning and shuddering through the mud and we had some bad moments." Beattie, looking over the side to see if the destroyer was still moving, noted that her speed was checked to about five knots, but by great good fortune she drove through without harm. In after days the professional Loire pilots declared that Green's feat of navigation that night was "without parallel" in the history of the port.

About this time yet another danger was averted. Away on the port quarter Ryder saw the dim shape of a small ship patrolling the entrance to the Charpentiers Channel. It was, as we now know, one of the two harbor patrol boats numbered 414 and 415. "We held our course as well as our breaths," Ryder said, "praying that we should go unnoticed." Their luck still held. We know today that the patrol boat did in fact observe them after they had passed, but, having no wireless, she was helpless to take any action, her attempts to attract attention by flashing her searchlight into the sky passing unnoticed.

The air raid had now completely stopped. Aircraft, indeed, were still flying, but they were high above the clouds and no one heard them now. The German searchlights had been dowsed. To the men who were stealing across the shoals nothing broke the stillness of the night except the murmur of the ships' engines moving through the unruffled sea. All hands were at action stations. In the motor launches the deck petrol tanks had been emptied and filled with sea water. The surgical dressings and the morphia had been laid out in each wheelhouse. The soldiers had prepared themselves, harnessed in their webbing equipment with their heavy loads of ammunition and grenades, and with their fighting knives strapped to their legs. The Bergen rucksacks carrying the explosives of the demolition men were laid out on deck ready to be picked

Bren Gun

up. Bren-gunners with stocks of 100-round magazines lay on
the deck. Officers waited on the bridge to take instructions
from the captain.

In the *Campbeltown* Copland, tall, erect, very cool and
self-contained, had summoned all the fourteen commando officers to a short final conference in the wardroom a little before midnight. They spoke in a matter-of-fact way about final
details of their tasks. It was just midnight when they finished
and Copland ordered, "Action stations, please, gentlemen."

They jumped up and went quietly to their places with
their men. Copland's place was on the fo'c'sle, where he was
to direct the disembarkation of the parties in their correct order. On the fo'c'sle with him was John Proctor, in the kilt, in
command of the two 3-inch mortars. Amidships the assault
and demolitions parties took up their positions under cover
of the steel fences erected for them, the assault parties out-
board, the demolition teams and their protection squads inboard. Leading on the starboard side, ready to land "like
lightning," was the assault party of the stalwart John Roderick, with Donald Roy's kilted party in the corresponding
position to port. Gunner Milne, the Laird's batman, close to
the signal deck, kept his eye musingly on that German ensign
showing darkly overhead. Etches, who was in charge of the
two demolition teams at the northern end of the dry dock,
was also close to the signal deck. Inboard also were the parties
of Chant, Hopwood, and Smalley. Down in the wardroom
were the demolition teams of the two Royal Ulster Riflemen,
Gerard Brett and Corran Purdon, looking wistfully at all the
bottles that were so soon to be blown to destruction. Burtenshaw, monocle in eye, wearing Beattie's cap and towering
above everyone, was in exalted good humor, humming
"There'll Always Be an England."

The naval officers and ratings were also already at their
action stations. On the bridge were Beattie and Tibbits, with
Montgomery as commando liaison officer. On the fo'c'sle,
with Proctor's mortars, was the ship's lone twelve-pounder,
manned by cooks and stewards, but with trained gun-captain
and layer. Gough, as first lieutenant, stood ready to control
the fire of the eight Oerlikons high on their "bandstand"
towers, the moment that Beattie should give the order to open
fire by the ringing of a bell. Petty Officer Newman, gunner's
mate, was at his hand. Down below, Warrant Engineer Locke
looked round the engine and boiler rooms. In the sick bay the
Canadian doctor, Surgeon-Lieutenant W. J. Winthrope,

(MGB 314)

(ML270) (torpedo) 7
Irwin

8 (ML160) (torpedo)
Boyd

H.M.S. CAMPBELTOWN

GROUP ONE
to land at Old Mole

GROUP TWO
to land in Old Entrance

(ML 447) 9
Platt, with Birney's
assault party for Old Mole

1 (ML 192)
Stephens, with Burn's assault party

(ML341) 10
Briault, with Hodgson's assault party;
transferred to No 15

2 (ML262)
Burt, with Woodcock (demolition)
and Morgan (Protection)

(ML457) 11
Collier, with Pritchard,
Walton and Watson

3 (ML267)
Beart, with Moss's h.q. party

(ML307) 12
Wallis, with Bradley (demolition)

4 (ML268)
Tillie, with Pennington (demolition)
and Jenkins (Protection)

(ML443) 13
Horlock, with Wilson,
Bassett-Wilson and Bonvin (demolition)
and Houghton (Protection)

5 (ML156) (torpedo)
Fenton, with Hooper's assault party

(ML306) 14
Henderson, with Swayne (demolition)
and Vanderwerve (Protection)

6 (ML177) (torpedo)
Rodier, with Haines's assault party

(ML446) 15
Falconar; took over from No 10

16 (ML298)
Nock, spare

17 (MTB 74)
Wynn

Figure 2. Order of battle for the attack.

waited. All else—mess-decks, cabins, galleys, stores, officers—
were empty, silent and abandoned. In the heart of the great
charge beneath the twelve-pounder the acid was inexorably
eating through the tensed copper wire.

Was it conceivable that they would have the luck to get
through unseen and unheard? Boyd, leading the starboard
column in ML 8, admits that, at this period, he was feeling
very apprehensive. "But I shall never forget," he recorded,
"the sweet smell of the countryside as we steamed upriver;
we could see both banks now and on the port hand could
even make out trees and hedges." They were within a few
hundred yards of the enemy.

The moon, that moon which the bombers had needed so
much, was now partially unveiled as the clouds began to dissipate. Under the clearer light, the two columns of little boats
and their big companion moved confidently forward up the
hushed river. At 1:20 A.M. the gunboat, now again in the van
for the final dash, passed the old disused tower of Les Morées
in midstream, almost exactly on time.

On that dark shore Captain Mecke, commander of the
antiaircraft brigade, had been following such events as he
could hear and see from his headquarters at St. Marc with
perplexity and some anxiety.

After the British bombing attack had developed at 11:30
he became considerably astonished at the unusual behavior of
the aircraft. Bombs fell only one at a time, with long intervals betwen. Not more than thirty altogether. Some aircraft
dropped no bombs at all. "The employment of so many aircraft"—which he estimated later at eighty—"and the determination with which the British pressed forward their attack
bore no relation to the number of bombs.

"Some aircraft," he noted, "flew on to Nantes."

As one after another they flew in, flying high and apparently aimlessly, the radar trace of their movements re-
sembling a spawn of eels, he became more and more suspicious. He formed the impression that the bombing raid was a
blind for some other purpose and he said to one of his staff
officers, "Some devilry is afoot." At midnight he made the
signal to all command posts of the Wehrmacht:

*The conduct of the enemy aircraft is inexplicable and in-
dicates suspicion of parachute landings.*

He noted that the night was not very dark, with no cloud
below 3200 feet, except for an occasional short rain squall,

and that surface visibility was fairly good up to three or four miles. By one o'clock the greater portion of the British aircraft had withdrawn and there remained only a few in the neighborhood, flying beyond the effective range of his guns. He had already given the order to cease fire and, in order to assist further aircraft in finding their way to St. Nazaire, he had also caused the searchlights to be switched off, and not to be employed again unless aircraft were visible by the naked eye or by glasses. But he also gave the order to his troops for a "continued and increased alert" and—a quite exceptional order for them—"to direct special attention seaward."

Perhaps as a consequence of this order, or perhaps, in his own words, "because he was bored with looking at the sky," Korvettenkapitän Burhenne, commanding 809 Naval Flak Battalion, from his headquarters on the east bank, turned his night glasses to the river and beheld to his astonishment a force of small ships moving up at moderate speed. As this was the concern of the Harbor Commander, he reported the fact direct to Kellermann's headquarters, but was given the answer:

"Don't be stupid. It's not your business. You would be better employed looking at the sky instead of the river."

He thereupon reported to his own superior, Mecke.

At 1:15 a lookout at St. Marc, or the naval signal station nearby, or both, reported the approach of a force of "about seventeen vessels" at extreme visual range. Three minutes later one of Mecke's staff telephoned to the Harbor Commander and asked, "Are you expecting any German ships to come into harbor?" The answer was in the negative.

At 1:20—the moment when Ryder passed Les Morées tower—Mecke made the signal to all concerned:

Achtung Landegefahr (Beware landing).

On receipt of this code word, the machinery for repelling an invasion in accordance with the Emergency Orders was put in force throughout the command. More particularly, all anti-aircraft guns switched to the defense of the shores and all available troops and crews of the minesweepers, harbor defense boats and tankers in St. Nazaire, many of whom were in their air-raid shelters, from which they were promptly routed out, became actuated in an infantry role as *Stosstrupps* (thrust troops). The most important of these were the spare hands of Mecke's own battalions—the watch off duty, the clerks, instructors, storemen and so on.

At the same time the commander of the coast-defense

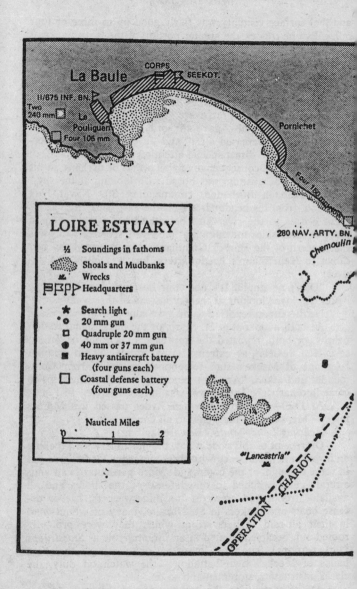

LOIRE ESTUARY

- ½   Soundings in fathoms
- Shoals and Mudbanks
- Wrecks
- Headquarters

- ★   Search light
- ⊙   20 mm gun
- ◻   Quadruple 20 mm gun
- ●   40 mm or 37 mm gun
- Heavy antiaircraft battery (four guns each)
- ◻   Coastal defense battery (four guns each)

Nautical Miles

0   1   2

La Baule

CORPS   SEEKDT.

II/675 INF. BN.

Two 240 mm

Le Pouliguen

Four 105 mm

Pornichet

Four 150 mm

280 NAV. ARTY. BN.

Chemoulin

2½

1¼

"Lancastria"

OPERATION CHARIOT

guns, Korvettenkapitän Dieckmann, who had become restless
at the sound of engines and who had come out immediately
at his headquarters at Chémoulin on receipt of the siting report at 1:15, gave the order to his batteries: "Stand by to attack naval targets."

Why the searchlights had not already been switched on
is not explained. According to the signal log, five minutes
elapsed before Mecke's order to illuminate was put into effect.
Those five minutes were of priceless value to the dim shapes
moving steadily onward under the misty moon.

Less than two miles to go. The luck was incredible.

At 1:22 the big five-foot searchlight BLAU 1, hard by
702 Battalion's headquarters, flashed out. The whole force
was brilliantly floodlit. In the cold, white beams the bow and
stern waves glittered and foamed. Towering over the little
ships, there was revealed the bulk of the German-seeming
Campbeltown, beginning to increase speed for her final burst.

Two German signal stations, their lamps winking
through the blaze of light, at once challenged—one from
right ahead in the dockyard area (in fact from the *Sperrbrecher* moored off the East Jetty), the other from a position on
the port beam. At the same time a few bursts were fired at the
van of the force from the Bofors guns at positions M16 and
M17 at Villés-Martin.

Now was the moment for Leading Seaman Pike to play
his part. For this critical eventuality Ryder had made careful
preparation and had given Pike instructions beforehand how
to act. He was to transmit in German a long, delaying mes-
sage and to give the "Morsename" or call signal of one of the
German torpedo boats on that coast, of which we knew several from documents found on the Vaagso raid. Further, as a
trump card, Ryder had been provided with the cartridges for
the current German Very light recognition signal, which we
also knew.

What Ryder had not been prepared for, however, was
being called up by two stations simultaneously. He would
have to think fast. Pike, who had been quick to grasp what
was needed of him, was standing ready at his elbow on the
bridge of the gunboat with his night signaling lamp, as the
harsh white light burst on them, and Ryder told him to answer first the station abeam of them.

"Make the call signal and then the delaying signal."

"Aye, aye, sir."

Pike complied. Standing up very prominently on the bridge and wearing a petty officer's cap which at that distance might give him an outline similar to a German's, he aligned his lamp on the challenging station, made the Morsename and then began the bogus signal: *Proceeding up harbor in accordance with orders. . . .*

It worked like magic. At the same moment, quite unaccountably, Mecke was advised by the Harbor Commander that the convoy was, after all, German. Firing stopped at once and several of the searchlights switched off. All hands on deck could see the German station acknowledging the signal word by word. Before Pike could complete the prearranged signal, however, it became imperative to deal with the *Sperrbrecher* station ahead, which continued to challenge. Ryder therefore interrupted Pike and ordered:

"Make the signal to 'wait.' "

Pike, cool and steady, complied, making "EB" followed by the Morsename.

"Now the station ahead. Call sign and same signal."

With some searchlights still glaring at them, Pike turned his signal lamp to the *Sperrbrecher*. He had scarcely begun, however, when the ships were again fired on, but still with obvious hesitation. Once more Ryder interrupted Pike and ordered him to make the signal for "ship being fired on by friendly forces."

This Pike made by directing the lamp vertically upwards, making two short flashes repeated three times, followed by the Morsename. On board *Campbeltown* Beattie made the same signal.

Again the firing ceased. Four precious minutes had been won. It was 1:27. Scarcely a mile to go. In another six minutes *Campbeltown* would be home.

13

"CAMPBELTOWN'S" ATTACK

The Germans, we know today, had been completely foxed. They did not conceive it credible that a British force could suddenly appear under their noses with such effrontery so far from home. Naturally enough, they supposed at first that this unheralded force was more probably a German one, perhaps seeking shelter after stress of battle, without having followed the proper procedure for obtaining permission to enter the port.

But the bluff was at an end. Had they been genuine, the approaching ships would have stopped when fired on. Every German gun that could bear had them in its sights and at about 1:28 the storm burst.

Ryder made one last attempt to gain time, playing what he hoped was his trump card. Raising the Very pistol in the air, he fired the recognition signal. It rose a few feet into the air and then fell sizzling into the water—for it was an aircraft cartridge, designed to be fired downwards. What the Germans noticed, however, was not its curious flight, but the fact that the red light was not the shade of red to which they were accustomed. The battle was on.

The British ships, too, were ready. Ordered to hold their fire till the last moment, they decided that the last moment had now come. On board the *Campbeltown*, Beattie had already ordered:

"Two hundred revolutions" (eighteen and a half knots) and to his yeoman of signals:

"Hoist battle ensigns."

The German colors were run down and as the masthead flag came to the signal deck, Gunner Milne, who had for so long been waiting for this moment, seized it, cut off a strip and gave it to the delighted Roy.

A moment later a German searchlight threw upon the mast a noose of light, which, traveling slowly upwards, came to rest on the white ensign—old, weather-stained and half-drooping in the windless air. All down the double column of motor launches, which had hitherto worn no colors, the white ensign was seen to break out astern.

Beattie sounded his bell to open fire. At once the eight Oerlikons, under the direction of Petty Officer Newman, burst into a shattering clamor. On the fo'c'sle Copland had softly ordered the twelve-pounder and the 3-inch mortars, a little ahead of him, to keep the searchlight on the port beam covered but not to fire. He now shouted, "Let her go!" Instantly gun and mortars opened fire. The Klaxon horns sounded all down the columns of the motor launches and in a moment the little boats were sparkling with gun flashes from twenty-four Oerlikons, from the four Hotchkiss guns of the torpedo craft and from Savage's little pom-pom in the gunboat. To this was added to brittle clatter of the Bren guns as the commandos joined in the common fire plan.

In a moment upwards of a hundred guns and innumerable small arms were firing within this small area, nearly all of them rapid-firing pieces, their orange flashes stabbing the white glare of the searchlights. Across this great pool of light, into which every lamp that the Germans possessed was now concentrating its shaft, there shot in all directions vivid streams of red, green and yellow tracer. They crisscrossed like lighted shuttles on some infernal loom, duplicated by their darting images on the still water. As orchestra to this spectacle there could be heard, above the drum-roll of machine gun and rifle, the prolonged bursts of Oerlikons, the repetitive thuds of Bofors, and the sharper cracks of Dieckmann's heavier coast-defense guns—75 mm., 150 mm., 170 mm. Gun blast and shellburst came almost instantaneously together, so short was the range. The rugged Boyd declared, "The weight of fire caught one's breath."

One might doubt whether in this raucous orchestra the heavier German coastal guns could bring their fire to bear upon the raiders at this stage, yet Dieckmann says that they did—even his 6-inch howitzers away at Chémoulin Point. Certainly the four 75-mm. guns at Le Pointeau could bear at all stages and during that night this battery fired no fewer than thirteen hundred rounds. But on any count the odds were unequal. It was a battle in which the German guns, firing from fixed and protected positions, and from behind their

own lights, fought against a quantity of heavy machine gun
half a dozen two- and three-pounders and a solitary twelve
pounder from exposed positions on moving platforms, firin
into a blinding white glare.

Yet the British gunners quickly established a temporar
superiority. Their only targets were the mere flashes of gun
or the direct glare of searchlights, against both of which it i
particularly difficult to lay or aim any weapon. Even by day
the most expert gunner would have been severely taxed t
secure direct hits on the actual guns themselves from th
water level. Yet, after a three or four minutes' duel, a definit
slackening of the enemy's fire was forced at the most critica
moment. Some guns ceased fire. Some searchlights went out
The Germans had been taken aback by the violence of ou
instant reply and although they recovered quickly, the relaxa
tion came at a moment when time was the most precious o
all elements. Not a single ship was mortally hit. Through th
whirlpool of light and the colored rain of shells and bullet
the raiders went undeviatingly ahead, moving faster now, th
seventeen ships preserving unbroken formation.

At this moment, the gunboat, with Green still keeping
careful check on navigation, came at last nearly abreast o
the long clasping, outer arms of the South Entrance. The mo
ment had nearly come for her to swing away to starboard t
make way for *Campbeltown*'s final dash. At that moment sh
came suddenly upon the enemy *Sperrbrecher* anchored in th
river, previously obscured but now revealed by the lights o
her own side. Her solid structure sprang out conspicuously
very close on the starboard bow. She opened fire at once o
the gunboat, but Able Seaman Savage, at the forward Vicker
pom-pom, plastered her from end to end with such accuracy
that she was at once temporarily silenced. Her dangerous
88-mm. gun was put out of action and its ready-use ammuni
tion set on fire. They passed so close to her that a man migh
almost have jumped on board.

Meanwhile, the main weight of the German fire was be
ing directed at the *Campbeltown*, clearly the main agent o
whatever mischief the British were up to. "Her sides," said
Newman, looking back from the gunboat, "seemed to be alive
with bursting shells." Beattie had begun to increase speed jus
before the action started, having discovered, as we have seen,
the inflexibility of the ship below about sixteen knots. She
must now, he knew, be able to answer the wheel instantaneous-

y. With the flood tide to help him, he intended to hit the caisson at about twenty knots.

High on the open bridge, Beattie, Tibbits, Montgomery, now in his full equipment ready for landing, the yeoman of signals and other ratings had been clearly revealed as soon as the Germans had illuminated the scene. They were, said Beattie, "too jolly conspicuous." He sent Tibbits down into the wheelhouse, immediately below the bridge, to take charge in case of trouble, and when the German fire began to get hot, and tracer-lit projectiles of all sorts were whistling about the bridge, he said:

"I think we'd all better go below; no point at all in getting killed."

Accordingly they all slipped down to the wheelhouse, where they had protection against small-arms fire overhead and on all sides, except for an open horizontal strip about a foot wide, which allowed them to see perfectly well ahead and on either beam. Here, therefore, they stood, with Chief Petty Officer Wellstead, the coxswain, at the wheel, the two telegraph men on either hand and the quartermaster to one side. Beattie was concentrating his mind on the changes in course which he would have to make at any minute and which he had already worked out in advance.

The moment that the full violence of the action broke loose Campbeltown began to take casualties. In the wheelhouse Wellstead was shot dead. The quartermaster jumped forward to take his place at the wheel but, almost immediately, he also fell. He attempted to continue steering while lying on the deck but he collapsed. Montgomery, nearest at hand, stepped instinctively over his body and grasped the wheel, but to his relief he felt Tibbits, who had come forward from behind, put his hand on his arm and move him aside, saying, 'I'll take it, old boy."

Beattie, unmoved, remained standing at the front of the wheelhouse, intent upon his task, pitting his eyes against the glare. The noise and the light were merely a nuisance. Montgomery, now standing at the back of the wheelhouse, with a few small splinter wounds in the leg, saw his solid, black, bearded profile stenciled against the brilliant light and exclaimed inwardly, "By God! the absolute Elizabethan!"

Ahead of them, the distance between them now shortening, Beattie was watching the gunboat firing vigorously to port with her little pom-pom. He was looking for the moment when she would sheer away to starboard for his final spurt. On either bow Boyd and Irwin were firing hard with their Hotchkiss guns. On his own decks Beattie could see the cooks and stewards serving the twelve-pounder just ahead of him— "and damned well, too." Amidships and astern, he could hear his eight Oerlikons.

A continuous stream of projectiles of all sorts was now striking the *Campbeltown*, but so violent was the sound of our own weapons that the ring of bullets on her hull and the crack of small shells was scarcely noticed; but when larger shells shook her from stem to stern none could be unaware, and what every survivor was to remember for ever afterwards was the unchecked flow of the darts of red and green tracer flashing and hissing across her deck and the quadruple whistle of the Bofors shells. Bullets penetrated her engine and boiler rooms, ricocheting from surface to surface like hornets, and Locke, the Warrant Engineer, ordered hands to take cover between the main engines of the condensers except for the throttle watchkeepers, Engine-Room Artificers Reay and Nelson, who stood unmoved at their valves throughout. High on the exposed bandstands two of the Oerlikons were knocked out and Sergeant Butler, lying behind the steel screens amidship, watched the ratings running up to replace their shipmates as they fell.

The group in the wheelhouse remained tensed and alert. The bodies of the coxswain and quartermaster lay at their feet. Beattie peered out through the slit into the glare as the minutes went by. "Can't see a bloody thing," he muttered to Tibbits. A moment later his vision was further obscured as the twelve-pounder sustained a direct hit from a large shell, her own crew and those of Proctor's mortars spread-eagled in death or wounds.

As the smoke cleared away Beattie saw revealed before him two stone arms with a strip of sea between. This must be the lock gate at last. He was shaping direct for the gap and he held his course to ram. Just in time, he saw that it was not the lock, but the long curving arms of the South Entrance. He ordered sharply:

"Hard astarboard!"

Tibbits acknowledged, "Wheel's hard astarboard, sir."

"Steer 055 degrees."

Scarcely had the destroyer swung to starboard than a German searchlight, swinging its beam, picked out for a fleeting moment the lighthouse at the tip of the Old Mole. This

Penhouet
Basin

a
M
B
A
C
Normandie Dock

c
b
c
a
b

Submarine Basin

Submarine
Pens

a
G
Old
Entrance

a

b
c

K

Anti-torpedo net

H.M.S. Campbeltown
MGB

MTB 7   MTB 8

Old Town
Old Mole

Avant-port

East Jetty

ST. NAZAIRE DOCKS

A: Northern winding-house
B. Northern caisson
C. Underground fuel tanks
D. The Bridge of Memories
E. Southern caisson
F. Southern winding-house
G. Swing bridge & lock
H. Pump house
K. Warehouses
L. Power station
M. Swing bridge
N. Forge de l'Ouest

a. Minesweepers
b. Harbor defense boats
c. Tugboats
d. Tankers

Sperrbrecher

was the aiming point for which Beattie had been looking.
From this point he had already worked out his course according to the distance he should find himself to be from the
mole. As he came abreast of it, he judged himself to be about
a cablelength away, and ordered:

"Port 25."

"Twenty-five of port wheel on, sir."

"Steer 345 degrees."

Before Tibbits had time to set the ship on this course,
however, Beattie made a correction. He must, he decided as
he looked again on the port beam, be only about half a cable
from the mole. He ordered quietly:

"Steer 350 degrees."

Tibbits swung the ship back five degrees to starboard.
Only seven hundred yards now.

"Stand by to ram."

Ahead of him Beattie saw the gunboat sheer away to
starboard. The moment had come.

Campbeltown was going fast now, making good twenty
knots, her bow wave splaying wide. Every German gun that
could bear was now converged upon her; not now those lower
down the river but those at point-blank range in the dockyard area itself—from the Old Mole, from either side of the
Normandie Dock, from the top of the submarine pens, from
the roofs of buildings—and from the east bank of the river.
Repeatedly hit, she was now suffering very heavy casualties,
among her sailors and soldiers alike, her decks spattered with
fallen bodies. To Copland it seemed as though they were the
converging point of one of those fountains in which illuminated jets pour continuously upon the center; how anyone in
those fiery minutes was left alive was always to pass his understanding. But miraculously *Campbeltown* escaped damage to
any vital part as she raced forward. The gunboat and the
motor launches of Boyd and Irwin were backing her up at
close quarters. Boyd's gunner, Able Seaman MacIver, observed a Bofors immediately to starboard of the caisson engaging the destroyer. With a steady hand, he caught it in the
sights of his Hotchkiss and silenced it with a direct hit.

Not till he was within two hundred yards did Beattie
see the great steel gate of the lock, discernible as an in-
distinct black line beyond the "spill" of the searchlights,
dead ahead. At the last moment an incendiary bomb, of the
nature of thermite, projected by no known agency, but conceivably dropped from one of our own aircraft, landed on the

forecastle and burst into flames. *Campbeltown* held steadily on her course. In the wheelhouse there was complete silence. Beattie and Montgomery propped themselves against the front of the wheelhouse, ready for the shock of impact. Throughout the ship every man braced himself; in the wardroom Brett's and Purdon's parties sat down on the deck and an unexploded shell, its red tracer burning in the base, shot through above their heads. Denser and denser grew the black line ahead. A momentary check told them that they had ripped through the anti-torpedo net. All hands could feel the wire dragging along the ship's bottom. The caisson was scarcely fifty yards away and only now could Beattie clearly see it. With extraordinary presence of mind, in order to hit the caisson in the center and in order to swing the ship's stern to starboard, so that the Old Entrance should not be blocked, he crisply ordered at this last moment:

"Port 20!"

Instantly Tibbits obeyed and at 1:34, with all her Oerlikons blazing at the enemy guns only a few yards away, with her fo'c'sle in flames, she crashed into the caisson.

She struck with such accuracy and force that her bows, up to the level of the caisson, crumpled back for a distance of thirty-six feet, leaving her fo'c'sle deck, which was higher than the caisson, actually projecting a foot beyond the inner face.

Beattie turned to Montgomery with a smile and said, "Well, there we are." Looking at his watch, he added, "Four minutes late."

14

THE DOCK SMASHERS

Beattie's achievement, executed with such cool precision, marks the attainment of the chief purpose of the expedition. There now began a medley of events difficult to describe in ordered sequence. The battle spread like a flame, to the whole scene by land and water. The motor launches, coming up astern of *Campbeltown,* pressed towards their designated landing places with the greatest daring, adding to the lurid scene the glow of their own conflagrations and the smoke and stench of burning petrol as one by one half their number burst into flames or blew up. The battle splintered into innumerable little actions. From the moment of committal command and control of the action was lost, partly through the very nature of the operation and partly through the failure of the gunboat's wireless, so that each boat and each group of soldiers pursued, or attempted to pursue, its predetermined part alone.

At the moment that *Campbeltown* crashes into the caisson, we may imagine Curtis's gunboat and the motor launches of Boyd and Irwin standing off to support her and the two columns of troop-carrying craft coming up close astern, with Platt leading the port column and Stephens the starboard. These beheld the bows of the destroyer erupting in flying timbers, smoke and flames. They saw the commandos leap to their feet on deck and, under a covering fire from the destroyer's Oerlikons overhead, begin to move forward. The guns of both sides began to concentrate their fire on this small area.

Campbeltown herself began to prepare for her last moments. Beattie, excited enough beneath his icy exterior, forgot to give the order to ring off the engines, and for a few minutes there was a little confusion in the engine and boiler rooms, accentuated by the darkness which now enveloped the whole ship below deck. The engines might have been required to hold the ship on the caisson, but Chief Engine-Room Artificer Howard went up on deck, found Gough in the storm of fire that crackled and flashed up there and got sanction to shut off steam. The ship was still being repeatedly hit and down below, where the engine-room staff were bearing themselves with exemplary courage, shells and explosive bullets were still penetrating. Stoker Petty Officer Pyke was going about quietly, maintaining machinery by torchlight. Engine-Room Artificer Nelson was killed while evacuating hands from the forward boiler room.

The first, the most imperative duty, however, was to disembark the commandos as rapidly as possible. Not till this had been done did Beattie give the order to abandon ship. Winthorpe's medical party, their hands more than full to the last minute, were routed out. Howard and Engine-Room Artificer Reay proceeded to scuttle ship by torchlight, opening the valves that would let in the sea and removing the condenser doors. To make assurance doubly sure, scuttling charges were fired under the direction of Hargreaves, the torpedo gunner. Finally Beattie and Gough then went round the ship to make sure that no one was left behind. Then they themselves went onto the upper deck while the ship, held fast by the bows on the caisson, was beginning to settle at the stern. About half the ship's company, according to plan, made their way forward to the fo'c'sle, which they found enveloped in acrid smoke pouring from the hole made by the mysterious incendiary. Led by Howard, they scrambled down the scaling ladders left by the commandos, and, suffering sharp casualties from the heavy machine-gun fire that was riddling the quayside, made their way to Curtis's gunboat in the Old Entrance.

The remainder, numbering about thirty and including Beattie himself, went aft. By this time Rodier, commanding ML 6, had with great coolness successfully landed Troop Sergeant-Major Haines and his party in the Old Entrance. On being hailed as he came out by Beattie, who was concerned at the difficulty of getting his wounded away safely, Rodier came alongside on the port quarter and took off Beattie's party.

Full of wounds, silent, empty and deserted by all except her dead, *Campbeltown* lay patiently waiting for the determined hour of sacrifice.

Meanwhile, her commandos had been taking heavy casualties before ever they landed. On the exposed fo'c'sle Proctor had been badly wounded when the twelve-pounder was knocked out and lay with his leg shattered and his kilt smouldering. Amidships, where lay the assault parties and some of the demolition teams, Chant, Etches, Sergeants Chamberlain, Jones, Davies, Corporals Johnson, Donaldson, O'Donnell and several more had been hit just before ramming.

The ship was a cauldron into which light and fire were being poured from all directions as though from hoses. To starboard the German guns were shooting from a few yards' range. The whole gun areas of Mecke's 703 and 809 Battalions were alight with jets of crackling venom, streaming through the searchlights' staring beams. The fo'c'sle was smothered in smoke from the incendiary, which had burned a large hole in the deck, penetrated the chief petty officers' mess and was threatening the great three-ton explosive charge immediately below, until a damage-control party arrested the danger.

Through this pall of smoke, confusing the searchlight glare, Gough, Tibbits and Copland at once hurried forward to direct the landings from the bows. Having seen that the way was clear to land on the caisson, the naval party began to fix iron-runged ladders over the side. Copland then ran back amidships, through the narrow gangways and into the well-deck, to call forward the assault parties. His path was choked with wounded sailors and unceremoniously he thrust them aside. He ordered; "Roderick off, Roy off." They went forward through the smoke and the colored darts, "with the awe-inspiring drumming of our own Oerlikons firing overhead," narrowly escaping falling into the gaping hole in the deck from which clouds of smoke continued to pour. As they came forward, they carried up their own bamboo ladders to supplement the ship's ladders, but several of them were smashed, either through enemy fire or by the heavy weights imposed on them. Roderick, adjured by Newman to be off "like lightning" to attack a gun position only a few yards away, was quickly over the side to starboard. Almost simultaneously, Roy's Scots were off on the port side, he and Tibbits cursing each other freely when the steel ladder jammed. Down they all went, carrying or supporting their wounded, collected themselves, then moved off at the double.

Very calm, though his slung rifle was shattered to pieces

on his shoulder, Copland took post on the swirling fo'c'sle, ordering off each of the parties in turn, with a word of encouragement for each, greeting many of them by name, and adding, "Just think of this as only another exercise." He might well, said John Roderick, "have been seeing us off on the local bus for all the concern that he was showing." When all were off he went in search of Beattie to report all troops disembarked. He found the bridge "a mass of twisted wreckage" and Beattie not there. He went about the ship, calling him by name. Not finding him, he searched the ship for wounded and got them over the side with Howard's party, to make their way to the gunboat. He put a tourniquet on Proctor's nearly severed leg and, finding it impossible to carry him down the damaged ladders, threw him over the side onto the caisson.

Then, accompanied by Corporal Cheetham, Lance-Corporal Fyfe (his wireless operator) and Private Hannon, he climbed down himself.

First Ashore

From this moment we must imagine the seven parties of the commandos, steel-helmeted, with whitened webbing, scattering to their several targets, moving at the double under heavy weights of arms or explosives, past tall cranes, buildings, railway trucks and piles of timber; now brilliantly illuminated by the searchlights, now in a moonlike gloom; sometimes unopposed, sometimes having to fight bitterly for their objectives. In the midst we see the handfuls of the commandos moving to their stations—Roderick scattering his enemies, Roy holding his bridge, the teams of destroyers fixing their charges.

John Roderick was a strapping young Welshman of twenty-three. At his side was John Stutchbury. Twelve NCOs and men made up their little assault force of Group 30, whose tasks were to destroy the group of light guns immediately to the southeast of the caisson, of which, as German maps now show, there were four, to establish a defensive position against counterattack, and to make an attempt to fire the underground oil fuel tanks.

Roderick's party was quickly away, clambering over the fallen bodies and leaving Corporal Donaldson mortally wounded on the deck. Impeded by the broken ladders, several swarmed down to the caisson by rope, Corporals Woodiwiss and Finch, Tommy-gunners, being the first of all the force to set foot on French soil, while the weapons of their comrades to cover them, opened fire against the bursts from the enemy positions to their right.

Clearly visible in the artificial light not many yards away there stood their first objective—a light gun in a sandbagged pit. Roderick and his men went straight at it, throwing hand grenades and then rushing in with Tommy guns and Brens blazing. A German grenade was kicked back by Woodiwiss to burst among the enemy, and it was Woodiwiss who clapped the sausage charge on the guns to sever the barrel. All six Germans of the detachment were left for dead.*

From this first success Roderick's men swept on to the next objective, which was a 37-mm. gun mounted on top of a formidable concrete bunker. This was position M70. As the only approach up to the gun platform was by a single stair-way, they were unable to assault it, but they silenced the gun with grenades skillfully thrown, killed the gun captain as he tried to come downstairs and, entering the bunker, killed three Luftwaffe men who had come to collect ammunition.

On again went the little band to the third gun (M10). This was a Bofors and they found it silent, for it was the gun that had been knocked out by Able Seaman MacIver, but Roderick's men, entering the bunker, destroyed the crew. Many Nissen-type huts were here and into these they hurled grenades.

There remained yet a fourth gun (No. 67), with a search-light beyond and here the historian finds some difficulty, for while the Germans admit officially that this gun and search-light were destroyed, "by parties landed by raft from the motor launches," no definite claim is made by Newman's men. Roderick's party, moving by small squads and giving covering fire to each other, was now extended and it is far more credible that it was one of these squads that accounted for the last targets. Whatever the truth, the simple fact remains that four guns and a searchlight were destroyed or silenced and a number of Germans exceeding Roderick's in strength were killed within a space of about twenty minutes.

By now Stutchbury, Sergeant Davies, Corporal Howarth

---

*In fact, three were killed, two wounded and one shammed death.

and Lance-Corporal Simpson had been wounded and the effective strength of the party reduced to ten or less. Yet the oil tanks were reached and incendiaries were thrown down their ventilators, though without effect.

By now the Germans had begun to collect themselves. The troops of 4 Works Company, whose headquarters was quite close, had almost certainly come into action. Beyond the gloom Roderick found resistance stiffening and it was only by great determination that his tiny band held on so long to fulfill their purpose of perimeter protection. Some time a little after 2:30 A.M. the appointed lookout reported having seen the green rain rocket which was the withdrawal signal from Newman's headquarters ashore. He was mistaken, for the mass of colored tracer in the rear confused him, but it was at about the expected time and, as events were to prove, it was apt to the occasion. Roderick gave the order to withdraw.

The little band began to move back, one party extricating itself at a time under covering fire from the remainder. Their way back lay across the caisson, but, since *Campbeltown*'s bows projected right across it, they had to clamber up once again onto the destroyer's fo'c'sle and down the other side. Roderick, last or nearly last, as he stepped again on that deck which he had left about an hour before, was aware of a strange sensation. The whole ship, littered with debris, her sides and works pitted and torn, smoke still issuing from the hole made by the incendiary, was enveloped in "an uncanny silence."

Passing on and crossing the fireswept dockyard, Roderick was bowled over like a rabbit with a bullet in the thigh.

Roy's Bridge

No less swift and successful was the performance of Roy's kilted team, detailed to the assault tasks on the western side of the dock. Disembarking on the port side of the destroyer's fo'c'sle, and assisting between them Sergeant Jones, who had been wounded on board, they made off by the way they had learned so well from the model, silent in their rubber boots and carrying bamboo scaling-ladders with them. Proctor having been so severely wounded, the Laird was now the only officer. They had not far to go for their first task, which was to silence the gun positions (64 and 65) on the roof of the big pumping station.

Before he could make his attack Roy saw the German teams in full flight across the shadowed dockyard, having escaped by an outside staircase. He called upon Sergeant Challington with his Tommy gun, but the gun jammed after a few rounds. Roy then lobbed two grenades on to the roof, and, following up quickly with Randall, found the guns deserted and he blew them without difficulty.

The Laird then turned and led off his assault party at the double to Bridge G over the Old Entrance, where he was to hold a vital bridgehead, through which the demolition teams, on completion of their tasks, would have to withdraw towards the designated reembarkation area at the Old Mole. He reached the bridge safely, finding no Germans there. His little party took post—thirteen men islanded in the heart of enemy territory.

To this position, extremely exposed and with only the flimsiest cover, they hung on nearly an hour and a half, suffering casualties to half their number from the unreachable guns on elevated positions on the far side of the Submarine Basin, particularly the two quadruple Oerlikons, and from the ships in the Submarine Basin. The whole of the German naval forces and establishments ashore were now dashing from their shelters and running to emergency action stations as the "Enemy Landing Alert" was circulated. Of these, the most troublesome were to be the five ships of the 16th Minesweeper Flotilla, and the four small harbor-defense ships, one of which scuttled herself to avoid capture. Further off the *Stosstrupps* of Mecke's brigade were already on their way to the scene.

Of all this, save for its results, Roy at Bridge G was unaware as he held onto his position and waited for the parties to eastward to come through. Sergeant Jones, Gunner Milne and Private McCormack had already been hit and now, throughout the long stand, Sergeant Challington, Lance-Corporal Sumner and Private Ashcroft were wounded also and Private Gwynn killed in circumstances to be painfully told before long.

Forty Feet Down

Thus the two assault parties carried out their tasks. The demolition teams were hard on their heels. Let us remind ourselves what the targets were they had been ordered to destroy. These numbered five. At the southern end of the dry-dock area was a group of three tasks entrusted to teams under officers of 5 Commando. Stuart Chant had the formidable task of destroying the big pump house; Christopher Smalley was to go for the winding-house where the machinery for moving the big southern caisson in and out of position was situated; Robert Burtenshaw was to destroy the caisson itself with magnetic "wreaths" and 18-pound charges if *Campbeltown* should fail to ram satisfactorily. The protection party for all these teams was provided by Hopwood, of the Essex Regiment.

At the northern end of the big dock, Etches, with Gerard Brett and young Corran Purdon, was charged with destroying the caisson at that end, and the winding-house associated with it. For these demolition teams the protection was provided by "Bung" Denison, of Roderick's Troop. All these five demolition tasks in the dry-dock area were under the control of Pritchard's friend, Bob Montgomery.

Stuart Chant, leader of the team ordained for the destruction of the pump house, was a young Gordon Highlander on the London Stock Exchange. Dark, good-looking and with a lively disposition, he was a rugby footballer of class. His team consisted of four quite outstanding sergeants, not of his own Commando, but of No. 1. Sergeant A. H. Dockerill, Royal Artillery, was a plumber from Ely and a former choir-boy of Ely Cathedral. His three comrades were all Norfolk men: Sergeant R. H. Butler, a village baker, and the two strapping Sergeants A. W. King and W. Chamberlain.

During *Campbeltown*'s approach Chant's party were lying behind their steel screens, face up and feet forward against the shock of impact. A moment before the destroyer rammed, a small shell burst beside Chant and Chamberlain, wounding them both. A sticky feeling running down his leg told Chant that he had been hit in the knee; splinters wounded his arm and fingers also. The bittersweet fumes of high explosive blew over him. He lay momentarily dazed, but an inner compulsion told him to rise and slip into his rucksack with its load of explosives. Three of the sergeants rose with him, but Chamberlain said, "Very sorry, sir, but I can't move."

Between them, however, they lifted up his hundred and eighty-nine pounds and half-carried him as they moved forward to disembark, together with Smalley's and Hopwood's teams. On the fo'c'sle Chant fell painfully into the smoking hole, as many others did, but was caught and held up by his rucksack and moved on, saying a word as he passed to the blanched Proctor. Then, heavily laden with their explosives, sledge hammers, axes and incendiaries, they scrambled, slid or fell down the scaling ladders on the port side. Somehow Chamberlain was got down and the team made for the pump house by the route printed on their minds through a scene vividly lit, but checkered by the dense angular shadows of the buildings, swaying from time to time as the searchlights swung their beams.

Chant was limping but could move fairly freely. They were right on Roy's heels, seeing the kilts flying just ahead. Without waiting for him to attack the German gunners on the roof of the pump house, they went straight for the entrance, but met an unexpected obstacle when they found it barred by a heavy steel door. Chant was momentarily at a loss, but at that moment Montgomery appeared and from the spare explosives that he carried he took out a small magnetic charge, clamped it on the door and stood back. Chant made to light the short length of safety fuse, but found it difficult to strike the fusee with his bleeding fingers. He was disconcerted to find his hands trembling and he said to Montgomery, "Bob, for God's sake help me light this bloody thing; the chaps will think I'm scared."

Montgomery complied, the door was blown in and Chant and his sergeants entered the pump house.

Chant's team had rehearsed over and over again, including provision for casualties. The task required two demolitions —the first, that of the great impeller pumps forty feet below ground, and the second, the electrical gear on the ground floor where they now stood, particularly the electric motors that drove the impeller pumps below, and the transformers. They flashed their torches around and, with the help of the glow coming in from the searchlights and the fires outside, they noted that everything was exactly as they had seen it in the King George V Dock at Southampton—the straight line of the motors, the transformers, the switch gear, the indicators, all laid out in orderly precision.

Chamberlain was by now weak and moving slowly. Chant was reluctant to take so heavy a man down the steep, zigzag staircase that led to the pumping chamber far below, but to ease the sergeant's chagrin, he said,

"Stay up here and do guard for us. Don't let anyone in."

The big sergeant lay down at the top of the stairs and

Figure 3. The four main pumps in the pumping chamber forty feet below ground. The figure of the man is included to indicate size. (By courtesy of Lieutenant-Colonel Chant.)

Chant started on the long descent below ground, Butler and Dockerill helping him down, with King following, and carrying between them Chamberlain's sixty pounds of explosive beside their own.

Utter darkness lay beneath them, a darkness that the torches at their belts penetrated only as a cold, unfocused beam. Below ground level a cold dampness at once struck their faces. Their blindfold exercises at Southampton came back vividly to them as they counted the steps, but these were not quite the same. The impulse to make haste was upon them, in check by the risk of losing balance and by thought of the results of taking a false step or of straying off the stairs on to the galleries that ran round the walls of the pit. Chant, limping down by jerks, fought the threat of giddiness.

At the foot of the long stairs, in the pumping chamber at last, their torches showed them that the impeller pumps were exactly as they knew they would be—four main pumps of the turbine impeller type and two subsidiary drainage pumps.

They looked rather like giant lifebelts, or huge inverted mushrooms. Inside these big steel ring castings were the fast-revolving vanes which impelled the water in or out of the deck. Standing up in the middle of each ring was the long, shining, steel shaft connecting with the motor that drove it far above at ground level. Each of the four sergeants was to blow up one of the main pumps and Chant himself the two subsidiaries, but Chant now took over Chamberlain's target, leaving the subsidiary pumps to be attacked collectively.

Not much need for torches now. They knew every step and every movement by heart. They wriggled out of their harnesses, laying them on the concrete floor, and took out the specially prepared plastic charges in their waterproof covers. These, reaching up and over the big circular tubes, they slapped and molded firmly onto the casting joints of the impeller pumps, which they knew from the Southampton dock engineers could not be replaced in less than a year. Disturbed by two deep muffled thuds overhead which shook them deep below, they were told by Chamberlain far above that it was "only Captain Donald blowing up the guns." They worked

Figure 4. Sectional view of underground pumping system. (By courtesy of Lieutenant-Colonel Chant.)

quickly and confidently. Dockerill was quietly singing "Blue
Birds over the White Cliffs of Dover" and the other two sergeants chatted casually in broad Norfolk. Their homely, easy
voices gave Chant a glow of affection, overcoming the pain
of his wound and the handicap of his lacerated fingers. He
heard one of them say:

"Nearly finished, sir. Can I help you?'"

"No, thanks, I'm all right."

The charges laid, out came the ring main. Together they
unrolled and laid it out, hands feeling forward to other hands
dimly seen in the checkered light. Out next came the cordtex
leads to connect each charge to the ring main by a clove
hitch. Chant, on No. 3 pump, heard successively reports of his
companions:

"No. 2 done, sir."

"No. 4 done, sir."

And finally, with a note of triumphant finality:

"No. 1 done, SIR!"

The subsidiary pumps were quickly connected likewise.
Finally, out came the two lengths of safety fuse, with igniters
and detonators already connected, to be crimped on to the
ring main.

A hundred and fifty pounds of high explosive was now
ready to be detonated at the touch of the duplicated percussion igniters. Three feet of safety fuse gave a delay of ninety
seconds, which would give a fit man ample time to run up
the stairs and out of the building. It was Chant's duty to fire
the charges himself, sending his sergeants up first and being
himself last man out. But he was wondering how on earth he
was going to get up those forty feet of steep stairs. His knee
was now slowing down all his movements. He therefore decided to keep Dockerill with him, sending King and Butler
upstairs with instructions to remove Chamberlain to safety
and to shout down when the way was clear.

He took one of the igniters and gave the other to Dockerill. Two long minutes passed in the underground darkness.
Dockerill continued humming his song. No other sounds were
audible and the battle above seemed far away. At last came
the expected shout from above and Chant, by prearrange-
ment, gave a simple "one-two-three" to Dockerill. Simultaneously they pulled their igniter pins and the slow fuse began
to burn along its three feet passage to the detonator and the
cordtex. Subaltern and sergeant turned and made for the

stairs. With Dockerill leading and Chant clinging tight to his
arm, they went up in the dark as fast as possible, Chant hop-
pining two or three steps at a time.

They arrived out into the bright light and the din and
Chant ordered his team to take cover behind the concrete
anti-blast wall opposite the door of the pump house, but
Montgomery was at hand and ordered them at once to cover
further off. They had no sooner reached it than the charges
went up, bursting in the confined space below with great violence—"a great roar of sound that cracked our eardrums," as
recorded by Copland, who was passing through not far away
—shaking the ground and throwing down a great concrete
block upon the very spot where they had lain just before.
Clouds of debris billowed out and bright showers of broken
glass burst outwards from the windows. The "great roar" impressed itself on the whole battlefield, heard with satisfaction
by both Ryder and Newman, both now ashore, and heard
even by the motor launches in the agony of their river battle.

It was not quite two o'clock.

Christopher Smalley, fresh at the nearby winding-house,
came up at a trot to make his report to Montgomery before
withdrawing to his last rendezvous. They exchanged quick
congratulations and Stuart Chant led his team back to the
pump house. They had now to go in again to destroy the
motors and electrical gear on the ground floor. Quickly in,
they found the building filled with clouds of smoke and dust,
the concrete floor caved in, two of the electric motors fallen
through it to the pumping chamber far below and the other
two lying at crazy angles. It was obvious to them all that the
place had already been sufficiently wrecked and that another
destructive explosion was unnecessary. Chant contented himself, therefore, with ordering King to smash the transformer
pipes and the gauges with his sledge hammer, which that
broad-shouldered sergeant did with relish and precision, and
as the oil poured out of the transformer pipes it was set on
fire with tar babies.

Thus, leaving the pump house completely destroyed and
burning fiercely, Chant and his sergeants set out to withdraw
according to plan, supporting between them their wounded
companion.

When all was done, Montgomery, having observed a
large shed at the side of the pump house, opened the door and
threw in an incendiary. There shot up, in the words of Copland, "a colossal burst of continuous yellow fire," adding yet

another to the series of fires that were now raging in the white beams of the searchlights.

Meanwhile Christopher Smalley and his small demolition team had had equal success in their attack upon the southern winding-house close by. Smalley, of the Manchester Regiment, was somewhat aloof, squarely built, had good looks and a heavy mustache. His little team consisted of Sergeant Bright, the miner, Corporal Howard, Bombardier W. Johnson and Corporal E. Johnson.

His was the nearest of the objectives to *Campbeltown*. Within the building he saw the two big wheels by which the caisson was moved and the motors that drove them. On these motors and on the spokes of the wheels he placed his charges, connected all up with cordtex, and, having had permission from Montgomery, pulled his igniters. There was no result. He reported to Montgomery and fresh igniters and safety fuse were fitted. These fired successfully and the whole building and all its machinery went up with a shattering concussion, the bricks and debris showering down upon the motor craft now in the Old Entrance and narrowly missing Ryder as he stood by the caisson watching *Campbeltown* sink.

Leaving it in ruins and blazing fiercely, Smalley went quickly to report to Montgomery, as we have seen, saying to him, "Bob, I have finished and I'm going to withdraw now." Returning to his team, he saw at that moment Burt's motor launch in the Old Entrance, disembarking his troops, and he decided to take this opportunity of effecting his withdrawal, instead of going to the Old Mole. He and his team ran to the quayside and embarked, but the boat was heavily engaged by the minesweepers and harbor defense boats in the Submarine Basin. The forward Oerlikon was jammed and Smalley took charge of it in an attempt to free it, but was almost immediately shot dead.

The Gate Crashers

These two teams had been fortunate to meet no enemy resistance and to suffer no casualties while at their work. A different experience awaited those who went out to attack the targets at the northern end of the dry dock—the far caisson and its winding-house.

Casualties had begun on board the *Campbeltown*. Etches himself, in control of both attacks, was hit four times, including wounds in both legs, and able to walk only very painfully; he could take no effective part and on Montgomery's orders he withdrew direct to Roy's bridgehead, crawling most of the way on hands and knees. On the other hand, Beattie having laid *Campbeltown* astride the caisson with such skill, there was no need for Burtenshaw's team to attack it and Montgomery accordingly sent them to reinforce Gerard Brett.

Corran Purdon, charged with destroying the winding-house, was another of the "babes" of the raid. Aged twenty and an Ulsterman, he was the son of Major-General Brooke Purdon, the doctor general. Lightly built, very fair and very good-looking, he had been in the last prewar batch of gentlemen cadets of Sandhurst. With him were four remarkable corporals, also of 12 Commando—Corporal "Johnny" Johnson, Gordon Highlanders, a tough, sandy-haired, humorous Aberdonian, who was badly wounded in the *Campbeltown* but with extraordinary courage and fortitude carried through his tasks; Corporal Ronald Chung, Royal Engineers, the redoubtable half-Chinese; Corporal Bob Hoyle, Lancashire Fusiliers, a North Countryman; and Corporal "Cab" Galloway, from the South.

To Corran Purdon, Gerard Brett stood in the position of an elder brother. Lean, spectacled, quiet-spoken, having something of the air of a kindly don, the archeologist came from Cirencester, had taken part in Byzantine excavations and was an assistant curator at the Victoria and Albert Museum in London. Brett's team, as might be expected from 12 Commando, had a strong Irish flavor. With only three exceptions, all were to be killed or wounded. To this band was now added Robert Burtenshaw's team from 5 Commando. His senior NCO, briefly noted already, was Sergeant F. A. Carr, the Regular sapper, quietly formidable, a model of devotion and integrity.

Having got up from their sitting position on the deck of the ward room, and Galloway having disembarrassed himself of the bookcase that had fallen on top of him when the destroyer rammed, Brett's and Purdon's teams, followed by Burtenshaw's, hitched themselves into their rucksacks, came up into the fury on deck and moved on up to the fo'c'sle. Coming to the smoke-shrouded hole on deck, Corporal Hoyle fell in. His trousers were ripped and burned off before he was pulled out and he went through all the rest of the action in his shirttails, his legs painfully burnt. Passing John Proctor, who waved cheerfully to them, they found Tibbits in the bows, standing erect to hold a ladder ready for them.

Behind them came Robert Burtenshaw. He was still wearing Beattie's cap, his monocle was in his eye and he was swinging a walking stick and humming quietly.

Thus on into the seething bows. Their tiny protection squad, under command of the massive Bung Denison, was from the start seriously depleted, for Corporal O'Donnell and Private Mattison had both been wounded in the legs on board ship. Thus Denison led on with only two companions. Behind him the three teams of destroyers scrambled down the shaky ladders, swung at a trot round Smalley's winding-house and past Chant's target, their heavy loads jolting on their backs, and so up the west side of the dock—a run of fully

Thompson

five hundred yards. In the dry dock itself, on their right, two large tankers under repair were clearly to be seen.

Not very far beyond the pump house small-arms fire was opened from the roof of a building on the protection squad as it led the way, but Denison and Private Elliott silenced it at once with a grenade and the Tommy gun. About a hundred yards further on, from a trench behind a crane on the dock side, a sharper fire was opened, wounding Elliott in the leg. Denison ran to the crane, to use it as cover, and, in textbook fashion, shot up the trench by Tommy gun while his two companions attacked with grenades, executing the little maneuver so effectively that when they rushed the trench, they found it full of dead. Denison then doubled forward to his allotted place beyond the caisson, his tiny squad taking up

positions to protect as best they could the demolition teams
from interference across Bridge M, and the wounded O'Donnell and Mattison limping up to play their parts.

Behind Denison the demolition teams were thudding up
soft-footed. Purdon and his four corporals made for their
winding-house on the left. Finding the entrance barred by a
heavy metal door Purdon tried unsuccessfully to shoot out the
lock, but Chung smashed it open with a sledge hammer and
they burst in. In no time at all they laid their charges on the
spokes of the big driving wheels and on the motors, just as
Smalley was doing to the south of them, Johnson, in great
pain, fulfilling his full part in the team drill. Sledge hammers
and insulated axes smashed up the electrical gear. When all
was connected up to the ring main, safety fuse and igniters
attached, they withdrew outside, waiting for Brett and Burtenshaw to blow their caisson first. Purdon sent Chung over to
report to Brett that he was ready, but the corporal found the
caisson under a storm of bullets that rang murderously upon
the steel deck, and returned, himself wounded.

For the two teams on the caisson were now carrying out
one of the most hazardous of all the tasks in the dockyard
area, under a violent fire which attacked them simultaneously
from several directions, but through which they pressed their
purpose with the utmost determination. In the dimly lit and
swiftly moving scene it is difficult after the years to perceive
the precise details with undeniable certainty, and to make out
the identity of each shadowy figure, but the main facts stand
out with an eloquence that is clear enough.

As Brett's team, with Burtenshaw's just behind, ran up
to the caisson, Brett himself was dropped, hit in both legs and
in the right arm. He was carried to the shelter of a wall,
whence he helped to direct the operation as best he could
from a sitting position. His team swarmed quickly over the
caisson and at the eastern end Corporals Wright and Reeves
killed with their pistols two Germans who suddenly appeared.
When Burtenshaw arrived very soon afterwards he saw Sergeant Deery struggling to open the hatch, or trap door, in
the middle of the caisson deck. He took charge of both teams
with casual and jaunty air, his tall, stooping figure striding in
the gloom.

In one particular, the caisson was found not to be identical with that of the King George V Dock. At either side of it
there were wide, deep scuppers and the whole of the steel sur-

face was decked over with timber, coated with tar and grit. With one important exception, however, the work went forward swiftly. The twelve eighteen-pound underwater charges were dropped over the northern side and secured by their cords to the handrail. The ring main was run out as the shadowy figures hurried soft-footed from end to end. The cordtex leads from the charges were tied to it with clove hitches. The safety fuses, with their detonators and igniters, were crimped on and laid out in duplicate at the western end.

Sergeant Frank Carr, having seen all this done, sought out Burtenshaw to report that the underwater charges were ready. He found him with Deery, still vainly trying to open the hatch which gave access to the interior of the caisson, where the wreaths had to be fastened magnetically to the inner walls and floors. Nothing that they could do would move it. Burtenshaw therefore ordered the sergeants to "clear the deck" while he tried, first with a magnetic "clam" and then with a wreath, to blow it open. Both attempts failed.

At that moment, aroused perhaps by the explosion itself, there burst upon them a murderous fire from all sides. The six Oerlikons on the towers to their left rear and the guns on the ships in the Penhouet Basin opened up. To their bursts was added a brisk small-arms fire from the nearer of the two tankers in the dry dock immediately below to their right. The explosive bullets and the shot burst and rang on the steel of the caisson with a venomous clangor. Brett was wounded a second time. Burtenshaw, also wounded, ordered the teams to take cover and several of them, including Carr, Lemon and Burtenshaw himself took refuge in the scuppers under the wooden decking on the dry dock side. From here they returned the fire of the ship in the dock with the only weapons they had—their pistols.

They very soon found, however, that this was no comfortable refuge, for the bullets from the tanker clanged about their ears. Burtenshaw ordered them all out, saying, "We've got to deal with those chaps." Out they scrambled, ran down to the dockside and emptied their pistols upon the tanker. Far more effective, however, was the action of two men from the protection party, who ran down the steeply sloping gangplank and, with their Tommy guns, silenced the crew with a few devastating bursts.

Sergeant Carr, leaving the dockside after the tanker had been silenced, looked about for the familiar, lanky figure of his officer, but could not find him. For somewhere in that stark dockyard scene Burtenshaw now lay dead.

While they had been silencing the tanker, a small party of Germans had attempted to attack them from the left rear. Burtenshaw, now also apparently wounded a second time, at once went to meet them, with one or two others. With their pistols alone they scattered the enemy, but Burtenshaw fell too, full of wounds and, we are told, still murmuring the words of that song which matched so well his gallant spirit. Corporal Blount was killed too.

Of this Carr knew nothing. Finding neither Burtenshaw nor Deery, the sergeant instinctively took matters into his own hands. He stepped again on the caisson and walked its full length but could see no one alive. He examined the cordtex ring main and the detonators to see if they had been damaged. Some others of the teams made another attempt to open the hatch. Seeing that it was unsuccessful, Carr took the decision that the underwater charges must now be blown. He knew well that, without the wreaths, it was unlikely that the caisson would be completely destroyed, but it would be severely damaged.

He cleared everyone off the caisson, walked back to the western side, took up both igniters, pulled the pins and withdrew. The two feet of safety fuse burnt through in its allotted sixty seconds and the detonating wave shot instantaneously through the whole assembly. A deep, thunderous boom sounded above the raucous din that animated the night, like some huge drum among clashing cymbals, and accompanied by a boiling and surge of the disturbed waters.

Carr walked back again onto the caisson to inspect the damage. There was little that he expected to observe visually, but above the din he clearly heard water coming through into the dry dock from each end of the caisson. He knew then that the gate had been damaged as much as could be hoped for and that its repair would be long and difficult.

On Brett's orders, what was left of the band withdrew, Brett himself being carried by Corporals Wright and Ferguson. Of these parties, Burtenshaw, Sergeants Ide and Beveridge, Corporals Chetwynd, Jones and Blount and Lance-Corporal Stokes were at some time killed and only a few of the remainder escaped without some wound.

The time had now come for the waiting Purdon and his corporals. About their performance there was no doubt whatever. As soon as the caisson-breakers had withdrawn, Purdon pulled the pins of his igniters. "It was," he recorded, "a memorable sight. The entire building seemed to rise several feet vertically before it exploded and disintegrated like a collapsed house of cards."

All the commandos' demolition objectives on the machinery of the great Normandie Dock had now been fulfilled with almost complete success in less than half an hour from the moment *Campbeltown* had rammed. Even if the destroyer herself should fail to blow up, it was now impossible to operate either of the caissons and impossible to pump out or refill the dock. The great Forme Ecluse was useless for certainly a year at least, useless to the *Tirpitz,* useless to every kind of ship. It was, indeed, to remain useless until long after the war was over. This feat is unique in military and naval annals. No other example exists of damage so vital and so far-reaching in its results being carried out so swiftly and with such economy of force. No guesswork, no "hundred per cent zone," no "permissible error," no "near misses" obscured the exactitude of the commandos' attack, for they placed their charges on those small, vital pinpoints which might never have been hit at all by projectiles launched from bomb rack or gun.

The achievement was not only the visible record of the daring of the men who performed it; it was also a triumph for the men, now at this moment about to die on the doorstep of fulfillment, who had planned it. It was Pritchard whose imagination, invention and fanatical persistence had built the way to this technical achievement, it was his midnight assiduity that had calculated every charge and written out every item of each man's task and load to the last fusee, and it was his patient and meticulous training that had taught each man precisely what to do. In the honors and memorials of the Charioteers his name, denied by death the award of any decoration, stands among the highest.*

Having thus completed all their tasks, the commandos of Group Three began their withdrawal according to plan, except for Smalley's team, whom we have already seen taking other

---

*The award of the DSC to Tibbits was made before it was known that he had been killed.

means. Their work was finished and they were now to re-embark for home again. The route for all parties, as we know,
lay through Donald Roy's bridgehead at the Old Entrance and
so to Newman's headquarters on the other side. Copland had
already passed through before on his way to organize the re-
embarkation at the Old Mole and with his passage occurred
a shameful incident of a type of which this book has, happily,
to record very few examples.

Crouching at his bridgehead, Roy had observed four
figures approaching, darting skillfully from cover to cover
and pursued by machine-gun fire from the minesweepers in
the basin. A dim blue pinpoint of light appeared and a voice
said, "Copland here." He answered, "Roy here; come
through."

Copland was feeling quietly exultant. He had observed
most of the dockyard tasks to have been brilliantly accom-

MP-40

plished. He said to Roy, "I must push on now to arrange the re-embarkation." As he began to move, there was a sharp burst of fire on the bridge and he called out the names of his men in turn. Cheetham did not answer, for he had been wounded at the last gap and was lying forty yards away. Copland said, "Bring him in, will you, Donald? I must get on."

Not much relishing the task, the Laird set off alone, found the corporal and supported him back to the bridgehead. There he told Private Gwynne, who had just had a finger shot off, to get the corporal back to the Regimental Aid Post beyond the bridge.

The two soldiers crossed the bridge safely, the corporal supported by the private. There, as they rounded the corner of a building, they ran head-on into a German Tommy-gun patrol. Unable to defend themselves, they were caught and stripped of their possessions. The Germans ordered the unsuspecting soldiers to run for it, one at a time. Gwynne was the first to go and as he ran the Germans riddled him with bullets in the back. This was the trick of shooting "an escaping prisoner."

Cheetham managed by a miracle to dive behind cover and somehow made his way in a shaken condition to Newman's now threatened headquarters.

Now one by one all the demolition teams came through the bridgehead, darting silently among the shadows, several of them carrying or supporting their wounded comrades, suffering further casualties as they came through, and giving their recognition signals to Roy, passed on, singly, across the fire-swept bridge. Chant, whose party was the first to arrive, found a safe means of crossing by climbing down to the substructure of the bridge and crossing underneath hand over hand. Many others followed him.

Chant then led his team to Newman's command post, now a very hot spot, with German parties firing into it from only thirty to forty yards away, found Colonel Charles beaming jovially, saluted and said:

"Task completed, sir. Pump house destroyed."

Brett and Purdon, both wounded, came through with the same reports of success. Etches had crawled through much earlier. Finally there came Montgomery, who had just blown up a railway truck, and who said:

"We're here, sir. All demolition tasks completed. Do I

now have to embark, or may I go and look for Bill Pritchard?"

Stanley Day, who was beside Newman, said, "Embark?
Just look in the river!"

15

THE RIVER BATTLE

The spectacle which met all eyes that turned to the river at that moment was one of the utmost desolation. The achievements of *Campbeltown* and of the commandos landed from her had found but two imitators among the motor launches that followed astern. From the chapters of success we turn to one in which, with surprise forfeited, failure, and failure of the most agonizing kind, was almost inevitable. Coming up under a murderous short-range fire from the automatic guns, the little, vulnerable craft met destruction one after another, either as they attempted to put in at their two appointed landing places, or as, frustrated and barred, they made their way out into mid-river. Not all, but sadly too many.

The great arena of light, overlaid with the complex of colored projectiles darting in every direction, was now punctuated by fierce orange conflagrations as the motor launches fell victims one by one to the enemy's guns. As they ignited, or blew up in violent explosions, pools of burning petrol spread far and wide, their flames licking the very surface of the water and trapping inexorably the shipwrecked men who were swept into them by the current. From these floating furnaces clouds of black smoke drifted slowly over the water in the almost windless air, disrupting the cold pattern of the searchlights. As a watching Frenchman recorded, "the sky itself seemed to be on fire."

This spectacle of flame and smoke and shellfire, of burned and drowning men, was, of course, the direct consequence of the enemy's loss of interest in what had been going on in the air. From the moment that the bombing stopped and Mecke made his tactical appreciation, only the grossest negligence by the Germans, or some extraordinary good chance could have saved the little wooden boats from the waiting guns. No one supposed for a moment that motor launches could assault fortified harbors. As soon as they had been spotted one would have thought, with Hughes-Hallett, that their death sentence had been pronounced. That they fought as they did, that some of them landed their troops and that eight out of the seventeen got to sea again past all the cannon to right and left of them—these facts are the measure of the men who stood on their bridges, who manned their little guns and who drove their highly inflammable engines.

In reading the record of these events in the river, it will not be easy to keep account of time, for much was happening simultaneously both by land and water. The river battle was taking place at the same time as the dockyard battle and while we have been reading of the exploits of Roy and Roderick, of Chant, Smalley, Burtenshaw, Brett and Purdon, we must know that a more deadly battle was proceeding in the river as the launches attempted against heavy odds to put the commando parties ashore.

There are seventeen little ships of whose fate and fortune we have to read, and, since things did not go as they were intended to do, each is a story to itself. These events took place more swiftly than the recording of them and as we read the exploits of each we must carry in the mind's eye the picture of the next one coming up fast astern of her, at less than a minute's interval. Thus the stories crowd into two focal points —the Old Entrance, hard by the caisson that *Campbeltown* has just rammed, where the starboard flotilla of motor launches is due to land the commandos for Newman's Group Two tasks in the center of the assault area; and the Old Mole, where the port column is to land those for Group One on the left. Sharing in the fortunes and misfortunes of both are those other craft not carrying troops—Curtis's gunboat, which was Ryder's headquarters ship throughout, Boyd's and Irwin's two torpedo-carrying boats in the van, Micky Wynn's little torpedo-boat, and the now single spare motor launch of young Sub-Lieutenant Nock in the rear. We shall read first of the affairs of those on the starboard flank and front, bearing in mind that those on the port hand were taking place simultaneously, and in due course we shall return again to the stage of the dockyard battle.

In the Old Entrance

After she had sheered off to starboard to make way for *Campbeltown*, the gunboat stood off, together with Irwin's ML 7, to give supporting fire to the destroyer and to the commando landing. At this stage, Ryder, through the complex of fixed and moving lights, could see only fitfully and imperfectly the two columns of motor launches coming up at speed astern of *Campbeltown*. Very soon he moved into the enclosed water of the Old Entrance, whence he could see nothing at all. Accordingly he was quite unaware of most of what is now to be narrated, until after this phase of the battle was all over.

Let us follow first the fortunes of the starboard column and the other craft that had business in the Old Entrance.

First Casualty

Leading the starboard column of troop-carrying boats was Lieutenant-Commander W. L. Stephens, an Ulsterman of thirty. He was to achieve an honorable notoriety as an escapist, which cost him imprisonment (with several other Charioteers) in the grim fastness of Colditz, from which also he escaped. He was carrying Michael Burn, Tom Peyton and the assault party that was intended to attack the group of targets at the swing bridge far away beyond the north end of the Normandie Dock.

First of the motor launches to come to grief, ML 192 was mortally hit even before *Campbeltown* rammed. When it was abeam of the Old Mole a shell tore a four-foot hole in the engine room, port side, threw the port engine completely off its bearings, damaged the starboard engine also and the Lockheed steering. A sheet of flame shot straight up into the air and the light craft was flung hard over to port, out of control. A second shell penetrated the petrol compartment and a third holed the boat on the waterline beneath the bridge.

Sheering across the front of the port column, the boat struck the East Jetty, two hundred yards south of the Old Mole on the star board bow, but bumped off before it was possible to get her troops ashore, the quay here standing fourteen feet above the deck. Stephens gave the order to abandon the burning ship. The wounded were put off on a Carley raft, but the boat herself was carried downstream by the strong current, which that night was to be the cause of many deaths from drowning. All but five of the commandos were lost by gunshot or drowning, including young Tom Peyton. Of the ship's company, Ordinary Seamen Hallett, Hale and Little and Motor Mechanic Snowball perished.

The only man to escape capture was Michael Burn. Entering the water, he sank like a rock under his heavy load of ammunition, but Lance-Corporal Young, Gordon Highlanders, seized him and towed him to the shore. On the quay the commando party became separated, but Burn quickly recovered and, by an astonishing effort, made his way entirely alone across the whole enemy-occupied dockyard area to his target area three quarters of a mile away. He found, however, that there was nothing he could do, for the gun towers that he was to attack were unoccupied; he made an attempt to set them on fire, but more he could not do alone. But it was a remarkable effort, exemplifying the nature of commando training. Copland visited him up here and he then made his way back through Roy's bridgehead, dragging a leg but jesting with Chant as he passed.

The Gallant Refusal

Coming up astern of Stephens was Lieutenant E. A. Burt, the young Scotland Yard detective.

In his ML 2 (262 of the Navy List) was the demolition party of Lieutenant Mark Woodcock, of 3 Commando, with Lieutenant R. F. Morgan in command of his protection squad, their task being the destruction of Bridge G and the two adjacent lock gates.

Burt came up in great style and, seeing Stephens ahead of him hit and flung over to port, increased to full speed to close up the line. Obliged, however, to take violent avoiding action and dazzled by the searchlights, he overshot his Old Entrance landing place and found himself a few hundred yards up the river before the landmarks disclosed to him his error.

Turning short round, he met Beart, next astern in the starboard column, who had made the same involuntary error, and he spoke to him over the loud-hailer and, proceeding, gained the Old Entrance under fire. It was about 1:45 A.M. and Rodier's boat, ML 6, was already there, made fast to port quarter of *Campbeltown* after having landed her troops. Maneuvering to avoid the loose ends of the broken torpedo net,

Burt successfully landed all his troops on the upstream side of the Old Entrance in accordance with his orders.

The moment they landed, however, the commandos came under a stinging fire from the 20-mm. guns of one of the harbor-defense ships immediately facing them in the Submarine Basin only one hundred and fifty yards away. They suffered casualties at once, Sergeant Hempstead being mortally wounded in the stomach. From the bridge of the motor launch Burt and Stoker Ball gave them covering fire with their stripped Lewis guns, but it was not enough. Morgan and Woodcock re-embarked, asking Burt to put them ashore on the downstream side. It was at this moment that Smalley and his party, having destroyed their winding-house, ran down and embarked.

As she maneuvered in the confined space of the Old Entrance for a fresh landing, the motor launch came under fire from the same *Hafenschutzboot* and a minesweeper. The microphone of Burt's loud-hailer was shot out of his hand. Smalley was killed trying to release the forward Oerlikon. Another burst of 20-mm. fire struck the after Oerlikon, killing Able Seaman Walker and severely wounding Sub-Lieutenant Hills and Able Seaman Martin.

To this "cannon-fire" the commandos replied as best they could with Bren guns and, while Burt conned the ship, Stoker Ball kept up a vivacious fire with his stripped Lewis from the wing of the bridge. "I never saw a man," recorded Ted Burt, "who laughed in action as he did." When the weapon in his hand was smashed by an explosive bullet, he merely made a salty jest.

Burt withdrew into open water and shaped course downriver under heavy fire, continuing to sustain casualties. He worked up to full speed until nearly abreast of the Old Mole and there he caught sight of Collier's boat, of the port column, disabled and under heavy fire after having skillfully landed its commandos. Burt immediately went to his assistance.

Dangerously lying stopped in the glare of the searchlights only a cable length off the tip of the bristling mole, the two friends spoke a few hurried words. Tom Collier, who had just given the order to abandon ship, was alone on the bridge of his dying craft, badly wounded, a leg shattered and nearly severed. To Burt's offer to take him off he gave an emphatic refusal. He would not endanger the other ship by another moment's delay. With the end of life immediately before him, he said quietly:

"I've had it, Ted. Get out quickly before the bastards get you too."

Burt gave the order "Full ahead together," but the Germans had seen him stop and did not miss their opportunity. Three shells hit the ship in quick succession—on the bridge itself, in the engine room and aft. The engines, steering gear and telegraphs were put out of action. Five commandos and Stoker Hollands were killed. Mark Woodcock fell, both legs shattered. Ball was hit in both legs also but hobbled aft in obedience to Burt's order to help Lieutenant E. C. A. Roberts rig the hand-steering gear.

Now out of control, ML 262, as well as Collier's a little way off, drifted out into mid-river and there, at approximately 2:45 A.M., with fourteen or more dead, with most of the others wounded with the ship on fire amidships and all guns out of action, Burt gave the order to abandon ship.

"In an exemplary manner by both Army and Navy alike," Burt tells us, all hands slipped over the side into the icy waters. Burt himself put the shattered Woodcock and Hills over the side on a splinter-mat, but both of them tried with their last strength to clamber on board again so that the mat could be used by others. The remaining wounded were put on the Carley rafts, to drift precariously with the current among patches of burning petrol. Burt himself drifted downstream until, by good fortune, he was carried on to Les Morées Tower, where he lost consciousness until he was picked up by the Germans next morning.

Three More

Very much the same fate befell the third of the troop-carrying MLs, commanded by Lieutenant E. H. Beart, a solicitor of about thirty-five. He had brought a rugger ball with him, hoping for a game on the quay while the commandos were about their business. He had on board Newman's tiny fighting reserve under Regimental Sergeant-Major Moss.

We have seen how Beart, following his predecessor, overran the Old Entrance. Turning about, he made into the Old Entrance after Burt had duly landed his commandos, but they also were repulsed and re-embarked. Maneuvering in the Old Entrance, Beart came under well directed fire. In a few minutes the ship was enveloped in flames and the order to abandon was given, Beart himself being mortally wounded.

The commandos, swimming or on Carley rafts, made for

shore in an attempt to carry out their mission. Here it was
that Moss, being on a Carley raft, saw a very young soldier
in the water. It was Private Diamond. Without hesitation, he
slipped off, and ordered Diamond to take his place. He then,
with others, towed or pushed the raft towards shore and in
doing so was, it seems, shot in the head and never seen again.
Out of the eleven commandos on board, only three survived.

Swifter still was the fate of Tillie's ship, No. 4 in the
column. Burt and Beart having overshot their mark, Tillie
was actually the first to shape course correctly and turn in
towards the Old Entrance. As he did so, however, he came
under heavy and accurate fire. In a moment the boat was a
mass of flaming petrol a little astern of *Campbeltown* and
after some minutes she blew up, spreading far and wide a
fountain of blazing petrol.

Tillie lived, but nearly all other hands on board were
lost. Of the seventeen commandos on board only Sergeant
Knowles and Lance-Corporal Parkes managed to swim ashore,
the remainder being drowned or overcome in the lake of
burning petrol that spread over the surface of the water.

Already we have seen the first four troop-carrying boats
in the starboard column completely destroyed—those of Tillie
and Stephens almost instantly, Beart's fairly soon also, Burt's
in a long-drawn trial of more than an hour. The fifth, commanded by the film actor, Lieutenant Leslie Fenton, was one
of the four torpedo MLs and was no less severely handled but
yet escaped destruction. He carried the assault party of Captain R. H. Hooper.

Very early in the action both Fenton and Hooper were
badly wounded by a direct hit from a shell on the bridge. Ob-
structed by the movements of ships in trouble ahead of him,
including two that crossed his bows sharply from port to
starboard, Fenton ordered "Hard astarboard," increased
speed, made a complete circle and shaped course again for the
Old Entrance. He then collapsed and handed over to Sub-
Lieutenant N. G. Machin, his first lieutenant, but Machin also
was badly hit, the Lockheed steering was knocked out and
one engine put out of action. After an attempt had been made
to torpedo the *Sperrbrecher*, the three badly wounded officers
held a painful conference, deciding that they had no other
course than to withdraw.

Somewhere about 2:30 A.M., after a long and bloody
fight, Fenton began limping painfully downstream on one en-

gine, using hand steering, and, successfully avoiding the fire of the big coast-defense guns, grained the open sea.

Mission Accomplished

Lieutenant Mark Rodier, commanding His Majesty's ML 177, was a dark, aquiline, officer of middle height, quiet and unassuming who spoke several languages and had a taste for classical music. He had under him three other officers, all sub-lieutenants—Frank Arkle, very young, W. J. Heaven, recently joined, and A. J. Toy, the engineer officer of his flotilla. Their ship was another of the four torpedo MLs, armed with a Hotchkiss instead of Oerlikons.

On board they had a particularly stouthearted detachment of fourteen assault commandos under the command of Troop Sergeant-Major Haines, the Kent farmer who had been ready to "tear off his stripes" to join the commandos. His tasks were to assist Hooper to silence the suspected waterside guns and then to come into Newman's reserve.

The scene that confronted Rodier's eyes as he followed close astern of Fenton was not one to be faced by the chicken-hearted. To port, to starboard and ahead, motor launches were on fire and drifting out of control, for the spectacles that we have seen in the starboard column were being duplicated to port. Already the agonized cries of men trapped in the pools of burning petrol, which were to be one of the memories of that night for British and Germans alike, were beginning to be heard. Wreckage, corpses, flames and drifting palls of smoke were starkly clear in the cold glare of the searchlights. These, the sudden waterspouts of burning shells and the swift streaks of colored tracer, "like red and green stitches on a piece of cloth," threatened the sixth launch with a like fate. Last of the troop-carrying boats in the starboard column, all that had gone before her seemed to have gone only to destruction.

Yet Rodier held firmly on his way. He saw Tillie blow up ahead, Stephens and Platt on fire to port, Fenton sheer away to starboard immediately ahead. Hit several times, but nowhere vitally, he sailed through the maelstrom, past the guns of the Old Mole blazing at him at a hundred yards range, past the wrecks of his friends, through the stream of projectiles that seemed to bar the way into the Old Entrance. This he slightly overshot, as Burt and Beart had done, but, quickly discovering his mistake, turned short round, steamed into the Old Entrance, first of the troop-carrying MLs to enter, and came alongside on the southern quay at about 1:40 A.M. He gave Haines the order to disembark and the commandos climbed quickly ashore and, in the words of the watching Arkle, "passed rapidly into the shadows," where we shall meet them again.

As he waited, Rodier saw Burt and Beart come and go and finally Micky Wynn arrive. Then, as we know, he was hailed by Beattie (or by Ryder) and stopped on the port quarter of *Campbeltown* to take off some thirty of her crew. His mission thus accomplished, he made out into midstream at 1:57 A.M. and began his return passage to the sea at fifteen knots with some forty to fifty men crowded into the small craft.

Drawing Fire

One more vessel, victim of sheer misfortune, made for the Old Entrance. This was the spare motor launch, No. 16, of Sub-Lieutenant N. R. Nock, youngest of all the ML commanders.

His main responsibility was to stand by to take off *Campbeltown*'s troops if she should get into trouble; otherwise, he was to maneuver to draw fire, to engage enemy guns and lights and to re-embark troops on the withdrawal. He certainly drew fire, and as he came up last of all he beheld the scenes of destruction almost at their climax. Young Bob Nock rode through it all unharmed, with Petty Officer Hambly a model of coolness at the wheel. Passing the Old Entrance, Nock found a "pool of darkness" and from there engaged enemy guns and lights with his Oerlikons for some while until he judged it time to make for the Old Entrance to pick up troops. But he found it empty; and the mole likewise. Moving out into the river again, he tried to pick up survivors who were heard crying out in the water on every hand, but caught fire when passing through one of the many pools of blazing petrol. He made downstream at full ahead under cover of smoke but was held in the searchlights and hit repeatedly. Ordinary Seaman Clear, who had been serving the forward Oerlikon almost continuously with great gallantry, was killed; so also were the two junior sub-lieutenants, Spraggon and Vardon-Patten, and Nock himself was wounded.

A little way down the river, under heavy fire, both engines blew up simultaneously, with severe casualties, and it was only through the cool handling of Hambly that the few survivors got away alive.

Newman and Ryder Land

As we have noted, Ryder himself had very little idea of what was happening in those first moments before he ordered Curtis to take the gunboat into the Old Entrance—and none of what happened in the river in the next hour. The dazzle of the searchlights, some fixed and concentrated on the vital area, others swinging and sweeping together with the bewildering network of tracers, gave him only a partial and uncertain picture of events as the MLs came up towards him, though he must have seen Tillie blow up quite close to him. Nor was he able to receive any wireless reports, for the gunboat's aerial had been shot away early and the emergency aerial failed of its purpose. Indeed the failure of communications was one of the minor lessons of the operation, as it is of so many others.

To Ryder, therefore, though under considerable strain, there seemed no cause for despondency. The gunboat herself, well handled by Dunstan Curtis, had behaved perfectly, in spite of the stoppage of the after Rolls gun and the two twin .5s. Able Seaman Savage, at the forward pom-pom, had given a first taste of his mettle and had sent a thrill through the whole ship when he had silenced the *Sperrbrecher* at close quarters. Then as the gunboat sheered away ahead of *Campbeltown* and circled, there had come the destroyer's triumphant crash upon the steel wall of the caisson.

As Curtis brought the gunboat back full circle again towards the Old Entrance, there ensued a sharp controversy on the bridge between Ryder and Newman. To the two friends at the time it seemed hot enough in the tension of the moment, but to us in detachment it does them both some honor rather than otherwise. "It was," said Newman afterwards, "the only time that Bob and I have ever had cross words."

Newman, fully accoutered, was on the bridge of the gunboat, itching to get ashore. His small headquarters staff, which the sailors referred to as his "bodyguard" stood by on the deck—Stanley Day his adjutant, Sergeant Steele his signal sergeant, trussed up like a chicken in his secret RT set; Terry, the War Office representative; Lance-Corporal Harrington; Peter Walker the ex-German specially sent by Mountbatten; and Murdoch and Kelly, the two Tommy-gunners, the last-named now in his kilt. Through the din of the mixed orchestra of artillery, the first distinctive notes of Tommy-gun fire ashore, as the men from *Campbeltown* sprang forward to their targets, came meaningly to their attentive ears. The shore battle was on.

Ryder, on the other hand, watching the fortunes and misfortunes of his little ships as they rode up, observed that the *Sperrbrecher,* although being roughly handled by every boat that passed her on either hand, had come to life again with plenty of spirit and was beginning to be troublesome; particularly, at that moment, to Fenton. Like the ships within the docks, she was a factor for which they had made no provision. The failure of the gunboat's wireless having left him no means of control, Ryder said to Newman:

"Charles, that ship has got to be sunk. I must find a torpedo ML at once."

Newman took immediate objection. "No," he said. "You simply must get me ashore first."

"Not until I have sunk that ship," Ryder replied.

"Look here, Bob, your job is to get me ashore, and as quickly as possible."

"It's also my job to sink that ship before she does any more damage."

"For heaven's sake, Bob, put me ashore first and sink your ship afterwards."

Ryder gave way with good spirit, for he realized that to Newman it was a matter of honor to be with his men, and in they went, immediately after Rodier. Curtis ran his gunboat safely into a wooden pier in the Old Entrance, downstream side, past the stern of the destroyer, Leading Seaman McKee bringing her alongside as though he were berthing at Gosport. The two leaders, so strong in friendship and courage, not to meet again for some three and a half years, shook hands and wished each other "good luck," and Newman's party, we are told by the observant McKee, "armed to the teeth, sprang over the side and away up the steps like young goats."

Having ordered Rodier by loud-hailer to take off *Campbeltown's* crew (as Beattie also did), Ryder ordered Curtis to maneuver the gunboat alongside the landing steps on the upstream side of the Old Entrance, with bows out. Here, soon afterwards, the remainder of *Campbeltown*'s crew, whom we have already seen scrambling down from the fo'c'sle after the commandos, came running down the steps, carrying or supporting their wounded, and having given the correct recognition signal as Curtis covered them, were taken on board, crowding it to excess.

About this time Micky Wynn came sailing in with his

motor torpedo boat, last ship of the force. He had had an anxious time coming up the river, for the idiosyncrasies of his craft had required him to move, in the rear of the force, by sudden darts alternating with dangerous stops. However, like Rodier and Nock, he had escaped trouble, except for a small shell that burst inside the engine room, putting the center of the five-engines out of action, and wounding Lovegrove all down his right leg. Covered with blood and oil, in great pain, weary from lost sleep, the motor mechanic was at this moment repairing the engine, with the help of the two stokers, Simmonds and A. W. Savage.

As he sailed into the Old Entrance, where for a brief space no fewer than five craft were collected, Wynn saw *Campbeltown* securely wedged into the caisson and he knew therefore that he would not be needed for his primary tasks. He came alongside the gunboat, and on Ryder's orders waited.

Ryder meanwhile landed. He had needed to satisfy himself at close quarters that *Campbeltown* was truly rammed and sinking: Wynn might still be needed to torpedo the destroyer if she had not struck properly nor been truly scuttled. He therefore set off along the quay, but he was not alone, for Leading Signalman Pike, having now no task, appointed himself bodyguard, and picking up a broken bayonet on the quayside, accompanied his commanding officer.

As they hurried along the quay a sharp challenge from a crouching figure with a Tommy gun halted them abruptly. It was one of Hopwood's protection squad, covering Smalley at his task on the winding-house. Ryder gave the password, which was his own name, and was passed by the sentry. He reached the caisson and hailed *Campbeltown,* but received no answer. He could see the fire burning on the fo'c'sle and there seemed no sign of life on board. He saw Rodier move off from the stern of the ship and he stepped forward and hailed again. The only answer was a burst of fire from behind him which struck the masonry of a small hut close to him. He and Pike dodged quickly into the lee of the hut and from there Ryder watched *Campbeltown* for several minutes. Then to his relief he saw clearly a series of small explosions along her port side and heard others on the starboard. These were the scuttling charges that Hargreaves and White had fired. The destroyer was already clearly sinking at the stern.

Satisfied, he turned to go, full of admiration for Beattie's performance and feeling a moment of exultation at the accomplishment of his main task. As he turned he was buffeted by the blast of a violent explosion as Smalley's winding-house went up, its debris spattering around him and his escort. A minute later there was a muffled roar and a shuddering of the earth as he saw a great flash from inside the big pump house, with sheets of splintered glass from the windows flashing like heliographs in the searchlight beams. Chant's work. Soon afterwards a like explosion took his eyes to the north as Purdon's winding-hut also went up.

Exhilarated by all this, he returned with Pike to the gunboat. Wynn, who had been having a quick drink with Curtis on the bridge, was waiting for his orders. Ryder told him to fire his *Scharnhorst* torpedoes at the outer lock gates of the Old Entrance.

"Aye, aye sir. Anything after that?"

"Yes, come back alongside and take off as many *Campbeltown* ratings as you can. Then straight back to Falmouth on your own at full speed. Make it forty knots, no less."

"Aye, aye sir."

Wynn maneuvered MTB 74 into position and Ryder watched with satisfaction the two torpedoes leap from their tubes through the airlike great flying-fish, hit the lock gates full pitch and then sink with a splash to the bottom. His center engine now repaired, Wynn embarked sixteen of *Campbeltown*'s ratings and took his little craft out on her last passage.

The gunboat followed him out not very long afterwards.

At the Old Mole

While the endeavors of those in the starboard column were thus being extinguished one by one, their fellows on the port column, who were due to land at the Old Mole with the commandos of Group One, were coming up abreast of them with no greater success but with better personal fortune; for five out of the seven were to get safely out to sea and three of them right home to England. Yet the mole was by far the more dangerous of the two landing places.

A small vessel that succeeded in making its way into the Old Entrance enjoyed a certain amount of protection, for it was partially enclosed by quays that stood well above the decks and the quays were not in enemy hands. The mole, however, was entirely exposed to fire and it was itself occupied by the enemy. It stood some twenty-five feet above water level at high tide and the only means of access was by the landing steps on the upstream or northern side of it, or else by the commandos' scaling ladders; on the downstream side there was a dangerous shelving beach.

At the tip of the mole, beside the stumpy lighthouse, a searchlight steadily poured out its beam in prolongation of the structure. Halfway along, a 20-mm. gun in a very strong concrete emplacement firing through embrasures, defied, otherwise than temporarily, all efforts to silence it by the very light weapons which were all that the Charioteers possessed. This very troublesome gun was Position 63 in the German dispositions. Immediately inland of the base of the mole another 20 mm., Position 62, mounted in or on top of a strong structure covered the deadly area between the mole and the Old Entrance. Landings on the mole were further hindered by parties of the enemy armed with hand grenades and submachine guns, dropping their grenades or firing their weapons straight down on the deck of any motor launch that attempted to come alongside.

There was therefore exceedingly small hope of any boat getting in, or of any troops being landed, until the enemy positions had been wiped out, though in one instance this was brilliantly achieved. In turn, there was not very much chance of wiping out these positions, or any other positions elsewhere, unless the assault parties of the commandos, powerfully armed for close-quarter fighting, were successfully landed; for the demolition teams, apart from their small protection squads, were armed only with pistols. This condition applied, of course, to both Groups at both landing places, but with far more force at the Old Mole, where the opposition to be overcome was immediately present. As events were to turn out, the loss of Birney's party in the flames of Platt's motor launch was perhaps the most critical of all, for it was Birney's task to attack the guns on the mole that were doing so much damage.

Let us remind ourselves that much of what is now to be recorded was occurring simultaneously with the events of the starboard column and occurring, moreover, more swiftly than we may read it; for the motor launches are fast upon each others' heels. All the landings and the attempts to land were over in a very few minutes. Even making allowance for those who overshot their mark, all such attempts were over within fifteen minutes of *Campbeltown's* ram at 1:34 A.M.

There is no substance in criticisms made shortly after the raid, owing to an understandable misreading of early reports, that the motor launches wrongly attempted to land on the southern or downstream side of the mole; all aimed correctly for the upstream side.

The Sergeant-Major's Vision

Ahead of the port column of troop-carrying boats was one of the torpedo motor launches, No. 7, commanded by Lieutenant C. B. S. Irwin, a professional Merchant Service seaman, with an Australian Number One, Lieutenant C. W. Wallach, and a New Zealand supernumerary, Sub-Lieutenant G. V. Fisher.

Six minutes after the destroyer had rammed, Irwin sustained a direct hit aft which put the steering gear out of action and damaged the auxiliary steering also. The boat began to drift, an easy target for the enemy, and after some ten minutes Irwin decided that he must withdraw. Successfully running the gauntlet of Dieckmann's heavy guns at the mouth of the estuary, he made good his passage back to the open sea.

A harsher fate befell the leading port motor launch that was carrying troops, No. 9. This was commanded by Lieutenant T. D. L. Platt, another experienced Merchant Service seaman. He was carrying the very important assault party, intended for attacking the Old Mole itself, of Captain David Birney, accompanied by Lieutenant W. C. Clibborn, and his troop sergeant-major, Ted Hewett. Below deck were Regimental Quartermaster-Sergeant Seaton and Corporal Crippin, the orderly room clerk, who had persuaded Newman to let them come at the last minute.

As Platt ran up towards the mole both his Oerlikons were knocked out and their crews, together with some commandos, were killed and Clibborn wounded. He put in on the upstream side of the mole, but stopped somewhat short of the landing steps, apparently aground, and was at once attacked from above by small arms and grenades. Only six commandos were now left who were fit for action, but in spite of this Birney was willing to go in if Platt could land him.

In a fresh attempt Platt went "Full astern." He got clear but had no sooner rung "Full ahead" again than the engine room received a direct hit and in a moment was a mass of flames. He drifted round to the south of the mole and there he put some of the wounded on a Carley raft and ordered the remaining commandos to swim ashore before giving the order to abandon ship.

Birney ordered a last-minute search of the ship and below deck one of them saw two prostrate figures awash in the rising water. They were Seaton and Crippin, almost certainly dead. Only Birney, Clibborn and Hewett were fit to swim. Throwing away his steel helmet, and standing on the gunwale, Birney ordered:

"Over the side, you two."

Had they been a little less prompt to obey Platt's order, they would have seen that help was at hand. Birney, only an average swimmer, was carried down the coast by the strong current and finally reached shore at the extremity of exhaustion. He stumbled up the beach for a few yards, collapsed and died a few hours later in a French house. Clibborn also drifted down and was beached off the Boulevard Wilson.

Now Hewett was a strong swimmer. All his life he had, in a quasi-mystical fashion, linked the act of swimming with the idea of the hope of salvation. The story of the Sea of Galilee held for him a powerful attraction. Now, cast into the icy flood, he had to fight for his life against the powerful current. One by one he got rid of the heavy loads that were weighing him down as he trod water—his sandbag full of Tommy-gun ammunition, his Colt, the hand grenades in his webbing pouches.

He kept his head, knowing, from the pull of the current, that he might have a long fight, though the shore was not far away. He struck out with all his strength, the cold penetrating him, the smell of drifting smoke and petrol assailing his senses, the missiles striking the water with a hiss about his head. In spite of his strength, he began to fail, his strokes feebler and the water entering his mouth. Very soon only the will for self-preservation kept him above water, but that will alone was not sufficient and he was in the last extremity when there appeared beside him the vision of Christ walking serenely upon the water. He spoke as He had spoken to the disciples, comfortable words that told the faint swimmer that there was nothing to fear. Hewett took the hand that was outstretched to him, as it had been to Peter, and struck out again with fresh strength. In a little while, now in darkness beyond the play of the searchlights, his hands struck a concrete wall. He reached out and grasped some material that he felt on the wall, but it came away in his hand, for it was seaweed. Again he was seized with an access of despair, as he dropped back into the water, but heard himself being told to go on. He grasped again at the wall, and his hand fell upon the rung of an iron ladder.

There the troop sergeant-major clung for a few moments. Then slowly he began to climb the ladder that went up the face of the quay. He reached the top, exhausted and sodden, and there a group of Germans was waiting for him. They seized him, threw him down on the quay, kicked him brutally, shouting angry imprecations, and drove him away.

The Perilous Rescue

It will suit the sequence of our story, since it concerns Platt's boat also, if we relate at this point the heartening narrative of the second of the torpedo motor launches that had been in the van during the approach. This was His Majesty's ML 160, commanded by Lieutenant Tom, or "Nero," Boyd, the robust, ruddy Hull trawler owner. Though tactically No. 8, he had in fact been in the van of the starboard column, as we have seen, ahead of Stephens. Having no troops, Boyd's business was to be prepared to torpedo any vessel that gave trouble, to give supporting fire to *Campbeltown* with his antique Hotchkiss, to draw fire and look for trouble. Nearly all these he accomplished.

Boyd had with him two officers—Sub-Lieutenant J. A. Tait, and Sub-Lieutenant J. G. Hall. His coxswain was Petty Officer L. S. Lamb, but the hand at the wheel throughout the operation was Able Seaman J. Glass. At the three-pounder Hotchkiss in the bows was Leading Seaman McIver and Petty Officer Motor Mechanic Walker was in charge of the engine room until he was painfully wounded in the face, when Stoker Petty Officer Rice took over.

We have already seen Boyd's boat giving supporting fire to *Campbeltown* and McIver disabling one of the shore guns immediately to starboard of the destroyer. Taking violent avoiding action against the shellfire, Boyd made off upstream to hunt for two 10,000-ton tankers that were said to be about. He could not find them (for they were actually in the dry dock itself) and accordingly he turned back "to see what we could do."

Reaching the heart of the conflict again, he observed a group of 20-mm. guns on top of a building inflicting a good deal of damage. Approaching to within two hundred yards of shore, he stopped, and gave it thirty rounds from the

Hotchkiss, the ship's company listening delighted as McIver
kept saying, "Och, that's hit the bastards again!"

The place becoming too hot to remain stopped, Boyd
moved on downstream and attacked with his torpedoes a
target near the avant port, which may have been the *Sperrbrecher,* but she was not sunk. Lamb kept crawling up from
the wheelhouse from time to time to see if he was all right,
but Tom Boyd indeed was never more so. Finding his steel
helmet too heavy, he changed into a very old and very flat
cap, known as his "fighting hat," which his crew preferred to
see him wear, as they had a legend that it brought them luck.
In this he felt more confident and kept saying, "By God, we're
still alive!"

Turning about, and running short of Hotchkiss ammunition, he fired a few rounds of old-fashioned "case" shot,
which has a shrapnel effect and with which the gun was
supplied. The motor launch was now being frequently hit.
There was a blinding crash and a cloud of smoke as a shell
penetrated the engine room. The engines cut out, the ship
was plunged into darkness and Boyd thought, "Well, this is
it."

But down below, Stoker Petty Officer Rice, realizing
that the cut was electrical, searched for the break with a
torch, found the battery leads severed, joined them up by
placing a jackknife across and the engines cut in again. Another hit penetrated one of the supplementary deck petrol
tanks, but only water came out and the square tank became
a round one.

It was about this time that, passing the Old Mole again
Boyd observed Platt's boat "smoking like hell and a red glow
from the engine room." As he approached Platt hailed him
and he went in without hesitation to his aid.

With the utmost boldness, Boyd put himself right alongside, between the burning ship and the mole under the very
nose of the enemy, and began to take off survivors. Petty
Officer Lamb and Able Seaman Lambert, one of Platt's
hands, though himself hit, went to and fro between the two
ships, carrying off the wounded one after another with flames
leaping from the doomed craft. The wounded commandos
on the Carley raft were rescued also.

Someone went below to search the ship and there found
and rescued two bodies in khaki with the water lapping round
them. They were Seaton and Crippin. Last of all came Platt,
having examined with Lamb every body that lay on the deck

to make sure that none was left who was living. In all some sixteen men in Platt's boat were killed or drowned, of whom about twelve were commandos and among whom were both his junior officers, Lieutenant H. S. Chambers and the Canadian Lieutenant G. MacNaughton Baker.

After this episode Boyd went astern into midstream and turned to begin his withdrawal. He had proceeded only a very short distance when he heard three men calling out in the water. He hesitated only for an agonizing moment. Then he gave the order to stop ship, himself seized one of the commando boarding ladders, hung it over the port guard rail, ran down it and pulled the men in. No sooner had he ordered "Full ahead together" than the ship was "heartily plastered" and several of the rescued commandos were severely wounded, one man having "a splinter through the chest and coming out the other side leaving a hole you could get your hand in," but nonetheless remaining conscious and talking sensibly until he died. Another burst of fire lit a fire astern, and a third hit the engine room again, but miraculously the boat escaped serious damage to any vital part.

At twenty past two, making only a moderate speed on one engine, but taking violent avoiding action, Nero Boyd proceded downstream through the bracketing waterspouts of Dieckmann's coast-defense guns, successfully making his way to the open sea and so home to England.

Another Landing

As we leave Boyd's action, we go back again to the movements of the port column and to the quick kaleidoscope of events that was taking place at about 1:36 A.M., there to witness an episode too much like that in which Mark Rodier had distinguished himself.

Next astern of Platt in the port column was ML No. 10, commanded by Lieutenant T. A. M. Collier. He carried a particularly important party—Pritchard himself with his squad of four, a demolition party under Lieutenant Philip Walton, whose task was to destroy the bridge and the lock gates at the northern end of the South Entrance, and their protection squad under Lieutenant "Tiger" Watson, very young and very small, who owed his nickname to the fond fancy of his parents in his infancy, but who was that night to prove himself a tiger indeed.

As they neared the harbor and battle began, Watson, kneeling at his Bren gun, spraying the German searchlights

and exasperated at their habit of switching off as soon·as he
had got their range, was conscious of nothing but exultation.
As they passed the *Sperrbrecher* he saw the burning ammunition and heard the screams of their wounded. He heard other
screams, however, from Platt's boat also, as accoutered and
ready to land, they approached very close to the mole. On
the mole itself he saw a party of Germans running landward.
"One couldn't possibly have missed them," he said, "but we
all assumed that they were surrendering to David Birney's
assault party, especially as they appeared to have their hands
up."

    At this moment Collier turned into port. Sub-Lieutenant
Hampshire and his bow party, however, who were to have
removed the port rail to ease the landing of the heavily laden
soldiers, all lay dead or wounded. With Platt backing out on
fire as he came in, Collier gained the mole, avoiding Platt on
his port hand and bringing his ship neatly to the foot of the
long steps that led upwards to the land. Clambering over the
rail, Watson's party first, followed by Walton's, followed by
Pritchard's, the soldiers were swiftly ashore.

    Collier, having thus accomplished the first part of his
mission, had no more to do until the signal was given for re-
embarkation of the commandos. He therefore made out into
midstream and maneuvered under heavy fire for about half
an hour, when, perhaps with the intention of awaiting the
return of his commandos under the defilade of the quay wall,
he swung in again towards the mole. But he was hit again and
again and, catching fire near the end of the mole, was obliged
to give the order to abandon ship. We have already seen how
his friend Ted Burt came in to his assistance, how, wounded
very badly, he refused it, and how, a little distance apart, the
two drifted out in flames and presently blew up. Eight of
Collier's ship's company were killed.

"Don't Go In"

    Despite Collier's success, the Old Mole was from the
first a very hot spot. The remaining four motor launches in
the port column were coming up fast on each other's heels at
less than a minute's interval, but only one of them got close
enough to land and all were forced to withdraw.

    The one exception was ML 12, immediately astern of
Collier, commanded by Lieutenant N. B. H. Wallis, an Australian. His troops were a small demolition party under

Captain E. W. Bradley, a young officer who had seen a good deal of service and who carried a cavalry trumpet on his back. With them were Edward Gilling, one of the journalists, who remained on the bridge throughout, and the extra doctor, Captain D. Paton.

Like Collier less than a minute before, Wallis passed Platt backing out from the mole on fire, and as he did so Platt called to him:

"Don't go in! It's impossible to land."

But Wallis, coming in at eighteen knots, was unable to conform. He succeeded in coming alongside, while Bradley shot down an enemy party attempting to drop grenades on them from above; but, missing the landing step in the confusion, Wallis found it impossible to land his troops at the twenty-five-feet-high quay wall. Backing and making another attempt, he appears to have grounded or struck an underground obstruction. Since the mole was in enemy hands and Bradley's small party was quite unsuitable to fight an opposed landing, the two officers reluctantly decided to abandon the attempt.

Firm and cool throughout, but with agonized self-questioning, Wallis pulled out, sailed over to the eastern bank to engage batteries and searchlights on that side and withdrew downriver at 2:30.

ML 13, commanded by Horlock, who had taken over at sea after the expedition left Falmouth, also failed to get in. Like others, Horlock was blinded by the searchlights, overshot his mark and on returning found the fire too hot to attempt a landing.

Henderson, in No. 15, also failed, attempting first the Old Mole, where he was covered with spray from near misses by heavy shells, and then the Old Entrance before withdrawing; but after regaining the open sea he was to be involved in a fight which was a minor epic in itself, recorded in Chapter 17.

Last of all, in ML 15, came Falconar, whom we have seen embark Briault's commandos while at sea. These were Hodgson's assault party and Barling's medical party. They were out of their proper order, although Falconar had caught up the main force just after making contact with *Sturgeon*.

Falconar also overshot the mole. He went about and was able to pick out the mole, but by this time he had no guns in action; his after Oerlikon, had had a direct hit, his

forward Oerlikon and both Lewis guns were jammed. Hodgson
was dead, killed outright in the approach, and Oughtred and
Sergeant Baron badly wounded.

In these circumstances it was useless, he properly decided, to attempt a landing, and he withdrew downriver, still
under heavy fire and with the tracers going right through the
hull from one side of the ship to the other where Barling was
attending the wounded below deck. Before reaching the facilities of a destroyer Oughtred was almost exsanguinated.

All these four boats successfully evaded the fire of the
heavy coast defense guns and gained the open sea.

Ryder's Withdrawal

During the greater part of the time that these things
were going on Ryder was still on board the little gunboat in
the partial shelter of the Old Entrance. The motor launches
came and went and last of all Wynn went. The sounds of battle crashed violently on every hand, but the greatest crashes
were the welcome roars of our own demolitions, adding to the
triumphant record of Beattie's performance. To Ryder, therefore, it seemed that the night was going well, for within the
enclosure of the Old Entrance he could see little of what was
occurring outside and the loss of wireless communications
prohibited any news reaching him.

Somewhere towards 2:30 A.M., therefore, after having
seen Wynn shoot his delayed-action torpedoes and leave for
home, he ordered Curtis to take the gunboat out, in order that
he might see how things were going at the Old Mole.

The spectacle that was revealed astounded and for a
moment dismayed him. "It was the only time," observed
Dunstan Curtis, "that I ever saw him momentarily at a loss."
The remains of five motor launches—those of Tillie, Stephens, Platt, Beart and Nock—were burning fiercely and
even while he looked a trickle of flame began to spread astern
of Wynn. Other boats could be seen withdrawing. The black
smoke of the conflagrations, the white smokefloats of boats
making their withdrawals, and the dust of the explosions
ashore drifted across the searchlight beams, while the noises
of the battles by land and by water made still more uncertain
the interpretation of a confused situation.

As he quickly appraised this sinister picture, still hop-
ing that the mole was in our possession, Ryder observed
Collier approaching it for the second time, under heavy fire.
He saw Collier's boat hit, burst into flames and begin to drift

away, and he saw also Burt come in "undaunted" to his aid. He therefore ordered Curtis to take the gunboat in immediately to their support.

At once the gunboat herself came under increased fire, from every quarter, but it was at this time that the skill and gallantry of Able Seaman Savage, and his No. 2, Able Seaman F. A. Smith, shone at their highest. Standing up in the bows at his pom-pom, completely exposed and with no gun shield, the burly, bearded seaman and his shipmate engaged, unmoved by the confusion of tracers that spun round them as in a web. While Curtis closed the mole to within about two hundred and fifty yards, Savage and Smith fought a duel with the specially dangerous gun 63 in the concrete emplacement on the mole itself. So steady was their shooting that they put one or more shells actually within the embrasure of the emplacement. The enemy gun was immediately silenced.

Curtis then directed Savage on to the searchlight that was throwing its beam dead ahead of the mole, but this proved too difficult a target; so also was the gun, silhouetted against the bizarre night skyline, on top of the building just inshore of the mole. A party of Germans was then seen to run down the mole to re-man the gun that had been silenced, but once again Savage put his little shells right inside.

Meantime the gunboat herself, now the last vessel left afloat on the whole scene, was under fire from all directions, and being repeatedly hit. Those on board her could see the colored traces converging upon them like the spokes of a wheel. With desolation over all the face of the water, there was clearly nothing more that Ryder could do at the mole and he ordered Curtis to return once more to the Old Entrance in an attempt to make contact with Newman ashore, and let him know that there were now no craft left to take his commandos home.

On arrival at the Old Entrance, however, he was dismayed to see a strange and uncertain battle going on. Someone had boarded the *Campbeltown* and was manning her Oerlikons. A fierce battle was going on across the Old Entrance, and Ryder clearly observed a figure fire several bursts from one of the destroyer's after bandstands before being shot dead itself. Was this little battle with Roderick's party recrossing the fo'c'sle? Or were the Germans themselves shooting at each other? Or was it perhaps some small commando party that had got ashore by swimming or by raft and was now bravely playing an impromptu part? For friend and foe were indistinguishable from one another. To Ryder, the only certainty was that the way in to the Old Entrance was now peremptorily barred.

While Savage continued to engage the enemy, pitting his little gun now against the difficult skyline targets beyond the Submarine Basin, Ryder looked regretfully round him. Crouching down on the bridge, he held a quick consultation with Green and Curtis, while the boat lay perilously stopped and shielded only by a smoke float.

It went very hard indeed with Ryder to leave Charles Newman and his commandos encircled by enemies ashore. But there seemed nothing more that could be done, and the means of communication were gone. Both points of embarkation were in enemy hands. The melancholy spectacle in the river showed no craft but themselves that were not on fire. The little gunboat was loaded down with wounded. Nearly every seaman had been hit and many of the wounded from *Campbeltown* had been hit a second time. It was scarcely possible to move on deck without treading on them. There was no one left to man even the two Bren guns mounted aft.

Regretfully, Ryder decided that there was no course open to him but to withdraw. The main purposes of the expedition had been brilliantly achieved. The secondary purposes had failed, but the slaughter of the small boats had been almost inevitable the moment surprise had been lost. He gave Curtis the order, and the little gunboat shot off downriver under the following beams of the searchlights and the pursuing shells at twenty-four knots.

The Plan That Went Awry

The outcome of all this effort, therefore, was that seven motor launches and many brave lives were lost in this river battle—and more are to be lost before our story is done—and that only a handful of commandos made a successful landing. Newman's own headquarters, Haines's party, the party of Pritchard, Watson and Walton, and the lone Michael Burn—only these got ashore from the launches and were able to advance, though Burt and Beart had very creditably landed their men also. The most grievous losses were those of the vessels carrying the assault troops. Had these got ashore—the parties of Birney, Hodgson, Burn and Hooper—

the results would almost certainly have been even more brilliant than they were.

Anyone could have foretold that such a fate was almost inevitable if the light wooden launches were to be called upon to face serious fire from the shore. They were never intended for this sort of purpose. Even so, they stood up wonderfully to the cannon fire of Oerlikons and even to the shells of Bofors. At such short ranges the Germans could scarcely miss. One is not quite sure how to account for the reports of heavier shellfire in the vicinity of the harbor, but no doubt this might have come from No. 2 battery of Dieckmann's 280 Battalion at Le Pointeau, which were 75-mm. guns on pedestal mountings with an all-round traverse. Their range to the Old Mole was less than three miles and they fired one thousand three hundred rounds that night. The 6.6-inch (17 cm.) battery at Pointe de l'Eve, we are told, could traverse round nearly as far as the *Sperrbrecher*.

One need not be surprised that there was a great deal of frustration and self-questioning among those who were prevented from attaining their objectives. The commandos were highly tuned and in that state of exaltation which we have noted. All felt bitterly disappointed and some felt angry at this deflation of high hopes. The motor-launch commanders felt no less keenly what appeared to some of them at the time to be a failure of their mission. One has but to read these pages, however, and those which follow, to be convinced that St. Nazaire provides no instance of any failures, but only of impossibilities.

The contrast with the success of *Campbeltown* and of the commandos landed from her is striking, and one may indeed consider that if, for this dangerous expedition undertaken at their own request, the Admiralty had made the effort to provide a second destroyer, according to the very first plan devised by the COHQ committee, there would likewise have been a still more brilliant result and a smaller loss of lives. Such speculations are by no means idle, for they point a lesson. At the same time, the greater lesson lies in the untimely loss of the bombing support. The tactical principle upon which the whole plan was based was that of surprise. Surprise might conceivably have been obtained if there had been no bombing at all, provided one could legitimately suppose that a first-class enemy was not on the alert in such highly sensitive waters; but it would have been virtually certain if, as planned, the enemy's attention had continued to be distracted by aircraft dropping anything, even, as Haydon had said, soda-water bottles, to mystify and alarm.

With this view the Germans themselves agreed, admitting, as Mecke says, that the air raid succeeded in distracting attention until that point was reached when its very peculiar nature, and finally the cessation of bombing, made it obvious to him that "some devilry" was afoot, calling for vigilance elsewhere than in the sky.

We have already seen that, after intense pressing at the last minute from COHQ, Bomber Command, overcoming some lukewarmness to an operation which heavily taxed their resources, requiring the attack to be sustained for four and a half hours, responded generously enough with sixty-two bombers. We have also seen, however, the inflexible restrictions that were imposed upon pilots, partly as a result of Cabinet directions. It was these restrictions that brought the efforts of pilots to nought and upset the conception and balance of the plan.

Willetts himself flew with the bombers, as did Hughes-Hallett. Sixty-two Wellingtons and Whitleys actually took off from England, all but three reached the target area. On arrival, however, they found ten-tenths cloud up to eight thousand feet, with bad icing conditions. In a report and commentary to the Director of Bombing subsequently Willetts records that, in consequence, only four aircraft actually bombed, and "a considerable number of aircraft were therefore flying over St. Nazaire before and during the operation without actually intervening."

He observed cogently that "an important omission from the plan was the action necessary should aircraft be dispatched from this country which, on arrival, found conditions such that aimed bombing could not be done." The target area, he adds, was clearly disclosed to pilots "by the flash of flak through the clouds" and he suggests that the sacrifice of surprise might have been mitigated had pilots been allowed to bomb on positions so estimated.

Two other facts, however, stand out. First, we know from the German naval staff's subsequent study of the battle and from Mecke's action report, that, except for scattered patches, there was no cloud below three thousand two hundred feet. Second, the notion of one bomb only per run from a considerable force of aircraft, which "pressed their attack with determination," was not good enough to fool so able and experienced a commander as Mecke.

Willetts returned sad at heart, and a squadron leader back in England next day said, almost in tears, "If you had only *told* us what it was all in aid of, we would have come down to nought feet and given them everything we had."

This, indeed, was what Newman had asked for, but been told that he could not have. But as a final note on this issue there remains the typical observation made to him by Mr. Churchill when the two met in after years. "The only person you can blame for the lack of air support," said Mr. Churchill, "is me."

Wellington

16

THE DOCKYARD BATTLE

That portion of the St. Nazaire docks lying between the Old Entrance and the new Southern Entrance, the scene of the commandos' confused and bitter fighting at close quarters, is divided into two parts. The dividing line is the broad Place de la Vieille Ville, which we shall call Old Town Place. About one hundred and twenty feet wide, it runs almost directly from the Old Mole to the modern town by way of Bridge D, that bridge which was to be graven in the minds of the commandos ever after as the "Bridge of Memories." The breadth and directness of Old Town Place provides a splendid field of fire for any weapons that command it, and a well-placed machine gun, stoutly manned, can make it impossible for any to traverse its length in daylight.

To the south of Old Town Place lies the Old Town itself, a dense concentration composed mainly of small buildings in narrow streets, but there are also a few larger buildings, such as the power station, to which, with Pritchard, we shall pay a fleeting and fruitless visit.

North of this broad and commanding dividing line lies an assembly of long warehouses and other sheds in parallel rows, with a hydraulic station among them. At the extreme north of this area, close to Roy's Bridge G, lie the offices of the dockyard roads and bridges engineer, which is the building that Newman has selected from air photographs as his battle headquarters.

This area, like all dockyard warehouse areas, is traversed and intersected by a system of railway loops and sidings, as indeed is the whole of the dockyard. On this night numbers of railway cars stand on these lines, and they are to afford valuable cover to the raiding commandos at a vital moment.

Charles Newman disembarked from the gunboat in the Old Entrance somewhere about 1:40 A.M. He was in high spirits and eager to get ashore. He had just seen Troop Sergeant-Major Haines disembark from Rodier's boat and the spectacle of *Campbeltown* rammed fast into her target. Though he might have seen Stephens and Tillie hit, he was quite unaware of the full malevolence of the fortune that was at that moment beginning to assail the motor launches. The signs were still fair and the Tommy guns ashore told Newman that his commandos were about their work.

Preceded by Murdoch and Kelly, his two Tommy-gunners, he sprang ashore at the wooden jetty on the south side of the Old Entrance. The soil of France! For two years he had trained for such a moment and dreamed of it. Then he went forward at a steady double followed by the remainder of his staff.

The brilliant light of the quayside, checkered by the sharp, black shadows of buildings, gave place gradually to a dimmer half-light, through which they moved apparently unseen by the enemy, beneath the streams of tracered projectiles that poured overhead. As he moved up to the building he had selected for his headquarters, close to Bridge G, Newman could see no sign of any of his commandos. He expected to see Moss already at the headquarters, but the sergeant-major at just about that moment slipped lifeless from the raft on which he had given up his position to Private Diamond.

Newman therefore found his headquarters apparently deserted, but on walking round it to find an entrance he "bumped helmets" round a corner with a German. It is characteristic of him that he instinctively said, "Sorry." The startled German, for his part, threw up his hands and began talking volubly. Instantly Terry, who spoke German, was upon him and Newman laughed ironically when he learned that his chosen headquarters was itself a German headquarters of some sort. Terry ordered the man to go in and bring out the others with their hands up, but at that moment the little party of seven came under dangerous fire from one of the minesweepers in the Submarine Basin which had spotted them, and accordingly they took cover behind the building.

As we have seen in earlier chapters, parties of Germans, roused out of their surprise, now began to come alive. They had reacted very quietly, as Germans always do. The first *Stosstrupps* of 703 Naval Flak Battalion, ordered out by

Figure 5. The German counterattack.

Mecke at 1:20, crossed Bridge D at 1:50, being rapidly joined by others and by the parties from 705 Battalion by way of the bridge just to the south, making a total of two hundred and eighty men from Mecke's brigade before very long. A detachment from 2 Works Company also arrived, but attempts by other Works Company troops to come down from the north were frustrated by Roderick and the party on the northern caisson. Other detachments were also on the move—those of naval shore establishments, the crews ashore of the tankers *Uckermark, Passat* and *Schledstadt,* and perhaps the Harbor Commander's guard company. Many of these were by no means troops of the best quality, Mecke's anti-aircraft troops being no doubt the best, but they added to the considerable superiority of numbers, for not more than a hundred and thirteen of Newman's men were landed effectively, some forty of whom were armed only with pistols.

Except in one instance which will shortly be related, the commandos had not the least difficulty in dealing with any of the troops that they met; what was much more serious to them than the superiority of numbers was the superior weight of fire from the fixed gun positions and from the minesweepers and harbor defense craft, some of them firing from extremely close quarters, to which were quickly added several machine guns. These weapons, particularly those of the ships in harbor and the hastily mounted machine guns, very soon began to turn their attention from the motor launches to the little parties of men that they now saw darting about in the searchlight beams or among the shadows of buildings and dumps and railway tracks. Later the quadruple 20 mm. beyond the Submarine Basin began to sweep this area with their more venomous fire and occasionally, from some unidentified battery, there came the sharp crump of an air-burst shell overhead.

With Moss and his important party missing, Newman was therefore very relieved when his tiny headquarters was augmented by the "special task party" of Troop Sergeant-Major Haines, which joined him soon after he had taken up his impromptu headquarters. The rugged little sergeant-major, in fact, had arrived before Newman and then moved off for his special task of silencing the guns reported to be on the sea wall between the mole and the Old Entrance. Finding none there, he reported to Newman in accordance with his orders. Standing to attention as on the parade ground, he listened as Newman told him:

"Stay near me in case I want you; because you are the only reserve I have now got."

He very soon did need him, for fire from one of the 20-mm. guns beyond the Submarine Basin and from machine guns mounted on the roof of the pens began to harass them. Newman called up Haines and said:

"We have simply got to stop those guns. What have you got you can take them on with?"

"I've got a 2-inch mortar, sir. No sights, but it's the only thing we've got."

With extraordinary unconcern, Haines took forward in his great hands a little 2-inch mortar, sitting it slap in the open near the quayside of the Submarine Basin just beyond the end of one of the warehouses. Here he knelt down and, taking the small bombs that were passed to him by a chain of hands, including Newman's, from behind the cover of the building, dropped them down the barrel of the mortar, to go soaring high into the air and onto the enemy positions only two hundred yards away. With the enemy fire plunging down on the very spot where he knelt, he successfully silenced one position after another, if only temporarily.

There then came against him one of the armed vessels in the basin, the flash of his mortar and the crump of its bombs being only too apparent. Coming close in, the ship made his position "a veritable death trap." Quite unperturbed, however, Haines leaped over to a Bren gun that some fallen comrade had left, and although the fire from the ship's machine guns was "cascading" in the very place where he was now lying, he sent a series of bursts so well directed that the ship ceased fire and sheered away.

All this time Newman was quite in ignorance of the progress of the battle elsewhere, for, as we know, he never succeeded in establishing wireless communication with Ryder, though the 38 set on the gunboat had its own independent rod aerial. Sergeant Steele opened up his own set immediately in the shelter of Newman's headquarter building, and almost at once heard Lance-Corporal Fyfe, Copland's signaler in the Normandie Dock area. But Newman was not interested in Copland. He kept anxiously asking, "Have you got the boat yet?" But Steele, swinging his dial from time to time, chanted "Newman calling Ryder—Newman calling Ryder" for over an hour without any effect, till at length there was disclosed a situation in which wireless could only too clearly have no value.

The Captain and the Corporals

The silence of the radio, however, was not matched by the din and clamor all around, and very soon sounds of fresh Tommy-gun fire on his left told Newman that something was afoot there also.

This was the party successfully landed at the Old Mole by Collier's ML 11, containing Philip Walton's team for destroying Bridge D, Watson's protection squad and Pritchard's demolition control team. Pritchard's tasks were to control the timings of the demolitions, to help where necessary and to attack targets of opportunity.

With Watson's squad leading, followed by Walton's, followed by Pritchard, this little band ran quickly up the steps to the landward end of the mole. Watson had orders that if his was the only squad to gain the mole he was to attack and hold it himself. He could probably have done so, had he not been led to believe that Birney had already arrived. As it was, he stopped to examine and empty his Tommy gun into what appeared to be a new gun position at the top of the steps, until the cry came up from Pritchard in the rear:

"What are you up to, Tiger? Get on!"

Without more ado, the three parties made straight for Bridge D, but very soon came under fire. In commando fashion they did not wait for each other's support, but made straight for their objectives independently. Pritchard, passing two bodies dead or wounded on the ground, reached Bridge D the first, having probably taken a different route from Watson and Walton and perhaps having seen the trouble into which they both ran.

Pritchard's party consisted of four corporals—I. L. Maclagan, a Royal Engineer Territorial, J. Deans and H. Shipton, all of 9 Commando, and S. Chetwynd, of 12 Commando. Approaching the lock of the Southern Entrance, they beheld before them the steel latticework swing bridge which was Walton's objective, looming in the half-darkness ahead of them like the ribs of some giant skeleton. There was no cover at all on the bare and open quay, except for a small concrete hut, about ten feet square, a few yards from the bridge. To this Pritchard and his corporals sprinted, dumping their rucksacks on its sheltered side—four men alone in the half-light with the enemy just across the bridge and all behind them also. Pritchard, looking round at once for prey, saw two ships berthed alongside each other against the quay of the Submarine Basin, forty yards to his right, and he whispered to Maclagan:

"Mac, I'm going to sink those two ships. Get out two five-lb. charges."

Under full observation from an enemy scarcely sixty yards away, the two men ran to the quayside, jumped onto the nearer ship, crossed to the second and lowered the charges between the two ships, three feet below water. They tied them to the rail of the ship, pulled the igniter pins and hurried back to the shelter of the hut.

Figure 6. Pritchard's party. Thick line shows probable route of party; thinner line, Pritchard and Maclagan; dotted line, Maclagan alone. Cross within circle is where Pritchard is believed to have been killed. Power station located at L.

There Pritchard gave instructions to the other three corporals, in the absence of Walton's party, to "do what you can" to the swing bridge, while he and Maclagan went round to visit, as he hoped, the other demolition parties in that area. He lingered a moment, however, listening for what he hoped for, and before they separated, smiled happily as the charges between the two ships blew up with a muffled roar, followed by a violent and prolonged hissing which told convincingly that the charges had been accurately laid against the ships' boiler rooms. When Newman passed there nearly two hours later he found the two ships sunk. They were the tugs *Champion* and *Pornic*.

Having accomplished this impromptu act, Pritchard and Maclagan, the tall Welshman and the smaller Scott, set out at a trot towards the South Entrance, going boldly and silently along the open lock side, in the half-light from the "spill" of the searchlight beams and from the moon that shone through the high cloud. But they passed in turn one lock gate after another, and the farther bridge likewise, disappointed to find no demolition parties yet arrived. At the most southerly gate they turned left to visit the power station that operated all these southern lock gates, close by on the edge of the Old Town. They could hear the trend of leather-soled boots but they saw no one.

At the power station Pritchard therefore decided that he must go back to find out what was happening. Together with his corporal, he turned about lefthanded and began trotting across the Old Town, making for Bridge D again, Maclagan on Pritchard's left. They passed through a labyrinth of small buildings, making their way through back yards and narrow streets.

They were nearly halfway across the Old Town when, at a sudden corner in the half-light, Pritchard ran straight into a German. The end came swiftly. At one second they met and in the next Pritchard had fallen backwards, possibly bayoneted, for no shot was fired by either. Maclagan took a quick pace forward and riddled the German with his Tommy gun.

He then dropped down on his knee beside his leader. Pritchard was breathing "terribly heavily" and for a few moments could not speak. Then he said:

"That you, Mac? Don't stop for me. Go straight back and report to HQ. That's an order." So far as we know, he never spoke again.

This order the corporal was desperately unwilling to

obey, but the tall, strapping Welshman was far too great a weight for his small frame. He resolved therefore to return to the concrete hut, send one of his comrades to headquarters, and bring the others to Pritchard's assistance.

He made his way back alone through the eerie, hostile streets and reached the concrete hut safely, but all that there was to be seen was a dead body. It was that of Philip Walton.

Still quite alone, therefore, in the heart of enemy territory, Maclagan continued on his way, across the dangerous and exposed Old Town Place, through the rows of warehouses and so to Newman's battle headquarters. There he asked for help to bring Pritchard in, but was told it was out of the question. At some time or other Corporal Deans and Corporal Chetwynd were also killed, Maclagan and Shipton being the only survivors of Pritchard's party.

Tiger's Teeth

Watson's tiny squad comprised young Sergeant Wickson, Lance-Corporal Grief, an irrepressible, ribald Cockney, Private Davidson and Private Lawson.

Coming up immediately behind them was Philip Walton the schoolmaster, with his demolition team for the critical Bridge D, consisting of Sergeant Dick Bradley, Sergeant Alf Searson, Corporal George Wheeler and Lance-Corporal Homer. Watson set off at a smart pace, too smart indeed for Walton's heavily laden demolition team, from whom they soon became separated. At the first group of buildings after passing the landward end of the mole, Watson saw in the half-light what appeared to be a group of French civilians. He shouted to them, as he had been instructed, *"Dedans vite"* (Inside quickly), and fired a burst from his Tommy gun over their heads as he ran. They disappeared, and he saw also a group of German soldiers running away into the Old Town —the second group that he had already seen to run away.

Full of confidence, therefore, he doubled along the broad open space of Old Town Place, but had gone only about one hundred and fifty yards before he met some Germans who did not run away. He called to them, *"Hände hoch!"* (Hands up!) But they answered him with a grenade and a similar summons. Himself a little way in front of his squad, he therefore dropped to the ground to engage them, his orders having been to keep the enemy occupied while the demolition team went on, then to disengage and join up again.

Disengagement became difficult, however, when a ma-

chine gun opened upon him from a rooftop to his left. He was
almost stunned by a grenade that fell and burst beside him.
With a metallic clang a litter tin attached to a lamppost just
above his head was riddled with bullets. Another bullet or
other projectile burst open his haversack of grenades and the
movement of scrabbling about to pick them up drew fresh
fire. From an emplacement beyond Bridge D another machine gun began spraying the area at random. Watson therefore lay low for a minute till the shooting stopped, then rose
quickly and darted back several yards to rejoin his squad, who
had taken cover behind a railway truck and who would have
shot him but for his blue pinpoint torch.

Watson was upset to find the demolition party here
also, but without Walton; they had seen him fall while running across Old Town Place, but in fact, unknown to all,
Walton was making his way to the bridge alone, there to die
in an attempt to lay his charges singlehanded at point-blank
range. The subsequent study of the battle by the German
naval staff reveals that German troops found charges actually
laid on his bridge, though whether by Walton or by one of
Pritchard's corporals who was killed we know not.

To Watson's urgent inquiries, Corporal Wheeler replied
that they had been unable to cross the road and that he
thought Walton must have been killed. Watson shouted for
his friend, without result and turned to question Sergeant
Bradley, when the sergeant was shot through the lung by the
rooftop machine gun. While bending down to administer
morphia, Watson himself was wounded in the buttock. Bradley was dragged under better cover, but before long he was
shot again.

Some reinforcement was clearly necessary for Watson's
tiny squad, but when he raised his Very-light pistol to fire
the required signal it was shot out of his hand. He therefore
sent Wheeler to run to Newman's HQ with the request for
help. He then attempted a new approach, moving half-right
through the sheds and warehouses north of him towards the
Submarine Basin, closely accompanied by Private Lawson.
He had nearly reached the quayside when he heard German
voices at the end of an alley between the warehouses, and,
instead of ignoring them, he hurled a grenade.

He was answered by a violent burst of machine-gun fire,
which enveloped him in clouds of dust from shattered bricks
at head level from the wall alongside him and from cement
stored in the warehouse. This brusque stoppage came from

Figure 7. Watson's route.

one of the ships of 16 Minesweeper Flotilla still berthed at the quayside only a few yards from him; he saw her outline clearly, heard her engine-room telegraph and heard the orders from her bridge. He saw also some cement bags lying in the road and thought in the half-light that they were his comrades. His calls to them brought no answer and the way ahead was blocked by wire. Frustrated a second time, he made his way back through the shadows to Newman's HQ, accompanied by the bewildered but obedient Lawson and pursued by the ship's machine gun.

Among all the clamor and the darting tracer Watson found Newman—who was not yet aware of the failure of the Old Mole landings—jovial, kind and reassuring.

"Hard luck, Tiger," he said. "You've done jolly well. I can let you have a couple more Tommy-gunners. Go back and have another shot."

Not much relishing this order, but determined to do his damnedest, the little officer, still accompanied by the faith-

ful Lawson, retraced his steps. "I was convinced," he said,
"that it meant certain death, but orders were orders." He
made contact again with Sergeant Wickson and the remainder
of the party and they turned about. His blood was up. Ob-
serving one man straggling, he shouted at him angrily:

"Do you want to live forever?"

The effect of this startling challenge was magical, and by
the time that they had all reassembled on the dangerous edge
of Old Town Place, they had all become charged with the
same ardor. They were at a point close to where they had
left Sergeant Bradley, of whom they could see no sign. What
they did see on that spot was a party of Germans standing
easy, and these they wiped out at a few yards' range.

While they were bracing themselves for the new effort, a
runner arrived from headquarters canceling the order and in-
structing them to assemble with the other parties, for it must
have been about now that Newman had seen Maclagan, had
learned from him that none of the demolition teams for the
Southern Entrance had yet arrived and had begun to realize
accordingly that these targets might be beyond accomplishment. Watson complied with mixed feelings, for from now till
the end he was in an angry mood, burning to have it out with
the enemy in atonement for the failure of his mission; but he
had done better than he knew, for his little fight had created
a valuable diversion, distracting enemy attention from what
was now a more vital area and keeping at bay superior forces
that would otherwise have been a danger to the remainder of
Newman's troops, who were now beginning steathily to muster
together.

The Happy Soldier

The sounds of Watson's fight had told Newman that
some at least of his troops had landed at the Old Mole and
were about their business. He had no reason yet to suppose
that the mole was not in our hands or that anything on the
left wing of the battle had gone seriously wrong. On the
contrary, one by one the explosions on his right flank and
rear began to tell their tale. He heard Purdon's and Smalley's
winding-houses go up, Chant's deep underground explosion in
the pump house, and the dull thud and boom of the northern
caisson's underwater burst. He felt tremendously exhilarated
and began to crack jokes with his staff. On the left, however,
no such detonations interrupted the unceasing crash and
clatter of guns and machine guns.

Apart from those who were already in his designated headquarters, parties of the enemy in this confused situation were extremely close to Newman's small team. One party was no more than twenty yards away, occasionally lobbing grenades, and small-arms fire seemed to be coming from every direction, besides the vicious air crumps from some unidentified battery from time to time. Mindful of the need of being personally out in the open with his men, Newman abandoned the idea of occupying his proposed headquarter house, and after some grenades had been thrown into it, took up a fresh position behind a shed near the quay (where Haines had fired his mortar), from which he could check the demolition parties as they came in and direct them, as he hoped, to the point of re-embarkation on the Old Mole.

One by one these parties began to come in, the young officers in charge of each—all of them wounded, though Montgomery only slightly—reporting personally. All those who could do so stood up and saluted as though on parade. Tremendously pleased with them all, Newman said, "Well done, old boy. Better move along now towards the mole and wait for Major Bill."

Copland came in very soon after, giving Newman the good news from the Normandie Dock area, and the less promising news of Burn's lone arrival far away at Bridge M. The time had therefore come to fire the rain rockets that were the signal for the withdrawal, but there were no rockets, for they had all been lost when Regimental Sergeant-Major Moss had gone down in the river. Newman therefore called upon Lance-Corporal Harrington to go out and take verbal withdrawal orders to Roderick, a quarter of a mile away, and to Roy. Harrington set out alone at the double. He crossed Roy's fireswept bridge after due challenge and reply, and swung to the right to traverse the dangerous no man's land beyond which lay the *Campbeltown*. On the way he was fortunate enough to meet Roderick, who, as we have seen, had already begun his withdrawal. The lance-corporal returned, passed the order to Roy also and reported back to his CO.

"When the situation is uncertain or confused, collect your forces." By the time that Roderick and Roy had completed their withdrawals, this maxim was being complied with. Newman and his commandos, now reduced by fatal casualties and by the re-embarkation of Smalley's party to something just under a hundred, of whom many were wounded, had collected loosely together in the warehouse area. Newman now knew that the main purpose of the expedition, as Haydon had set it out, had been achieved. The situation on the left was dubious, but, so far, no more than that. The general impression on his buoyant mind, therefore, was that the operation was developing favorably. Of the fate of the motor launches he had little or no knowledge, for where he stood the warehouses and railway trucks acted as a baffle to any view of the river.

Thus when Copland said that he would "push along" to organize the re-embarkation, for which the parties from the north were now ready, Newman said, "I'll come with you, Bill."

Together they made their way southeastward through the ranked warehouses, keeping to the selvage of black shadow that bordered the buildings under the harsh, white beams. Emerging from the buildings and coming to a line of railway cars, they had their first glimpse of the river north of the mole and were all brought up standing.

Struck with consternation, Newman exclaimed:

"Good heavens, Bill! Surely those aren't ours!"

Nothing, in the recorded words of Copland, more exactly resembled a scene from the *Inferno*. The river itself was on fire. Close in to the mole the hulks of burned-out motor launches still glowed red on the water, while in the night beyond, seemingly suspended in the air, there blazed a sea of burning petrol which had spread outwards from each burning ship or had been splayed far and wide like so many fountains of fire as other craft blew up. From this floating furnace a pall of black smoke, frustrating the glare of the searchlights, rolled indolently towards the northwest in the almost still air, minged with the white withdrawal smoke of the escaping launches. From out this curtain of smoke shot the burning trails of cannon fire from the batteries at Mindin Point beyond. In all this forbidding scene there was no sign of life, nor of movement, except the leaping flames and slowly drifting smoke. And on the Old Mole itself the still-glaring searchlight at its tip and the emplaced gun halfway along its length, firing far downstream on some target that they could not see, betrayed to the watching officers in whose hands the pier still remained.

For a moment they both gazed in silence, the import of the scene only too apparent. Then, with a little, wry laugh, Newman said:

"Well, Bill, there goes our transport!"

The first requirement was to rally, consolidate and organize for the new situation. Copland set briskly to work to reform the little force, choosing as the rallying ground the loop in the railway one hundred and fifty yards north of the Old Mole, where there was some field of fire and where a few railway cars gave a little protection. Using the well-armed assault troops to form protective screens, he put out Roy on the southern flank, whence increasing fire was being directed from the Old Town, and Haines to the west, where stood the ranks of warehouses.

Here at this rallying point an extraordinary situation existed. Until the commandos were re-formed, both sides were in considerable confusion. Often only a few yards from each other, friend was not instinctively distinguishable from foe. The winking blue torches, the white webbing and the occasional kilt proved their value but were not infallible. The tread of boots and the shouted orders likewise gave clear indication of German presence, but no one knew who was on the other side of a building nor who had thrown a grenade. In Newman's words, the enemy "were shooting at us round corners." The gaunt dockyard reverberated to the bursts of Tommy and Bren gun, the explosions of hand grenades, the crack of rifle and pistol and the answering fire of the enemy, echoing among the warehouses and accented by the cries of the wounded of both sides.

Steadily augmented in numbers, the Germans were now on all sides of them, except to the north, probing forward with caution, but were kept at bay by fire from troops far more highly trained in the use of infantry close-quarters weapons at night.

Virtually surrounded and their means of withdrawal gone, the commandos nonetheless intended to retain the initiative as long as possible. Newman himself, with the responsibility for men's lives on his shoulders, alone had a moment's doubt. They had, he reflected, accomplished the major part of their mission. To satisfy his mind, he sought a second opinion, calling Bill Copland into a short conference. Did Copland think, he asked, that they ought "to call it a day"?

"Certainly not, Colonel. We'll fight our way out."

Nothing pleased Newman more. He had a quick plan to divide his force up into groups of about twenty, fight their way out of the dockyard, through the town, into the open country beyond and try to make their way in pairs to Spain and thence to Gibraltar.

He told Copland and Day his plan, a grenade exploding at their feet as they talked. Copland then moved off to divide the force into detachments of twenty and brought the group leaders to Newman for their orders. Newman's own words vividly illustrate this moment. "The scene at the Old Mole," he said, "is hard to describe. There were flames and smoke everywhere. Some wounded Germans were screaming down an alley and small-arms fire was coming from all the buildings around us. Our own chaps were forming a perimeter round the Old Mole; some railway trucks gave them cover and from behind these they were coolly returning the fire with ever-decreasing ammunition. When the group leaders came up to me for my orders, they saluted and grinned. I told them that, as usual, there was no transport to take us home, and that we should fight our way into the town and from there to open country. No one seemed at all surprised."

Their shortest route into the town was by Old Town Place and Bridge D, two hundred yards away, but this broad, open approach was so covered by enemy fire that it would be rash to attempt it. The route decided upon, therefore, was through the area of sheds and warehouses to the north of them, and thence back along the quayside of the Submarine Basin, which Watson had already attempted, this route being chosen because by any other they would have to pass between warehouses with the enemy on both sides of them, for the whole of the warehouse area was now alive with Germans. It was a run of some six hundred and fifty yards, which would have to be undertaken by the wounded also.

Copland marshaled the force into their groups. Making a final round of the positions, accompanied by Private Fahy, he found a party of Germans trying to break through a weak point, and saw them scatter with casualties as Fahy opened up on them with his Tommy gun.

Then, when all was ready, Copland reported to his colonel.

Break-out

Some time after 3 A.M. this extraordinary column, encumbered with wounded, short of ammunition, began its dash straight through the serried rows of buildings thronged with enemies. They were fewer than a hundred now, a third of

them armed with pistols only and nearly one man in three
wounded.

They moved by bounds, keeping to the shadowed ways
at the edges of the long warehouses and halting from time to
time to squat in some dark patch and collect together—
sometimes to rush some open stretch by parties under covering fire, or to overcome some point of enemy resistance or to
give time for the straggling wounded to catch up. These,
obedient to the precept that the lame must not impede operations, fell out to await the inevitable when they could no
longer keep up. Gerard Brett, with manifold wounds, could
move no further than the first twenty or thirty yards and, giving his Colt to a man who had lost his own, he sank down in
a warehouse.

Throughout the whole route, from concealed positions a
few yards away in the dark, a ragged fire, now feeble, now
bursting into an angry challenge, was sprayed upon the silent-
footed column.

Stumbling through a bomb crater made that night by the
RAF, they ran the gauntlet through the warehouse roads,
turning left, right and left again, and reaching the approach to
the old headquarters building. Contact with Burn had somehow been lost at the first or second turn and Donald Roy was
now in the van, a splendid figure in his kilt, a grenade in
either hand, now striding along in the middle of the road. As
he led, Day and Haines served as whips to the field under
Copland's mastership, running up and down the column to
bid Roy slow down or quicken up, to urge forward any strag-
glers and to keep the column closed up. Somewhere always
in the van was to be seen the figure of Newman, still cracking
jokes, never taking cover, always on his feet and directing
fire or calling out, "Keep going, lads!"

Reaching the Submarine Basin, the commandos swung
boldly left handed along the quay. An hour earlier this route
would have been impossible, but the minesweepers had now
moved from their berths at the quayside and, appreciating
that the attack might be directed against the submarines, had
taken up positions in front of the pens. In their place, however, the commandos met the fire of the guns across the
water on their right, while on their left small-arms fire assaulted them at a few yards range from the sheds. Halted by
one troublesome party, Copland took a squad right into the
shed to silence them.

Watson trying to rush a rifleman who was firing at close

range from round a corner, was hit in the left arm, the bullet shattering the humerus. He sank to the ground and prepared to shoot it out with his Colt, but Roderick appeared, killed the German, administered morphia to Watson and began to carry him, but Tiger called in pain to put him down. Hopwood was there, too, and together they put him down at the side of the road. Very quietly, ignoring the boy's cry of "Hoppy, what the hell are you doing with my gun?" Hopwood slipped his Colt off its lanyard.

Roy, meanwhile, was sweeping along to the southern extremity of the Submarine Basin. At the end of the quay came the most dangerous place of all—the wide, open stretch of Old Town Place, which, turning right, they must cross before reaching Bridge D. At Newman's order they halted accordingly in the pale moon shadows aslant the buildings on their left hand, while Newman himself, accompanied by Roy and Haines, darted across the open space for a quick reconnaissance from the buildings opposite. Immediately they came under fire from a machine gun in a pillbox beyond the Southern Entrance, commanding the open way by which they must all go.

There lay the girdered Bridge D, gaunt and ghostly in the curious light. It was barely seventy yards away. Beyond it the German machine guns looked down from roof and window. Astride it on the far side, and stretching along the quayside, lay a line of enemy riflemen, last remaining elements of the German naval troops.

No means of indirect approach to the bridge was at hand, no cover, no opportunity for finesse. Haines, at his own suggestion, sited a Bren gun to give a little covering fire. Then Newman called to his waiting soldiers:

"Away you go, lads!"

The commandos went for it, moving at a steady double as a hurricane of fire burst upon them from beyond the bridge. The astonished Germans, quite in the dark about the purposes of all these confounding occurrences, shot high and wide, as they had done all that night. A violent storm of bullets swept over the commandos' heads.

Donald Roy made on right in the middle of the road, Newman now beside him. Close behind him were Sergeant Rennie, Denison, Montgomery and Haines. They saw the German riflemen athwart the bridge scramble to their feet and retire. They passed the ships that Pritchard had sunk, passed Philip Walton's dead body and swept over the Bridge of

Memories, their rubber boots thudding on the hollow road while the bullets rang and sparked on the steelwork or whistled overhead into the night. To all those who took part it was the most inspiring moment of the night. In the pages of British history there have been many glorious charges, but, on its smaller scale and in its more modest intent, the break-out of the commandos at St. Nazaire ranks high among them as a manifestation of soldierly purpose and of the will and determination to defy odds.

As they reached the end of the bridge Sergeant Rennie fell, shot in the knee. A German grenade hit Corran Purdon in leg and shoulder, bowling him over on top of Day. At that moment Copland went straight for the pillbox, emptying his magazine into the slit and others followed his example. Roy, seeing a German run out from behind it, attacked him with a grenade. He ran to a roadside pit with Denison, Haines and a sergeant to attack with fire another machine gun in action from a window a little way up the street. A motorcycle combination, carrying machine-gunners, came suddenly from round a corner at a crossroads. Every commando in sight opened fire and the Germans, riddled with bullets, crashed into a café wall. Further up the road what appeared to be an armored car drove up very fast, spitting out fire at random in every direction and taking station at a crossroads a hundred and fifty yards ahead, thus barring further progress by that route.

So, about a hundred yards beyond the bridge, ended the commandos' dockyard battle. For the motorcycle combination and the armored vehicle gave notice of the arrival of the first troops of the German Army. They were units of 679 Infantry Brigade, a partially motorized formation, consisting of one or more infantry companies, half a company of machine-gunners, two companies of 559 Construction Battalion and probably a unit of the 333 Division's artillery regiment. The brigade commander himself arrived in the town about this time and took over command of the operations at 4:30 A.M. These troops had arrived too late to mar the splendor of the commandos' break-out from the dockyard, but just in the nick of time to stop them from getting any further. Had they been fifteen minutes later, all the commandos who were fit enough would have made their way through the town and into the marsh country beyond, for once over the bridge, there were no more naval troops to oppose them.

Capture

Immediately after having crossed the bridge, the little force, deflected by the armored car, turned left and soon broke up into separate parties. Copland, finding a lorry parked at the roadside, seized the opportunity for escape, but inside the cab the only switch he found to work was the one for the headlights, which illuminated Denison, who gave vent to the familiar wartime cry: "Put out those bloody lights!"

From this point all becomes confused as the small parties of commandos, with no maps and not knowing which direction to take, made their way through the streets, sticking close

Figure 8. The commandos break out. Dotted ring shows the reorganization area. Rail lines shown in part only.

to the shadows of walls. All over the town the Germans were now rushing in reinforcements, uncertain what was afoot, believing that the raid was the spearhead of an invasion. Armored cars or machine guns were being posted at every road intersection. Newman squeezed into a doorway to avoid an armored car that shot past. Everywhere the Germans were shooting promiscuously at any object that moved, frequently firing at each other, as the watching commandos observed.

To avoid all these patrols and pickets, now being augmented each minute, the British began to forsake the streets, and to engage in what they were afterwards to term the "St. Nazaire Obstacle Race," clambering over walls, passing through one back yard after another, even going through houses from front to back. Private Hannon dropped over a wall into a chicken-run, awakening the startled fowls to a premature reveille. Newman also dropped into a chicken-run and, going head-first through a window, entered a parlor with the breakfast things already laid out on a blue-checked cloth, and so passed through the house to the front door.

By now, however, time was running out. It was somewhere about 4 A.M. and only two hours of darkness remained in which to find lying-up places for the day. Ammunition was very short and, with every street corner now picketed by the enemy and every street swept by fire, effective progress became difficult. Worst of all was the condition of the wounded. By now about three men out of every four had been hit. All but a few had kept up but were now weak from loss of blood and fatigue. Etches and many others were nearly done. Here and there small parties, becoming broken off from their main groups, began to seek shelter in cellars and outhouses.

Michael Burn and Rifleman Bushe were surprisingly caught in the boiler room of a ship in the docks. Very few of them had any luck.

Donald Roy, at the head of a party, seeking water for the wounded who were with him, called at a building which unfortunately turned out to be a police station, and the police, after stalling him, had a squad of German bayonets round in in a few minutes, for the French police, under orders to collaborate with the invaders, were nearly as dangerous to escapers as the Germans themselves.

Newman himself, with about fifteen others, found refuge in a large cellar equipped as an air-raid shelter, with eighteen palliasses. Of them all, only himself, Copland, Day and Steele were unwounded. Steele was posted as lookout near the head of the stairs and wounds were dressed as far as possible. Here Newman intended to stay until night, when they would set out in pairs for the open country. "But I also decided," he said, "that if we were found in the cellar I should surrender, as the wounded were in a pretty bad way and a single grenade flung down the stairs would see the lot off."

They were indeed discovered, the commander of 679 Brigade having ordered a systematic search. Newman himself at once dashed upstairs and offered surrender. Roughly handled, the party was frog-marched across the road and taken into the house immediately across the road, which turned out, to the amusement of Newman, to be the German headquarters. Under heavy guard, they were stripped of their weapons and interrogated by a German officer without much success.

While this was going on one of the commandos had some occasion to take out his fighting knife, which they all wore strapped to their legs inside their trousers and which, as we have noted earlier, they scarcely thought of as weapons, the British instinct (and, one thinks, the German too) being averse to the use of the knife as a soldier's weapon. The interrogating officer, who was what Newman called an "officer type," observed this action and flew into a rage. Why had they not surrendered all their weapons? They were then all stripped naked under the muzzles of Tommy guns and lined up against a wall. "I really thought," said Newman, "that that was going to be the end of things." At that moment, however, another German officer appeared who was not an "officer type," and he quietly gave orders for the prisoners to resume their clothes.

Back in the dockyard Chant lay by the quay, unable to rise. Wounded a second time in the legs, he had been bowled over in the dockyard battle. Sergeant Butler and Private Brown, of the Argylls, had come to his aid and carried him onward as far as the Submarine Basin, but there he had bidden them leave him. He lay in "the weird half-light" looking straight across to the submarine pens and watching the Germans moving about and manning their weapons on the housetops. A dazed young soldier whom he did not know came and sat down beside him.

There they were found in the morning by a German patrol, who came up to them, Tommy guns leveled, and, shouted, "Herauf! Herauf!" (Get up! Get up!). The young soldier, prompted by Chant, obeyed and was immediately shot dead. They turned to Chant and again ordered "Herauf!

Herauf!" Chant, mad with anger but helpless, pointed to his injured leg. One of the Germans then noticed the stars on his shoulders, and said *"Offizier."* They searched him, taking all his personal possessions, and carried him to a café at a corner of Old Town Place, where Gerard Brett and several other wounded or dying prisoners already lay.

Not far from here Roderick, Hopwood, Sergeant Searson and one or two others, all wounded before or during the break-out (Roderick had been hit a second time), were lying up in a warehouse stored with bags of cement. They all managed to climb to the top of a pile of bags high off the ground and for some hours they avoided capture, watching the German search parties at work.

It was not until 10:30 in the morning that a German, on a higher level than they, looking out from a shed across the dock road, saw, through a bomb-splinter hole in the wall of their warehouse, the bandaged and bloody head of one of the commandos. In next to no time the place was alive with Germans. The wounded men were roughly manhandled to the ground, searched, lined up against a wall, and, like Newman's party, thought that "they had had it." Again, however, some responsible German intervened and instead of being shot they were hustled off to a ship in the Submarine Basin before rejoining their comrades in captivity.

Thus, little by little, what was left of the commandos began to come together again. "It was just like a reunion," Newman recorded. "In spite of personal misfortunes our spirits were high. We never gave in to the Jerries. We all felt that a good job of work had been done, and as each newcomer arrived we pieced the story together. What we were all waiting for, and straining our ears to hear, was the big bang of *Campbeltown* going up in the air."

Not all, however, could maintain this high note. Many were wounded very badly. Wherever the wounded lay, the camera-mad Germans gathered round, clicking from all angles and stepping over bodies to take close-ups. Private McCormack, grievously wounded in the head, lay in an open space in St. Nazaire town, with his head between his kilted legs, dying. The Germans gathered round him in crowds, jeering and laughing, while their cameras clicked. One of these pictures was published throughout Europe in the German armed forces magazine as a whole-page picture with the derisory title "Picture of a British Commando."

17

NOT THE SIX HUNDRED

While the commandos were fighting their dockyard battle and trying to effect their "withdrawal by land," the little motor craft of Ryder's force, or what was left of them, had begun their withdrawal by sea. For some of them the fighting had by no means been ended.

Seven of the seventeen craft we have already seen lost in flames in the immediate neighborhood of the docks—those of Stephens, Platt, Burt, Beart, Tillie, Collier, and Nock. The remaining ten, which include Curtis's gunboat and "Wynn's Weapons," have begun their homeward journeys, setting course at full speed for the open sea. There they are to make rendezvous at Point Y, twenty-five sea miles from St. Nazaire, with their escorting destroyers *Tynedale* and *Atherstone*, with whom they parted company at 8 P.M. It was intended that, having assembled at Point Y, the force should be well on its way home before first light, which was at 5:48 A.M.

Tweedie and Jenks, commanding *Tynedale* and *Atherstone* respectively, had passed an anxious night, having had no news at all of what was happening in the river. All that they had heard on the air, picked up between 2:18 and 3:25, were the "leaving" signals wirelessed by only five of the MLs. Their anxiety had been added to by the knowledge that the five small German destroyers of the 5th Torpedo Boat Flotilla, which had left St. Nazaire early that night as a result of the signal from U 593, were somewhere in the vicinity and might be encountered at any minute.

While the destroyers waited, the ten remaining motor craft, passing beyond range of the small, rapid-firing flak guns in the harbor area, came under fire from the heavier and more dangerous guns of the coastwise batteries. With the exception of the 75-mm. battery at Pointe de l'Eve, which was not manned, all these batteries engaged them hotly, even the big 9.5-inch guns on railway mountings at La Baule. The 6.6-inch battery at Pointe de l'Eve fired no fewer than four hundred rounds that night, mostly in this withdrawal phase, their shells of about a hundred and ten pounds splashing up great fountains of water as they detonated on the surface. Yet all but two of the withdrawing craft successfully ran the gauntlet.

The first of the unfortunate two was Mark Rodier.

Death of Rodier

Having accomplished his mission of landing the assault party of Troop Sergeant-Major Haines in the Old Entrance and having taken on board Sam Beattie and some thirty or more of *Campbeltown*'s crew, Rodier set off down the river at three minutes to two. As he emerged again into the blinding arena of searchlights, the enemy guns turned upon him again, but Rodier successfully took avoiding action.

Beattie joined him on the little bridge and suggested to him a course to steer. They began a lighthearted discussion on trivial subjects, such as the schools they had been to. Off the tip of the East Jetty some "floating shapes" were seen, and, thinking it a pity to take home his torpedoes, Rodier fired them, but with uncertain result. Then, at full speed and making white smoke astern with his chlorosulphonic acid equipment, he passed successfully out of reach of the rapid-firing, short-range weapons in the harbor area. The boat was crowded but Winthrop, *Campbeltown*'s doctor, helped by Hargreaves, the torpedo-gunner, continued to dress and attend to the wounded both above and below deck.

Very soon, however, they were picked up again by the searchlights lower down the river and came under fire from Dieckmann's 75-mm. and 6.6-inch guns. Rodier took evasive action as he was straddled with increasing accuracy. The end came after they had gone some three miles. A shell from the 75-mm. guns at Le Pointeau on the eastern shore hit the boat on the port side of the engine room, lifting one engine bodily on top of the other and stopping both. Toy, the Flotilla Engineer Officer, went below at once. Beattie left the bridge and went down also. He had no sooner left than another shell hit the bridge direct. Rodier was mortally wounded and died a few minutes afterwards. The same shell wounded Frank Arkle.

The engine room was now on fire, burning fiercely, and the sprayer mechanism for fire-fighting had also been put out of action. Toy, who had come up momentarily, at once returned to the blazing compartment but was never seen again. Locke, *Campbeltown*'s Warrant Engineer, was able partially to repair the extinguisher mechanism. The flames amidships divided the crowded ship into two, but the ship's company continued to fight the fire for some three hours. At length, when all means had failed and the fire had spread throughout the boat, the order to abandon ship was given at about 5 A.M. One Carley raft had been damaged, but a few of the wounded ratings were got away on the other, and the remainder of those alive entered the icy water, in which they remained for four and a half hours, many of them succumbing to the ordeal.

All *Campbeltown*'s officers were lost except Beattie and Locke, among those who perished being Tibbits, to whose skill and resourcefulness the success of the raid was so much due. Salter, one of the stewards of *Campbeltown*, was terribly burned about the head as he was caught in a pool of blazing petrol. At 9:30 A.M. the survivors were picked up by a German patrol trawler.

The End of "Wynn's Weapons"

Some twenty minutes or more after Rodier had left the Old Entrance, Wynn also left. After having fired his delayed-action torpedoes into the outer lock gates of that entrance, he had stood by for further orders from Ryder and had been a witness of the little fight between Savage and the Old Mole pillbox. Like Rodier's ML, the MTB was very overcrowded, carrying, in addition to her own small crew of ten, some sixteen hands she had taken from the *Campbeltown* and the ten others had she had stopped to rescue from the water on her way in. Lovegrove had restored to life the damaged center engine and the little torpedo boat shot off at high speed, making smoke to cover her withdrawal.

She had now no weapons but her speed and a few light machine guns. After going only a few hundred yards she was hit in the stern and a small fire resulted, but, under the impetus of her five engines, she was soon racing over the Loire at forty knots, her forefoot high out of the water, her stern settled down into the froth of her wake, and throwing out high on either hand great wings of flying spray. At such speed she was a very difficult target for any gun to hit and as she flew down the river she had no need to resort to evasive action. Very soon the searchlights and the guns gave up the

hunt and in a minute she was racing ahead through the gray
dark, the open sea only a few miles away.

With a clear course before her, nothing seemed able to
stay the utmost gallop of her 3600 horses. Spurred up to
forty-four knots, she flashed through six long sea miles in nine
minutes. The rendezvous with the Wrens drew nearer at every
beat of her engines.

But the course was not clear. Directly ahead of her in
the gray pallor of the night, there appeared the forms of two
men on a Carley raft. Impossible to avoid cutting right
through them or capsizing them by the boat's violent wash.
Operating the engine-room telegraph himself, Wynn pulled
the lever immediately to "Stop" and then to "Slow Astern."

With her extraordinary knack of pulling up with a few
yards, the MTB stopped right alongside the raft. Within a
matter of seconds, before the shipwrecked men could be
hauled on board, she was brilliantly illuminated by a searchlight. In another few seconds she was struck amidships by a
heavy shell and Wynn was blown unconscious from the bridge
into the charthouse. For some minutes he lay there and when
he began to recover consciousness, his senses were dimly
aware that all the world was red. Instinctively he reached his
hand up for the methyl bromide fire extinguisher and at the
same moment he became aware of a dim figure struggling to
make its way to him through the enveloping red clouds. It
was Lovegrove.

The boat was on fire from stem to stern, the petrol-red
flames roaring and the boat's timbers crackling like rifles. All
hands had abandoned ship. Lovegrove, however, looking
about for his captain, could not see him. In pain from his own
wounds, he went back to look for him. Fighting his way
through the flames, he saw the recumbent figure in the charthouse, with the left eye hanging out of its socket. He ran in,
lifted Wynn to his feet, half-carried him up on deck, and then,
putting his arms round him, pulled him into the water and
swam with him to a Carley float. There he supported him for
nearly twelve hours, lashing him to the float or holding on to
him himself.

Through his blurred vision Wynn could see that some
thirty men were crowding round the raft as it was carried
downstream, either on it or clinging to its lifelines or to each
other. The water was bitterly cold, and one by one, as their
strength failed, men let go their grasp and slipped into death,
drifting off with the swift current of the Loire. One of these

was the New Zealander Arthur O'Connor, Wynn's Number One and his dear friend. As the night wore on he heard O'Connor call out to him:

"Good-by, Mick, I'm leaving you now."

Wynn called back to him, "Don't be a bloody fool, Arthur. Hang on!"

But all the answer he got from the night was:

"It's lovely, Mick. I am going. Cheerio."

The night wore on, and at dawn the survivors on the raft realized that they had been carried out to sea. They observed also that only four of them were left—Wynn, Lovegrove, Petty Officer Robert Ward, the coxswain, and Stoker William Savage. Lovegrove and Savage therefore climbed up on the raft and between them they pulled up Wynn. Then they tried to get Ward, but he would not come. He made a last effort to swim with them, pushing the raft in front of him, but after a little while suddenly sank beneath the water.

A little while before, Able Seaman Leonard Denison, one of the most resourceful of hands, had successfully swum out to some concrete structure in the river mouth, although wounded, and found safety there. All the rest of the thirty-six souls on the boat were lost.

The long morning of Saturday, the twenty-eighth, dragged on as the raft drifted in the currents, but Lovegrove remained full of spirit to the end, and when at long last a German gunboat appeared at two o'clock in the afternoon and approached them he actually drew his revolver and only with the greatest difficulty was restrained by Wynn from using it against the Germans. No doubt they were all three by now somewhat delirious. Taken on board by the Germans, they were generously treated by a chivalrous captain, whose final act before landing them earned Wynn's lasting gratitude. Knowing that, once ashore, officers and men would be permanently separated, he allowed them some little time together in private.

The Last Fight

In personnel, the losses of Rodier's and Wynn's boats were the most grievous of all, for they accounted for at least sixty per cent of the naval fatal casualties. But the account is nearly closed. Nine craft have now been lost, but, of these, three have accomplished their missions in full. The circumstances in which the tenth met her end deserve that we should look at her more closely.

His Majesty's ML 306 was commanded by Lieutenant Ian B. Henderson, RNVR, who in peace was an underwriting member of Lloyds. He had a young wife and small family to whom he was devoted. He was fair-complexioned, but premature baldness made him seem older than his thirty years. Number One to Henderson was Sub-Lieutenant P. J. C. Dark, a student of both anthropology and art.

The commandos whom Ian Henderson was carrying were a demolition party under Lieutenant R. O. C. Swayne, of the Herefordshire Regiment and 1 Commando, and their protection squad under Lieutenant J. Vanderwerve of 2 Commando. Swayne had played rugger for Oxford, but missed his Blue, and had been a member of the University Air Squadron until he received a bad concussion in a crash. He was an old hand at the commando game, having taken part in the very first little tryout raid on the French coast in June, 1940, his patrol being the first to inflict German casualties, and in the semi-abortive raid on the Channel Isles the next month. Of the noncommissioned ranks, the most outstanding —and, indeed, one of the most remarkable characters in the whole of our story—was Sergeant Tom Durrant, the swarthy, intense Royal Engineer.

We have already seen Henderson take up ML 306 in the port column in all the blaze of the searchlights in an attempt to land at the Old Mole. Circling, he attempted the Old Entrance also, but so heavy and continuous was the flow of tracer across it that it seemed to Swayne as though "the way was being barred by lighted chains." The boat was hit several times by 20-mm. fire and her decks were splashed with spray from larger shell bursts that narrowly missed her. Philip Dark was slightly wounded in the leg and Durrant was slightly wounded also. Regretfully, Henderson set course for Point Y at eighteen knots under cover of white smoke.

Swayne, standing on the bridge beside him, very bitter at this let-down of tuned-up hopes, felt nonetheless bound to accept his decision absolutely. But he had to face a very obvious feeling of resentment among his troops. Durrant was cold and sullen and all the team very grumbly, saying to each other, "What have we come here for?"

As they entered the arcs of fire of Dieckmann's coast-defense batteries lower down the estuary, they were engaged continuously by heavy pieces and drenched with spray from water-bursts of "near misses." But they successfully evaded it all by frequent changes of course and speed which taxed the promptitude of Leading Seaman Sargent at the wheel and Petty Officer Bennett in the engine room. Thus they made their way safely out to sea. They were much ahead of time for the rendezvous at Y with *Tynedale* and *Atherstone* and reduced speed first to "Three Quarters" and then to "Slow." Henderson therefore said to Philip Dark, who had been clearing up the ship and whose injured leg was now stiffening:

"There's no point in hanging about here; we might get caught by a German patrol any minute. I shall go on to the next rendezvous. You'd better go below and rest your leg."

And when Dark offered to relieve him on the bridge he answered: "Oh no; I can go on for days at this sort of thing."

Dark accordingly went down into the little wardroom, lay down on a couch and took his boots off. He was never to put them on again.

A little before 5:30 in the morning, when forty-five miles out to sea, while it was still very dark, and with a light sea mist resting on the water, Dark was summoned urgently to the bridge. He went instantly, in his sea stockings. He was followed by Swayne, who was, however, merely taking up some bully beef sandwiches to the naval officers on the bridge. He found Henderson and Dark puzzled by some white streaks on the water that could be faintly seen some little distance off ahead. Swayne's flippant suggestion that they might be caused by a large fish was not well received and he went below again. The commandos and hands below were drinking cocoa and eating sandwiches.

A minute later Dark came down and asked Swayne to return to the bridge at once, very quietly. Swayne was still eating a sandwich. When he arrived on the bridge Henderson said nothing but handed him his night glasses and pointed ahead. Swayne put up the glasses and there, fine on the port bow, he saw the outlines, faint but distinct, of three or more German destroyers, coming towards them on a nearly parallel course. His sandwich turned to dust in his mouth.

"Those," said Henderson, "are some of your fish."

They were, in fact, the five ships of Schmidt's 5th TBD Flotilla, which, as we know, had put to sea the evening before on orders from Naval Group Command West as the result of the report from U 593. Schmidt had put out his paravanes to search for the suspected mines and was about a hundred miles out to sea when he was astonished to receive the wireless sig-

nal "Enemy landing at St. Nazaire." He was ordered to return
at once and to endeavor to intercept the raiding craft or their
escorts as they withdrew.

Henderson immediately stopped ship and asked Swayne
to bring his men and Vanderwerve's to action stations as
quietly as possible. No talking. Swayne went below and
passed the order to Vanderwerve and Durrant. The sergeant
nodded and had the men moving at once, collecting their
arms. Swayne went back to the bridge and watched the German ships looming larger and larger.

"What will you do?" he asked Henderson in a whisper.

"Keep as quiet as possible and hope they won't see us,"
Henderson answered.

"And if they do see us?"

"We shall have to fight, of course."

A featherweight launch against a steel ship of eight hundred tons. A handful of machine guns against high explosive
of three 4.1-inch guns, three 20 mms. and two Hotchkisses.
A speed twice their own. Quietly the word was passed along
the little deck.

It was very cold. A bright phosphorescence lit the disturbed waters at bow and stern as the German ships came
on. Another minute and they were right on the port beam,
barely a hundred yards away.

In the motor launch hands could even hear the German
voices. The forward Oerlikon was still jammed, but the after
gun stood ready, manned by Ordinary Seaman Garner and
Batteson and controlled by Pat Landy, wearing a white submarine frock. Amidships, between the bridge and the mast,
Able Seaman Alder manned the little twin Lewis guns on
their high, exposed antiaircraft mounting. Just abaft the mast,
among the commandos, Sergeant Durrant and Chappell, the
sandy-haired Corporal Evans and Corporals Llewellyn and
Salisbury were manning the four Bren guns, crouching low
behind the deck petrol tanks. Manning Tommy guns were
Vanderwerve, Sergeant Gallagher and the remainder of their
squad. Down in the engine room Bennett and Butcher, having no idea what was afoot, stood by attentively with their
engines stopped.

The German ships appeared quite blind to the presence
of the little motor launch. Two of them passed ghostlike into
the night behind them, the silence broken only by the German
voices and the swish of the bright bow waves. The third ship,
the *Jaguar,* came abeam and began to pass likewise. The little

group on the bridge of the ML held their breath, scarcely believing their luck.

On board the *Jaguar*, meanwhile, Kapitänleutnant F. K. Paul reported by radio to Schmidt, in *Seeadler*, that he had observed a "shadow" on his port hand. Schmidt did not at first credit him, but when Paul repeated his suspicion, ordered him to investigate.

Thus, when the German was on his extreme port quarter, Henderson observed him to swing out of line and begin to come round astern. The next moment the night was violently ripped apart by the white blaze of *Jaguar*'s main port searchlight. The solitary motor launch stood instantaneously revealed, illuminated with so fierce a glare that all on board her felt as though suddenly stripped naked. Above them the White Ensign hung clearly displayed.

Henderson immediately ordered, "Slow ahead together."

Almost simultaneously the two ships opened fire on each other, and in the very first burst the German's searchlight was put out, the tinkling of the shattered glass clearly audible on the ML. There was a moment or two's darkness before he switched on a second searchlight, the fusillade continuing meantime. The German did not bring his main 4-inch armament to bear for such apparently easy meat, but his heavy machine guns soon caused casualties on Henderson's exposed deck and tore through his wooden hull. Paul counted upon an obvious surrender in such a hopeless case and he was eager to capture a prize rather than to sink.

Continuing her circular movement, *Jaguar* came up on Henderson's starboard hand at a range of only a hundred yards, still keeping the ML fully illuminated and under fire. A burst hit a small group of soldiers amidships, wounding several of them and kindling a small fire on the bridge. When nearly full on Henderson's starboard beam, she bore round still harder to port, closing the ML bows-on. Henderson, seeing her bows suddenly looming high and near, realized that she was bearing down to ram. He ordered "Hard aport!" in the nick of time. Sergeant swung the wheel over. The *Jaguar*, instead of ramming, struck the ML a glancing blow that caused no material damage, but it rocked the little craft so violently that Vanderwerve, who had just been wounded in the head while blazing away with a Tommy gun, was thrown overboard together with Ordinary Seaman Rees and two others; Vanderwerve was never seen again and Rees, sucked underwater, had his toes taken off by the propellers.

As they recovered from the impact, hands on the motor launch saw the bows of the destroyer poised above them like a huge carving knife. The fo'c'sle rails were crowded with Germans shouting excitedly and pouring down a shower of small-arms fire. The motor launch replied instantly. Ammunition ran low and hands repeatedly went below for replenishment. Every minute added to their casualties. Vanderwerve, Llewellyn and Tomblin were dead, Durrant, Bishop, Hopkins, Chappell and several others wounded.

After the attempt at ramming, the *Jaguar*, apprehending from the movement at the ML's after Oerlikon that Henderson might drop a depth charge at these close quarters, sheered sharply off to starboard and then began again to circle the motor launch. "I was," said Paul, "very angry." When the range had opened to about fifty yards, enabling his guns to depress onto the ML, he opened fire again, now using his Hotchkiss guns as well as his 20 mms. A shell burst in the wheelhouse, wounding Sargent at the wheel, and he staggered up to the bridge, clutching his stomach. Another knocked out the only remaining Oerlikon, killing Garner and wounding Sergeant Gallagher at his Tommy gun. Landy, perhaps somewhat earlier, was shot in the back by a bullet. Alder was badly hit at his twin Lewis abaft the bridge and Durrant, though now wounded a third time, stood up and, calling for more ammunition, took over. Down in the engine room Bennett said to Butcher, "I had better go up and see what's happening," but on reaching the deck he was at once mortally wounded in the stomach and head.

Henderson watched the *Jaguar* continue her circling movement and come round on his port hand. Philip Dark was beside him on the bridge and the wounded Sargent lay in pain at their feet. When square on his port beam, the destroyer, according to British reports, fired her 4.1-inch aramament. The shell hit the bridge direct, mortally wounding Henderson, killing Sargent and miraculously missing Dark but throwing him unconscious into the starboard corner.

There was a moment's deathly hush. Swayne, the only officer of either Service left unhurt, coming up from below at that moment with ammunition, looked around upon a scene of desolation. The ship reeked of high explosive. The deck was covered with prostrate forms and by the pallid light of approaching dawn he saw the dark bulk of the bigger ship closing in upon them again in a tighter circle.

It looked, thought Swayne, as though they were nearly

finished. The German certainly thought so. He hailed them in English, calling upon them to surrender and shouting, "Stop shooting! Don't shoot!"

Immediately everything came to life again. Durrant, shot through with manifold wounds, opened fire once more with his twin Lewis, followed by Evans. The Welshman was shouting angry abuse at the Germans as fire was resumed. Stoker Butcher, having come up after the order to stop engines, was immediately hit in the leg. The enemy ship was now barely thirty yards away. Seeing no other course to take, Swayne started along the deck, scrambling over the crowded prostrate forms to get out the small dinghy. He passed Durrant, covered in blood but still standing up to his Lewis, gripping it with what little life and strength remained to him. He struggled aft to the dinghy and began to unship the gear that was stowed in it, but found it full of holes. *Jaguar* now came virtually alongside, only a few yards away, and Paul, high on his bridge, again called down to them to surrender.

He was answered by Durrant. Lying half collapsed across his gun, the dying sergeant fired a burst straight up at the German bridge. It ripped across the small navigational table within an inch of the German captain.

Disconcerted and astonished, *Jaguar* went astern. At such close quarters she could not depress her guns down on to the ML; but when the range had opened far enough, she resumed firing and went ahead again. Once more Durrant was hit. His body was riddled with bullets—in both arms, both legs, stomach, chest and head. In terrible agony, he collapsed on deck.

It was time to stop, Swayne decided. There was no longer any means of continuing the fight. Out of twenty-eight all hands of both Services, not less than twenty were dead or wounded. Dark had recovered consciousness, but he was very shaken and his face was covered with blood from small wounds in the nose and forehead. It was now daylight and the destroyer was alongside, towering over them. Swayne, standing up by the dinghy, called out in English, and then in French, "I'm afraid we can't go on."

There was a moment's dead silence. The German commander looked down in astonishment upon the shattered boat, its deck carpeted with dead and wounded men. Fearing that the British might "play a Richard Grenville," he said in English:

"You must not play any funny tricks."

Swayne answered, "No, I give you my word of honor."

Thus ended this astonishing fight, which the motor launch had sustained, it is said, nearly a full hour—from the pitch dark of soon after 5:30 to the daylight of 6:30. Leaving their dead where they had fallen, her survivors climbed or were carried on board the enemy destroyer. Ian Henderson, still just alive but completely unconscious, was brought up with them. Like Wynn and his companions, they were fortunate enough to fall into the hands of Germans of honorable behavior. Kapitänleutnant Paul treated them with consideration and chivalry. The wardroom and officers' cabins were given over to the wounded and officers' sheets were torn up for extra wound dressings.

Tom Durrant was dying. "The amount of pain he suffered and bore so well," Dark said, "was incredible for any human being." Because of a wound deep in the belly, Dark had to refuse him water, for which he was crying out. Bennett also was dying and Able Seaman Sparkes had compound fractures of both legs.

Paul, who spoke fairly good English, invited Swayne to his cabin for a drink, and when Swayne refused, said, "I don't want to question you." Thinking that it might be best not to offend an enemy obviously so well disposed, Swayne agreed. When they had gone to his cabin the German said:

"I wanted to compliment you on your brave fight. You had no chance, of course. Besides, I knew you would need a drink." It was a pity, he said to his prisoner, that the Germans and the British should be fighting each other.

Dark, still in his sea stockings, was also well received by the first lieutenant, Oberleutnant Heilig, who invited him into his cabin to wash the blood from his face and to have a drink. They conversed in French. Afterwards, as he had had a year's medical training and as the German ship carried no doctor, Dark was asked to treat the German wounded, "after you have seen to your own." There were few medical supplies and no morphia, but fortunately the British officers carried morphine ampoules. Assisted by the German first-aid hand, Dark therefore did what little he could, and he put a tourniquet on Ordinary Seaman Shephard's shattered leg. He noticed the German upper deck soiled with blood, especially below the bridge, and he treated four of their wounded before a new excitement distracted the attention of all as the German crew were ordered again to action stations.

Swayne had been given license by Paul to be on the

upper deck for a short time and it was with mixed feelings that, at a little after 6:30 A.M., he saw the silhouette of HMS *Tynedale* on the horizon. By such a narrow margin had ML 306 failed to reach the safety of her protection. The motor launch, which had been made fast, was now cast off. Swayne wondered what it would feel like to be shot up by one's own friends and thought what a strange paradox it would be to cheer on the shelling of oneself. Hopefully he asked Paul if he intended to fight; but the German said no, he was fast enough to make port. Unfortunately, he was right. Separated from the rest of his flotilla, he did not engage in the brief action that had just taken place between *Tynedale* and Schmidt's leading ships.

Thus the survivors sailed once more up the Loire and came at last to St. Nazaire, anchoring not from from *Campbeltown*. There, as they went over the side under guard, Paul paid them the signal honor of calling his ship's company to attention and himself coming to the salute.

About a week later a German officer called on Newman in the prison camp at Rennes and said that he wished to bring to his notice the gallant conduct of a sergeant in a captured motorboat, "as you may wish to recommend him for a high award."*

"I Don't Call That Failure"

The tally of losses is complete. Except for a few "write-offs," there is nothing more to enter on the debit side. Ryder, whom we have left a long time ago in the harbor area, had no knowledge at all of these last three entries but had already seen and heard enough to have grounds for qualified satisfaction.

The gunboat left the Old Entrance, a little before 3 A.M. it was high time she did so. The only one of the raiding craft now left in the harbor area, every German gun was waiting for her. Only by a miracle had she so far escaped any vital damage, for she was riddled with holes, littered with debris, laden down with wounded men in every inch of her space, her decks slippery with blood. Dropping a smoke-float, Curtis ordered full speed ahead and quickly worked up to twenty-four

---

*The above account is compiled mainly from the narratives and personal interrogations of Swayne, Dark and Paul, together with several other testimonies. While differences on some points of detail persist, the main features of the action have been reconciled. Paul does not agree that at any time he used his 4.1-inch guns.

knots on his three engines, those on the bridge noting with satisfaction that the enemy at once opened fire on the flames and sparks emitted by the float.

On ordering Sub-Lieutenant Worsley to check the guns' ammunition and their readiness for action on the withdrawal, Curtis was distressed to learn that Able Seaman Savage and Able Seaman F. A. Smith lay dead at the forward pom-pom that they had served so well. At what precise stage they were killed is uncertain, but the burly bearded figure and his ship-mate had that night, in their exposed positions, given a stir-ring example of devotion.

The pom-pom, now the gunboat's only weapon, was taken over by Able Seaman A. Sadler and Ordinary Seaman H. A. Boswell. As the gunboat sped out, searchlights and guns from both sides of the river concentrated on her. Though the group of officers assembled round Ryder on the little bridge remained unhurt, every single seaman on the gunboat had by this time been wounded and many of *Campbeltown*'s wounded on board her had been hit again. It was scarcely possible to move anywhere without treading on the prostrate forms. In these conditions Curtis ordered Leading Seaman McKee, the coxswain, to help Worsley with the casualties, while he him-self and Ryder took alternate tricks at the wheel. There was little that could be done beyond first aid, the administration of morphia and some attempt at making men comfortable in the cramped quarters. No lights could be allowed below deck because of the innumerable holes in the ship's hull, and the first-aid party worked as best they could by the light of torches. To this work CERA Howard also gave his hand, together with Gordon Holman, who, his journalist's task for-gotten, was throughout a conspicuous example of calm and comforting devotion.

By speed, smoke and the tactics of evasion, the gunboat successfully sped through the storm of fire from the flak bat-teries in the harbor area. She also avoided the more dan-gerous fire of the big guns in the estuary, the fountains of water from their shell bursts spraying her decks as she slipped between them. Gaining the open sea, she fought her last en-gagement; one of the German patrol boats at the mouth of the estuary attacked her out of the dark, sending a burst through her deck petrol tanks. Every man held his breath, waiting for the sheet of flame, but although the tank was full no harm ensued. Sadler and Boswell then put the enemy ship to flight with a fire burning on his deck.

Rendezvous Y was reached at 4:30 A.M., but, like Henderson, Ryder decided that it was unwise to loiter, and he ordered Curtis to proceed on course. At daybreak they sighted the badly damaged Fenton (No. 5) and immediately afterwards Falconar (No. 15). At almost the same moment they were cheered by sighting *Tynedale* and *Atherstone*.

The two destroyers had just come from a brief encounter with the four leading ships of Schmidt's flotilla. The British destroyers had been patrolling on a southwesterly course parallel with the withdrawal route from Y, five miles apart, and looking out for the returning motor launches, when, at 6:29 A.M., the enemy ships had been sighted in line ahead to the westward by *Tynedale*. She altered to southward to close *Atherstone* and protect the MLs, and the enemy altered to starboard. Six minutes later *Tynedale* came under the concentrated fire of the enemy and a running action ensued for nine minutes, both sides scoring hits. *Tynedale* then made smoke and the enemy did not press the action.

The two British destroyers were now therefore in company with the gunboat and the three MLs. Fenton's was sinking and she was accordingly abandoned, her crew and her commandos (Hooper's party) being taken on board by *Atherstone*. At the same time the wounded from Platt's and Falconar's boats were transferred to *Tynedale*. As Ryder and his small headquarters staff returned to *Atherstone*, he saw the gunboat covered with scars—one engine badly damaged, water coming through the many wounds in her hull, her pumps out of action, an improvised chain of buckets struggling to keep down the level of rising water, the petrol running out of the deck tanks that had just been hit, her speed reduced to ten knots and her decks crowded with the patient human wreckage of the battle. For these also it was time to be taken to the comfort of the destroyer, but the task was accomplished only with great difficulty and distress, for the injured lay closely packed together and men were slipping on blood as they attempted to move.

As Bob Ryder quitted forever the gunboat's bloody deck and climbed to *Atherstone*'s bridge, he realized that he was completely exhausted physically and emotionally and was beginning to feel that flat reaction which is quite commonly experienced by men who have come out of a harrowing action, even when the results are known to have been achieved. Though he had not seen *Campbeltown* actually blow up, he knew that the demolitions of the pump house and winding

gears were of themselves sufficient to immobilize the Normandie Dock for a long time to come. He knew, however,
that the assault on the Old Mole had been a failure, and he
felt very distressed at having been obliged to leave Charles
Newman and his commandos to their fate.

It was in this mood that Ryder mounted to *Atherstone*'s
bridge, to be greeted by Robin Jenks, her commanding officer,
who gave him a chair and ordered coffee. Jenks had naturally
been on tiptoe to learn the fortunes of the expedition and had
suffered acute disappointment when an officer from a motor
launch that had had a very rough time had given him a
pessimistic report, saying that no boats could get in and that
no objectives could have been gained. Jenks, therefore, ob-
serving Ryder's silence and fatigue, and fearing the worst,
observed a solicitous silence also. After a time, however, he
could stand the uncertainty no longer and said to Ryder:

"I'm sorry it was a failure, sir."

Beaufighter

Ryder, without any change of expression, answered with a quiet incisiveness:

"Well, I personally saw *Campbeltown* firmly wedged in the lock gates and her fuses fired—objective No. 1. I was nearly killed by a piece of masonry from the pumping station blown up by the commandos—objective No. 2. I saw Wynn fire his torpedoes at the foot of the old lock gates—objective No. 3. I don't see why you should call that a failure."

In the fine spring morning the remnant of the force moved on at a painful eight knots, slowed down by the damaged craft. At eight o'clock a Heinkel 115 dropped out of the sky, but the pilot would not face the formidable concentration of fire from the force and contented himself with sinking Fenton's waterlogged wreck, now some distance away. A little later the appearance of a Beaufighter from 19 Group Coastal Command cheered them all and when a Junkers 88 also appeared the British pilot attacked it with such ferocity that he rammed the German in the air and the two went locked to death. Twenty-two sorties were to be flown that Saturday from St. Eval and Praedannock by Beaufighters, Blenheims and Hudsons of 19 Group, under Air Vice-Marshal Geoffrey Bromet, and in the numerous air encounters that took place five enemy aircraft were shot down for the loss of two of our own.

Soon afterwards, they sighted the two additional destroyers that Forbes had sent to their support—the *Cleveland* and the *Brocklesby*. Command then passed from Ryder to Commander G. B. Sayer (*Cleveland*), who was Ryder's senior. He decided, both on the grounds of safety and in the interest of the wounded, many of whom would die unless hurried to hospital, that the three motor craft that were holding them back so seriously, though seaworthy enough to get back at their own speed, must be scuttled. Thus the motor launches of Irwin and Falconar and Curtis's little gunboat, passed quietly to an honorable sleep.

It was a sad moment for Dunstan Curtis and for all that little ship's company, who looked forward with pride to taking their ship home; but it was as well that this step was taken, for, unknown to Ryder and his friends, a hundred German aircraft were then bombing up at Rennes to attack the remnants of the audacious force that had set the German High Command by the ears. After *Brocklesby* had shot down a

Junkers 88, the destroyers' twenty-five knots took them safely home at last.

Meanwhile, unknown at first to Ryder, three other motor launches, having failed to make contact with the destroyers at Rendezvous Y, were making their way home alone in accordance with orders. These were the boats of Boyd, Wallis and Horlock. This little force, pushing far out to the westward and thence north up the meridian of eight degrees west, made a most creditable passage, shooting down on the way a Heinkel 111 by the combined fire of their Oerlikons (thus making a total of seven enemy aircraft shot down as an extra dividend for the operation) and seeing off a Blohm & Voss seaplane. These three boats, together with Briault's, which we have seen return much earlier on account of engine defects, were the only ones to return home out of the eighteen small motor craft that had set sail from Falmouth two and a half days before.

> *They that had fought so well*
> *Came thro' the jaws of Death,*
> *Out of the mouth of Hell,*
> *All that was left of them,*
> * Left of six hundred.*

18

HAVOC

If, in the manner of their coming, the Charioteers did not win the surprise that they had wished for, they certainly accomplished it in dramatic fashion after their exit. It was one of the kinder ironies of chance that only those who were left behind in captivity were to be the delighted witnesses of the fulfillment of their work.

While Ryder and his companions were sailing home, while Wynn and Lovegrove and Stoker William Savage were drifting out to sea on their Carley float, while Beattie and the survivors of Rodier's unhappy boat were immersed in the bitter waters, an air of crisis hung over St. Nazaire, undispelled by the Saturday's early morning light. The Germans were ill at ease, having no idea of the purpose of the raid. There in the stark light they now saw *Campbeltown*, securely jammed into the gate of the big lock. There for all to see were the demolished pump house and winding gears. These, three small sunken ships, wrecked guns, the burned out Forge de l'Ouest and some seventy-six corpses were the visible evidence of the havoc so far.

Nor did the shooting stop when Newman's men at last surrendered. Desultory shots cracked and ricocheted about the town. Here and there the patriot French had begun to take out their few hidden arms, believing that the British invasion had begun. The Nazairiens began making Mr. Churchill's V sign, to be instantly suppressed whenever observed by the Germans. The *patron* of the Old Town café where Chant and Brett had lain, coming out to wave and shout his good wishes as the British wounded were carried away, was immediately hustled inside by the Germans.

German Army troops continued to pour in, mingling with the bluejackets and white moleskin trousers of the sea-

He 111

going sailors on the town side of the docks and with Mecke's
field-gray naval units beyond. What all these troops were
does not clearly appear from the available German documents, but maps show a continuous girdle of troop positions
all round the town and Burhenne declares, somewhat improb-
ably, that no fewer than six thousand troops arrived on the
east side of the river, where he was stationed. Other troops
of 333 Division were also hastily redeployed in various areas.
The town of St. Nazaire itself was placed in a stage of siege,
all exits being closed, tram and train services stopped, crossroads picketed by machine guns, and the docks sealed off to
the French except for a few specialist workmen. The infantry
brigade instituted an intensive house-to-house search of the
town to ferret out any hidden commandos who, for a long
time, were believed, by reason of the continued desultory
firing, to be still lurking in concealment with the connivance
of the French. Meanwhile, from the beaches and from the
sea, the naval forces were collecting the living and the dead
from the wrecked motor launches, and as the bright March
sun rose higher it appeared to the Germans that the situation
was under control.

As one may suppose, the Germans lost no time in boarding *Campbeltown*. A group of very senior officers and many
technical specialists, to the number of about thirty, climbed
on board by the ladders that the commandos had left and
carried out an examination. It is said that the Admiral-Superintendent of the dockyard himself arrived and, immediately
suspecting the existence of an explosive charge, ordered a

search to be made; but none was found, so shrewdly had it been concealed in its steel and concrete jacket. On being so informed, he said, we are told, "Well, the British must be very stupid if they think we can't deal with this." For the problem of disengaging the destroyer from the caisson was not one of serious engineering difficulty. It was apparent that she would sink in the lock entrance if simply towed out, and the methods to be adopted for getting her clear without immobilizing the dock for longer than necessary were being discussed. The acting Harbor Commander also visited the ship, but neither he nor the Admiral-Superintendent stayed very long. Mecke also came, driving up from his headquarters at St. Marc, and he took some photographs.

But these were by no means the only visitors. Orders had been given for a cordon to be placed round the dock, but either the order was never carried out or the cordon was ignored. For the word very quickly flew that here were plenty of cigarettes and chocolates to be had for the taking and a throng of curious sightseers of all sorts began to arrive by car and on foot—the submarine commanders, the gun position officers, officers of the naval shore staff and so on. And their lady friends. Looking for souvenirs, they roamed the littered upper deck from the shattered bows, where the displaced twelve-pounder stood precariously by the big hole in the fo'c'sle, on past the tangles of twisted metal, underneath the bandstands where the Oerlikons had been so bravely served, and so down the steep incline towards the sunken stern, where the falling tide lapped quietly on the quarter-deck. They penetrated to the darker chaos below, where the officers' sherry lay spilled and wasted in the wardroom, where the butter was plastered on the mirrors, where broken glass, cigarettes, clothing and little personal things littered the cabins and the mess decks and where the inert corpses indifferently lay.

While this tour of his ship was being made Beattie, blanketed and barefoot, was brought ashore in St. Nazaire with the other survivors of Rodier's boat. It was probably some time after ten o'clock and he was disappointed to see *Campbeltown* still intact on the caisson. The latest possible computed time for Tibbits's fuses to act was 9:30. What had gone wrong? He supposed that the Germans had discovered the arrangements and found some way of disarming the fuses, though he thought that Tibbits had provided against that contingency also. He had no opportunity, however, to stand and stare and was hurried on, very cold, to some German office,

where he was taken for interrogation by a pleasant-mannered
German Intelligence officer, who spoke English well. The
Intelligence officer got nothing out of Beattie, but he was
persuasively talkative, and he remarked:

"Your people obviously did not know what a hefty thing
that lock gate is. It was really useless trying to smash it with
a flimsy destroyer."

At that precise moment the glass from the window
crashed to the floor, as the room, and indeed, the whole town,
was shaken by a thunderous explosion sustained for several
seconds.

"That, I hope, is the proof," observed Beattie dryly as
the vibrations began to abate, "that we did not underestimate
the strength of the gate."

The interrogation was brought to an abrupt close.

This heartening evidence of their success was heard, or
even seen, by nearly all the Charioteers who had now been
swept up. The time, as nearly as can be judged, was 10:35
A.M.; not earlier. Between them, Beattie and Tibbits had done
better than either could know. *Campbeltown* erupted with an
enormous flash and a column of black smoke. Under the
impact of this blast, reinforced by the hammer-blow of the
inrushing sea, the great one-hundred-and-sixty-ton caisson
burst open inwards. The sea poured like a tidal wave into the
empty dock. The northern caisson, the inner face of which
had not been destroyed by Brett and Burtenshaw, held, but
the two tankers that lay inside the dock—*Schledstadt* and
Passat—were flung against the dock walls and damaged and
the sunken stern half of HMS *Campbeltown*, cut off as by a
giant saw, was swept inside by the force of the flood. Of the
rest of her nothing remained but the fragments that were
flung far and wide. All the Germans on board the destroyer—
men and women—went with her. So, too, did large numbers
of those who clustered about her on land, dismembered by
the violence of that blast.

How shall one explain the fact that this explosion took
place so long after the extreme limit of time expected of its
fuses? Not one fuse, but at least three. Under normal func-
tioning, they should have burned through at 7 A.M. Even
under the extreme expected tolerance, they should have acted
by 9 A.M. When they did act, they were nearly four hours
overdue.

There persists a belief in St. Nazaire that a British officer,
either voluntarily or involuntarily, went back on board and,

in a deed of self-immolation, refired the quiescent charge. Workmen are said to have seen one or more go on board. The finger of surmise points at once to Pritchard. He understood the charging and the fusing of the explosive ship. He had the professional competence.

Did Pritchard die in the Old Town where Maclagan saw him fall? No shot was fired and the corporal did not know by what weapon he had been struck. Had he only been very badly winded? Or had the wound been not a fatal one?

If there is any truth in the legend, it would, of course, explain the delayed explosion; but it is a legend not easy to sustain. For Bill Pritchard lies buried in the cemetery at Escoublac. Had anyone else gone back on board the destroyer, it is difficult to explain how, without the requisite gear, which he is unlikely to have carried, and in the presence of the Germans, he could have fired the great charge. It was recognized that these fuses were of an experimental and uncertain nature in regard to their timing and we can do no more than suppose that some unknown factor of temperature, moisture or material led to an excessive delay in the action of the acid on the copper. Yet it remains very odd that all the fuses should have been so long delayed without failing altogether, and even a man so little given to fanciful speculation as Hughes-Hallett thinks that "some hero" may have gone back on board and immolated himself.

An alternative interpretation of this persistent French legend is that some one or two British officers, on being ordered or invited by the Germans to go on board, did so in order to encourage the belief that the destroyer was not armed with a deadly change. That is entirely possible, but there is no positive evidence.

Whatever may be the truth in this matter, nothing detracts from the brilliance of the demolition plans conceived and carried out by Nigel Tibbits, which so conclusively prevented the enemy, for all the remaining years of the war, from using against our most vital convoy route the most dangerous ship that they possessed. And to the memory of Pritchard we owe a like acknowledgment for those acts of demolition against the operating machinery which would have put the big dock out of action for at least a year even if *Campbeltown* had never blown up.

"It was from this moment," said Monsieur Grimaud, one of the assistant mayors, in his report to Paris, "that a state of tension became apparent between the Germans, unnerved by the surprise of the night and the explosion of the morning, and population, who had now recovered from their astonishment and were becoming ironically amused at the events which were unfolding themselves before them like a surprising motion picture."

The great, black cloud of *Campbeltown*'s explosion, drawing all eyes to the sky, dissipated idly in the hush of astonishment that followed, while fragments of metal clattered down on roof and road over a radius of a mile. It was a very severe shock to the Germans. Men ran to the scene, to stand horror-stricken not only at the towering column of smoke, the shattered gate, the swirling waters, the crashing ships, but also at the spectacle of human flesh and bones showered over all the devastated scene.

Gradually the Germans' discipline and order re-established itself, but their unease showed itself in a tightening of their grip. Scattered shooting was still going on, believed by the Germans to be coming from commandos not yet discovered, and the bullets were still whistling about the streets, and in the country also, when Newman and his friends were lorried off to La Baule. As late as six o'clock that evening Dieckmann, driving back to his coast-defense guns after a visit to Admiral Lindenau's headquarters in Nantes, was shot at as he passed through St. Nazaire.

By Sunday a superficial calm was restored but with no easing of the tension. The episode now appeared to be over. But at about four o'clock that Monday afternoon another heavy explosion shook the surroundings and threw the whole place once more into confusion and consternation. In a great shower of smoke and water the outer gate of the Old Entrance blew up, as one of Wynn's torpedoes exploded.

A new anger seized the Germans, an anger the more dangerous because they were completely mystified. What was this big charge that had gone up under water, and who the devil had placed it there? It was two and a half days since all the British had been rounded up. Had the inhabitants been conniving with the British in these acts of destruction? A search of all houses and an examination of identity cards were set on foot. Orders were issued to the mayor that all cafés must be shut at 9 P.M. Patrols were sent out through the streets, where the French were gathering in small groups and discussing with animation the extraordinary events. They

were very well aware of the dangerous temper of the
Germans. The threatening looks and the peremptory commands told their own story. The news that a furious Hitler
had ordered an immediate inquiry on the spot had already
set the Germans on edge. Like the Charioteers' fuses, a cor-
rosive acid was inexorably at work, ready at the appointed
moment to release the springs of an emotional explosion.

An hour later the second of Wynn's torpedoes blew up.
Tumult burst throughout the dockyard. A group of
French workmen, fearful of German suspicions and reprisals,
threw down their tools and ran for Bridge M at the northern
end of the Submarine Basin. There they were met by German
troops, who, supposing this to be an organized rising, opened
fire on them, driving them to take refuge in trenches and
shelters where they remained far into the night. The fever
spread quickly through the port, as everywhere the Germans
began to fire upon bewildered parties of Frenchmen.

It is very unusual for German troops to lose their heads,
but they did so on this occasion. The mysteriousness of these
events, the troubled and uncertain atmosphere, the renewal
of shooting by a few Frenchmen, to whom every explosion
was a new song of hope, the kindling of fires in the Old
Town and in the Loire and Penhoët docks threw them into
a state of angry bewilderment. Unnerved and acting on sudden impulse, on what official orders we know not, they began,
with the fall of night, to shoot at any sign of movement,
imagining British commandos about to spring on them from
every shadow. Inevitably German soon began to shoot German in the confusion of the night, each thus believing that
he was being attacked by an enemy. Sohler, hurrying in by
car from La Baule to ensure the safety of his submarines
from the reported civilian rising, was repeatedly fired at on
his way and the officer accompanying him wounded.

At 8:30 P.M. squalls of musketry, machine-gun fire and
even grenades broke out in the neighborhood of the Boulevard de l'Océan. The streets were filled with troops and
naval ratings, circulating in small parties, seemingly under
no orders, engaging each other and the French. They emptied
their magazines into houses and into the hospital. They
opened fire on passengers arriving at the railway station
from Nantes. They fired at every head that appeared at a
window and at the reflections of the flashes of their own
rifles.

Before midnight this panic shooting had died down in the main town, but new outbursts began in the Old Town and at Penhoët. A chance bullet, breaking the high tension electric cables, plunged the whole town in darkness. The water supply stopped also; and these occurrences served only to give further emphasis to the enemy's conviction that a concerted rising was taking place.

It was upon the Old Town that the German hand fell heaviest. After their search parties had combed the houses, the inhabitants were thrown out without notice, locked up in the German blockhouses, to be thence conveyed, to the number of one thousand five hundred, to the prison camp at Savenay, while their houses were ransacked. At about eleven o'clock a fog mercifully descended and silence gradually returned, but during that night sixteen French men, women and children, from the ages of five to seventy-six, were killed and twenty-six wounded.

A little after midnight squads of the *Feldgendarmerie* entered the houses of the mayor and the four asisstant mayors and, standing over them with sub-machine-guns as they dressed, carried them off under Leutnant Mayer to the Collège de Saint-Louis, where the office of the military administration was installed. They found themselves in front of a cold and forbidding Prussian colonel who had arrived that evening from Army headquarters at Angers. He spoke to the Frenchmen very fast in a harsh and menacing tone, charging them that the civilian population had been attacking the Germans and threatening them that if these acts continued tomorrow one-tenth of the persons in the quarter responsible would be shot without hearing.

As a result of this threat, the unfortunate officials spent the rest of the night preparing a proclamation to the town, turning printers out of their beds, searching for billposters, and directing where the posters should be displayed so that they could not be defaced by the public. The mayoral authorities stoutly denied that any citizens had attacked the Germans, but there is small reason to doubt that many patriotic Frenchmen, convinced that deliverance by their allies was at hand, brought out such weapons as they may have managed to hide and set fire to installations in the docks.

Throughout France the impact of the news of the Raid was immense. In spite of the mendacious accounts circulated by the Nazis and their Vichy lackeys, the hearts of all loyal Frenchmen rejoiced in the shining prowess of the deed and saw in it the first hope that the long night would have an end.

In the German hierarchy there was a terrific row. Hitler was extremely angry. What enraged him as much as the loss of the Nomandie Dock was that British forces had succeeded in penetrating German defenses and actually landing on territory that he held. The very day after the raid he took the extraordinary step of ordering Field-Marshal von Rundstedt, Commander-in-Chief of all German forces in western Europe, to conduct a personal inquiry immediately. This von Rundstedt accordingly did at St. Nazaire on March 31.

He reported that there was no fault to find with the German conduct of the action and that no blame could be assigned to anyone for the British landing. But Hitler was far from satisfied. On his orders General Jodl, Director of Operations of the supreme command of all the armed forces, visited von Rundstedt three days later "to examine further the failure to repel the enemy" and the inquiry, under pressure, very soon shaped itself into one of those violent quarrels between the army and the navy which are so familiar a picture in German military archives. Hitler declared that the measures taken to detect Ryder's forces at sea were quite inadequate and critical interest became forcused at once on that crucial encounter between Ryder and U 593, when, as we have seen, the Naval Group Command West had been misled, by Ryder's change of course and by the submarine's faulty report, into thinking that the British force was merely returning from laying mines or else was on its way to Gibraltar. It was this assumption that led Group Command West to order 5 TBD Flotilla to sea to make an exploratory sweep. "An imminent attack from the sea on a port of the French west coast was never anticipated."

This probing into naval affairs, or the manner in which it was done, lit the fires of wrath in Grand Admiral Raeder, the Commander-in-Chief, who wrote personally to Field-Marshall Keitel:

I have heard with the greatest displeasure of your signal to C-in-C West on the subject of the St. Nazaire inquiry and the questionnaire that has been drafted at your express wish. I have not been informed at any stage of the proceeding, although the greater part of the questions are within my province and are my personal responsibility. You have not once informed me of the

instructions you were issuing. This procedure is against
all military custom. I must therefore insist on an expla-
nation and apology from you.

As far as official records go, he does not seem to have
received that apology.

In the official report the factors contributing to the successful British penetration of the Loire were set out as:

Failure to anticipate the repetition of small raids such
as that on Zeebrugge.

The diversionary bombing raid (which did at first divert
attention).

The incorrect conclusion drawn from the report of
U 593.

Lack of aerial reconnaissance.

Inadequate patrolling of the estuary and the absence
of wireless on the patrol boats.

The existence of only one naval radar station, which had
been diverted to an antiaircraft rôle.

Examining the British plan and performance, the Germans acknowledged that the principle of a diversionary air
attack was sound. Mecke (who was awarded the Knight's
Cross by Hitler) stated in his report that had the RAF been
able to continue bombing he had little doubt but that the
raiders would have penetrated entirely unobserved. It was
admitted that the chief object of the raid had been achieved
and it was described as an operation cleverly planned to the
last detail and boldly carried out. The failure of the subsidiary objects was attributed to the "half measures" adopted
by the British, "who always fight shy of shedding blood even
when the target is important enough to justify it." Had the
operation been planned on the larger scale of Zeebrugge, em-
ploying more men and larger ships capable of withstanding
heavy antiaircraft fire with equanimity, the raid would without doubt have been a complete success in all its objectives.
These tactical criticisms, however, were based on an entire
misconception of the very factors that had confronted Forbes
—lack of suitable ships and the difficulty of an undetected
approach.

19

THE CAPTIVE AND FREE

Of all these later happenings most of the captured charioteers knew nothing until years afterwards. As they gradually came together in small parties on that Saturday morning, some very roughly handled, others treated decently, they greeted each other with the utmost cheerfulness. Exhausted, bedraggled, badges and shoulder straps ripped off by Germans rapacious for souvenirs, they had nonetheless not lost their spirit.

As the commandos of the dockyard battle were gradually gleaned by the Germans, a still larger harvest was being gathered in from the sea. Gunshot, drowned or burned to death in the cruel petrol fires, the dead were brought in for burial. All down the estuary others were rescued, or washed ashore, miraculously alive after long immersion. Some of these, including Beattie and Burt, were stripped of their wet clothing and rubbed down, but provided with nothing more than a blanket to wrap around themselves and in this exiguous cover, barefoot, they were required to endure the long day and journey before them.

There now began for the Charioteers a long trek to the trying and squalid life of a prisoner of war. But, so long as they were together, they were no ordinary prisoners. For a long time they were specially guarded and kept separate from all others. So important were they considered that a few days later Hilter sent his own interpreter, the celebrated Dr. Schmidt, to interrogate them. There grew up a pride in their brotherhood one with another in one of the most daring of exploits, a pride which was shown not least in their bearing and discipline as prisoners.

As far as can be gathered from the scattered and inexact records, a total of two hundred, perhaps a few more, were taken prisoner. The dead have in all official accounts been reported as 144, but in point of fact they reached a total of 169—a proportion of more than one man in four of all the 611 who sailed (not 630 as officially recorded). This was an extremely high proportion of fatal casualties for any operation; yet, in the harsh accountancy of war, a low price for the high results achieved. By far the greater number— probably more than three quarters—were killed in the river battle and the withdrawal. The commando losses amounted to 64 and the naval losses to 105, fully two thirds of the naval losses being accounted for in the two sinkings of the crowded boats of Rodier and Wynn during the withdrawal.

The enemy casualties, as given by the German naval staff, amounted to 42 killed, plus the hundred or more (almost certainly far more) admitted as blown up in the *Campbeltown*, and 127 wounded. To these are to be added a few army losses. According to Mecke, all the German losses, except for a few wounded and except for the deaths incurred in *Campbeltown*'s explosion, were inflicted by the commandos ashore, but this is not easy to accept. If the German figures are accepted, the losses in men were thus pretty much the same on both sides, although the losses of an assaulting force are usually expected to be the higher. It is not, however, by such figures that the merits and value of the action are to be measured; though we may note as a matter of interest that the British losses at St. Nazaine were proportionately more than twice as heavy as those in the Zeebrugge Raid.*

At La Baule the captive Charioteers came together in two main parties. The able and the slightly wounded were driven away to the large Brittany of Rennes, where they were shut up in a prison camp of unspeakable filthiness (Stalag 133) used for French colonial prisoners of war. The main body of the wounded, to the number of about ninety, were taken to the German naval hospital that had been established in the *de luxe* Hermitage Hotel at La Baule. The conditions for the British wounded however, were anything but *de luxe*. Their beds were the floor. The place was crammed with the British and German wounded, the medical staff inadequate for the emergency and, as was not uncommon in German hospitals, poorly supplied with anesthetics. All but the most

---

*At Zeebrugge the fatal casualties numbered 195 out of a total of 1,784 officers and men in the assaulting forces.

severe operations—even the removal of Wynn's eye—were carried out without anesthesia. All the time, day and night, German Tommy-gunners paraded up and down between the rows of prostrate forms. They even followed the stretcher cases up to the operating theater and when the patient revived after his ordeal there was the Tommy-gunners still.

On Wednesday—four days after the raid—there took place a ceremonial burial of the dead of both sides, organized by the Germans with honorable decorum. The British were invited to send a party and all who were able to walk turned out in the best shape they could. From the pile of clothes, which had been taken away from them, the least spoiled items were picked out. The sailors borrowed razors from the commandos. All hatless, and most without jackets, a party of some twenty paraded under Hopwood, and marched as smartly as they were able into a field at Escoublac, adjacent to La Baule. For a brief space all hostilities were forgotten in an act of mutual homage and respect. The Germans provided a generous wreath. The British dead lay in a long trench in a double row of coffins, and beside this common grave stood one more coffin, covered with the Union Flag. The German coffins were similarly disposed. Services were then conducted by Protestant and Roman Catholic chaplains, but unfortunately the British were not able to understand a word. Six British sailors and soldiers then advanced and lowered into the grave the remaining coffin. Hopwood let fall the wreath and three volleys of musketry were fired. "It was," Dark recorded, "all extremely impressive and our hearts were filled with twisted and unintelligible emotions."

This field of graves was the beginning of a cemetery which during the next three years was to be much expanded by British dead, particularly of the Royal Air Force, and there it still is.

As they became well enough, the wounded were moved on, also to Rennes, and were put into St. Vincent's Hospital, a very stark, and cheerless hospital for French colonial troops, where they received devoted care from the French doctors, ill-provided though they were with the barest necessities, and from the warmhearted native orderlies—Senegalese, Moroccans, Cambodians and others—all themselves prisoners. Thence all but a few moved on into Germany, to a prison camp at Westertimke, near Bremen, known as Marlag-Milag; until, the Germans deciding to break them up, officers and men, navy and army were sent away to separate camps.

There we must leave the main body of these gentlemen, continually plotting their escapes, often succeeding, but nearly always being caught again. The more persistent escapists were sent off to the notorious punishment castle of Colditz—Stephens, Purdon, Wynn and Morgan. Michael Burn was sent there, too. Even from there, however, Stephens escaped successfully at last, in company with Major Ronnie Littledale, of the 60th Rifles, who was later killed in the Normandy campaign. Disguised as French workmen, they escaped from the formidable prison under cover of music from the camp band, made their way to Switzerland and crossed the border near Singen, existing for the last two days on apples, and evading "with the skin of their teeth" the German sentry on the very edge of the frontier.

Even more remarkable, perhaps, was the successful escape made by Sergeants Alf Searson and Dick Bradley, old friends of 2 Commando and members of Walton's demolition squad, and Private Jimmy Brown, of 5 Commando. All had made several attempts before, learning by experience the tricks of the trade, and they were fortunate to have in Bradley a a man who spoke good enough German. On their third attempt Searson and Bradley had come within an ace of success, reaching the Swiss frontier where the Rhine joins it, but at the very last moment had stumbled into a German frontier patrol hut. Nonetheless, Searson was already thinking about the next attempt, for, as they waited for an escort to take them away, he carefully studied the frontier and noted the dispositions and movements of the German sentries.

The last time they were joined by Brown, friend of previous attempts. They had now been moved to a camp at Gross-Zeidel, far away in the southwest corner of Poland, six hundred miles from Switzerland, but they set out again on Trafalgar Day, 1943, making designedly for the very spot where they had before been. Going openly by train the greater part of the way, they survived extraordinary encounters, boldly asking the way of a German sentry, who challenged them on the roadside at midnight, coolly going back for an English novel which Bradley had left at the office of a burgomaster where they had bluffed their way out after arrest on suspicion, giving deliberately stupid answers to a German sergeant-major who took them for recruits. Finally, on October 25, crossing a ploughed field in stockinged feet, creeping from shadow to shadow, they slipped across the frontier at the very spot where they had been captured last time.

To escape is honorable and the duty of all prisoners of war. To avoid capture and to fight again is still more honorable. Not all who landed at St. Nazaire fell into enemy hands. Five commandos succeded in avoiding capture and in obeying Newman's order to make their way to Gibraltar.

These achievements were carried out by three separate groups, and two of them originated from the cellar of a bombed shop in St. Nazaire, where six men had concealed themselves. These were Troop Sergeant-Major Haines, Sergeant Challington (Camerons), Lance-Corporal Howarth (Grenadier Guards), Corporal Wright, the RE diarist, Corporal Douglas (Liverpool Scottish), and Private Harding (Gloucesters). All but Douglas and Harding were pretty sharply wounded, Wright bleeding profusely from a calf partly shot away. They stayed in the cellar all that Saturday in considerable pain and with very little to eat, and narrowly escaping discovery as a German search party went through the ruins overhead. By good fortune some civilian trousers and a jacket were found for Challington, who had no hope of escape in the kilt, and a jacket for Haines.

Haines decided that that night they should make their way out in pairs, but Wright, knowing that he would seriously hold back other people and that he was too badly injured to go alone, walked out after dark and gave himself up. Haines and Challington, both with leg wounds, set off painfully together, the first to leave, and succeeded in making their way into the country but had the bad luck to run into a party of Germans.

Howarth, who had been with Roderick's assault party and twice hit, was the next to leave. Going alone and reaching open country, he was befriended by a French family who gave him a bath and put him to bed, and a day or two later an English-speaking schoolmaster, Monsieur Barratte, at great personal risk, took him to his own house in St. Nazaire and afterwards accompanied him by train as far as Bordeaux. Going on from there alone into unoccupied France, Howarth fell into the hands of the Vichy police and spent eight months in confinement before he made his escape.

Last to leave the cellar were Douglas and Harding, who had both been members of Haine's own assault party. Still in uniform, they rolled up their battledress trousers, opened the

collars of their blouses and sailed safely through the Germans
at the street barriers put up at the entrances to the town,
Douglas painfully aware of the corporal's stripes on his sleeve.
Marching by night, they reached La Roche Bernard, where,
near the end of their tether, they barely escaped capture by a
German flak battery. Chance led them to a kindly French
butcher and he in turn passed them to an American lady, who
gave them clothes, money and bicycles. Making their way to
Loches, they were befriended by a French lawyer, who provided them with faked papers and, together with his wife,
took them all the way to Marseilles, where an escape organization took charge of them.

Perhaps the most colorful of the evaders' experiences,
however, was that which befell Corporal George Wheeler and
Lance-Corporal R. Sims. Wheeler, wiry, spectacled, dark-
haired, an honors degree man in economics, has already been
briefly seen with Philip Walton's demolition team. He could
speak schoolboy French. Sims, well set up, robust, of simple
character, was a young Canadian, a Regular soldier in the
Somerset Light Infantry. These two took refuge together in
a small cavity beneath a house in St. Nazaire just as day was
breaking on Saturday.

That night, they crept out into the moonlight, and
reached the outskirts of the town. There they passed a dance
café where the Germans were noisily celebrating. Regretting
having left their grenades behind, they fingered their Colts,
sorely tempted to break up the party, but thought better of
it.

Just before daylight, they reached the little village of
L'Immaculée Conception and lay up in a haystack, where
they were discovered by Monsieur Guillaume Francis, who,
astonished and alarmed though he was, took them to his
house, and together with friends whom he summoned, generously provided them out of their little store with food and
two hundred and fifty francs each and clothed them with old
"Sunday best" black jackets, green with antiquity, and pin-
stripe trousers, but no civilian boots. He took away their
pistols. "Not safe for you, my friends," he said, "but might
be useful to me one day."

The two men went on that night but, bedeviled by the
uncertainty of where to go and by the lack of a map, went
to and fro for two nights, still only a very little way out of
St. Nazaire, trying to find a way round the marsh that

stretched for thirty square miles inland from the town. At the little village of St. André des Eaux, however, they were given a calendar map issued by a firm of agricultural implement manufacturers; these were issued separately for each district, showing every lane and cart track. "After that," Wheeler said, "it was easy. Wherever we went, all we had to do was to ask for the P.T.T. calendar."

Receiving much contrary advice on the best direction to take, they knew, however, that they must avoid Germans and large towns and travel by remote byways. Finally they made their way round the north of the big marsh and struck east, never certain whether it was best to march by night or by day, sleeping in hayricks, barns or open woods, incongruous figures in their black suits and commando boots, often very hungry, often generously fed, experiencing the oddest encounters and many close shaves, frequently wet to the skin but always determined to press on. To Wheeler, one of their greatest dangers was Sims's passion for smoking; he thought nothing of accosting a startled French man on a lonely road to ask for a cigarette.

Not all the French were friendly; some hostile, some frightened, many highly suspicious of the identities of these shabby and weather-soiled apparitions. It was as well for the refugees' peace of mind that they did not know that the Germans were on their trail and had circulated descriptions emphasizing their boots and Wheeler's spectacles. Except for these few instances, however, the two young soldiers found that the words *"évadés de St. Nazaire"* were a magic password to the hearts of Frenchmen; for everywhere the news of the great deed had brought hope and rejoicing.

To their surprise, they crossed the Loire without being challenged at a bridge seven miles from Angers. They were getting very footsore as they pressed on through the drenching rain over a country well trodden by English armies of old and through antique places haunted by the ghosts of French kings. At the tiny village of Pouant a very pro-British farmer wept when they left. The most serious of all obstacles was before them—the Line of Demarcation between occupied and unoccupied France, under strong surveillance by German guards.

Having learnt that the Line of Demarcation in this area was the River Creuse, they were taken by a Frenchwoman to the house of a gamekeeper in the Forêt de Guerches, a mile and a half from the river. Here the Frenchwoman and the

gamekeeper's two daughters, pretty and vivacious, held a
feminine council of war and "made a plan," based, as all
good plans should be, on accurate knowledge of the enemy's
movements and habits. The French here knew that all the
German cyclist patrols on the riverside roads came in to
change guard on the bridge at Leugny at midday.

The two girls, carrying towels, left on their bicycles the
next day at 11:30, followed by the two soldiers. They met
on the riverside road. All was clear; the last German patrol
had passed.

"Take off your jackets," the girls said, "and give them
to us."

They did so and the girls turned left and rode away to
Leugny, a quarter of a mile away, while the soldiers watched
from the screen of roadside trees. After a minute or two they
saw the girls dismount by the sentry with a great flurry of
skits and begin talking to him.

This was their cue. Wheeler and Sims crossed the road
and waded into the river, ice cold from the winter snows.
Looking to their left they saw the French girls still flirting
with the sentry. Scrambling out on the far bank they hurried
to conceal themselves among the trees and no sooner had
they done so than the girls, with a great business of flying
skirts, displays of leg and waves of the arm, mounted un-
steadily and rode across the bridge.

In a few minutes the girls rode up, restored to them
their dry jackets and gave them the towels, with which the
men dried themselves as best they could, and waved them
a cheerful good-by.

We cannot stay too long to follow this adventurous and
well contrived evasion of the two commandos. The worst
was over. The next day, April 14, after having marched about
two hundred and fifty miles, they arrived at Azay-le-Ferron
and were welcomed with open arms, by Monsieur Maurice
Génichon and his wife at their small château. Their rags
were stripped off, good clothes and shoes given them; a hot
bath was followed by a memorable dinner that ended with
green Chartreuse and then real beds in private suites, the
enjoyment of the warm hospitality of Monsieur and Madame
Génichon enhanced by their excellent English.

Next morning, overcoming with the utmost difficulty a
nervous reluctance to traveling openly in public transport,
they were put on a bus to Châteauroux by Monsieur Génichon, fell in by chance with a sterling and resourceful

Belgian youth named Gilbert Mahun, who was himself trying to get to England, traveled with him by train down to Toulouse, and there, once more by fortunate chance, met Monsieur Pierre Uhlmann and his American wife and through their agency were put in touch with an escape organization which took them, with many a near squeak, over the Pyrenees and thence to Gibraltar.

Regaining England, Wheeler, Sims, Douglas, Harding and Howarth rejoined their units and fought again in the great campaigns that led at last to victory.

The last scene of all is fittingly presented by Micky Wynn. Repatriated on medical grounds, he was barred by the rules of war from bearing arms again against the Germans, but he was determined to fulfill one ambition. At the time when our armies were sweeping victoriously into Germany he persuaded the Admiralty to send him on a mission for rehabilitation of released naval prisoners of war. He insinuated himself into the area of the Canadian Army, made contact with the Guards' Armored Division and, wearing the white ensign, rode in a leading tank into the Marlag-Milag prison camp, to release his gallant shipmate, Bill Lovegrove.

Join the Allies on the Road to Victory
BANTAM WAR BOOKS

These action-packed books recount the most important events of World War II. Specially commissioned maps, diagrams and illustrations allow you to follow these true stories of brave men and gallantry in action.

Join the Allies on the Road to Victory
BANTAM WAR BOOKS

These action-packed books recount the most important events of World War II. Specially commissioned maps, diagrams and illustrations allow you to follow these true stories of brave men and gallantry in action.

☐	13806	AMERICAN GUERILLA IN THE PHILIPPINES Wolfert	$2.50
☐	13582	BLACK THURSDAY Caidin	$2.50
☐	20472	BATTLE FOR GUADALCANAL Griffith	$2.95
☐	13581	COMMANDO FORCE 133 Strutton	$2.50
☐	13469	DEFEAT IN THE EAST Thorwald	$2.50
☐	13568	FULL CIRCLE Johnson	$2.50
☐	12670	HUNDRED DAYS OF LT. MACHORTON Machorton W. Maule	$2.25
☐	13014	BRAZEN CHARIOTS Crisp	$2.25
☐	12666	COAST WATCHERS Feldt	$2.25
☐	13121	THE GERMAN RAIDER ATLANTIS Frank & Rogge	$2.25

*Cannot be sold to Canadian Residents.

Buy them at your local bookstore or use this handy coupon: